ISBN 978-1-332-96787-2
PIBN 10444431

This book is a reproduction of an important historical work. Forgotten Books uses
state-of-the-art technology to digitally reconstruct the work, preserving the original format
whilst repairing imperfections present in the aged copy. In rare cases, an imperfection in
the original, such as a blemish or missing page, may be replicated in our edition. We do,
however, repair the vast majority of imperfections successfully; any imperfections that
remain are intentionally left to preserve the state of such historical works.

1 MONTH OF
FREE
READING

at
www.ForgottenBooks.com

By purchasing this book you are eligible for one month membership to ForgottenBooks.com, giving you unlimited access to our entire collection of over 1,000,000 titles via our web site and mobile apps.

To claim your free month visit:
www.forgottenbooks.com/free444431

THE
PENTATEUCH,

Bible. O. T.

OR THE FIVE BOOKS OF MOSES.

(SCHOOL AND FAMILY EDITION.)

PUBLISHED BY

ADOLPH MOSES AND ISAAC S. MOSES.

MILWAUKEE, WIS.

1884.

PRICE, 30 CENTS.

GENESIS,

CALLED THE FIRST BOOK OF MOSES.

CHAPTER I.

IN the beginning God created the heaven and the earth.

2 And the earth was without form, and void ; and darkness was upon the face of the deep. And the spirit of God moved upon the face of the waters.

3 And God said, Let there be light : and there was light.

4 And God saw the light that it was good, and God divided the light from the darkness.

5 And God called the light Day, and the darkness he called Night. And it was evening and it was morning, the first day.

6 And God said, Let there be a firmament in the midst of the waters, and let it divide the waters from the waters.

7 And God made the firmament, and divided the waters which were under the firmament from the waters which were above the firmament : and it was so.

8 And God called the firmament Heaven. And it was evening and it was morning, the second day.

9 And God said, Let the waters under the heaven be gathered together unto one place, and let the dry land appear : and it was so.

10 And God called the dry land Earth ; and the gathering together of the waters called he Sea : and God saw that it was good.

11 And God said, Let the earth bring forth grass, the herb yielding seed, and the fruit tree yielding fruit after its kind, whose seed is in itself, upon the earth : and it was so.

12 And the earth brought forth grass, and herb yielding seed after his kind, and the tree yielding fruit, whose seed was in itself, after his kind : and God saw that it was good.

13 And it was evening and it was morning, the third day.

14 And God said, Let there be lights in the firmament of the heaven to divide the day from the night ; and let them be for signs, and for seasons, and for days, and years :

15 And let them be for lights in the firmament of the heaven to give light upon the earth : and it was so.

16 And God made two great lights ; the greater light to rule the day, and the lesser light to rule the night : he made the stars also.

17 And God set them in the firmament of the heaven to give light upon the earth.

18 And to rule over the day and over the night, and to divide the light from the darkness : and God saw that it was good.

19 And it was evening and it was morning, the fourth day.

20 And God said, Let the waters bring forth abundantly the moving creature that hath life, and fowl that

may fly above the earth in the open firmament of heaven:

21 And God created great whales, and every living creature that moveth, which the waters brought forth abundantly, after their kind, and every winged fowl after his kind : and God saw that it was good.

22 And God blessed them, saying, Be fruitful, and multiply, and fill the waters in the seas, and let fowl multiply on the earth.

23 And it was evening and it was morning, the fifth day.

24 And God said, Let the earth bring forth the living creature after his kind, cattle, and creeping things, and beasts of the earth after his kind : and it was so :

25 And God made the beast of the earth after his kind, and cattle after their kind, and every thing that creepeth upon the earth after his kind : and God saw that it was good.

26 And God said, Let us make man in our image, after our likeness : and let them have dominion over the fish of the sea, and over the fowl of the air, and over the cattle, and over all the earth, and over every creeping thing that creepeth upon the earth.

27 So God created man in his own image, in the image of God created he him ; male and female he created them.

28 And God blessed them, and God said unto them, Be fruitful and multiply and replenish the earth, and subdue it : and have dominion over the fish of the sea, and over the fowl of the air, and over every living thing that moveth upon the earth.

29 And God said, Behold, I have given you every herb bearing seed, which is upon the face of all the earth, and every tree, in the which is the fruit of a tree yielding seed ; to you it shall be for meat.

30 And to every beast of the earth, and to every fowl of the air, and to every thing that creepeth upon the earth, wherein there is life, I have given every herb for meat : and it was so.

31 And God saw every thing that he had made, and, behold, it was very good. And it was evening and it was morning, the sixth day.

CHAPTER II.

THUS the heavens and the earth were finished, and all their host.

2 And on the seventh day God ended his work which he had made ; and he rested on the seventh day from all his work which he had made.

3 And God blessed the seventh day, and sanctified it : because that in it he had rested from all his work which God created and made.

4 These are the generations of the heavens and of the earth when they were created, in the day that the LORD God made the earth and the heavens.

5 And every plant of the field before it was in the earth, and every herb of the field before it grew : for the LORD God had not caused it to rain upon the earth, and there was not a man to till the ground.

6 But there went up a mist from the earth, and watered the whole face of the ground.

7 And the LORD God formed man of the dust of the ground, he breathed into him the breath of life ; and man became a living soul.

8 And the LORD God planted a

garden eastward in Eden ; and there he put the man whom he had formed.

9 And out of the ground made the LORD God to grow every tree that is pleasant to the sight, and good for food ; the tree of life also in the midst of the garden, and the tree of knowledge of good and evil.

10 And a river went out of Eden to water the garden ; and from thence it was parted, and became into four heads.

11 The name of the first is Pison : that is it which compasseth the whole land of Havilah, where there is gold ;

12 And the gold of that land is good : there is bdellium and the onix stone.

13 And the name of the second river is Gihon : the same is it that compasseth the whole land of Ethiopia.

14 And the name of the third river is Hiddekel : that is it which goeth toward the east of Assyria. And the fourth river is Euphrates.

15 And the LORD God took the man, and put him into the garden of Eden to work in it and to keep it.

16 And the LORD God commanded the man, saying, Of every tree of the garden thou mayest freely eat :

17 But of the tree of the knowledge of good and evil, thou shalt not eat of it ; for in the day that thou eatest thereof, thou shalt surely die.

18 And the LORD God said, It is not good that the man should be alone : I will make him a help meet for him.

19 And out of the ground the LORD God formed every beast of the field, and every fowl of the air ; and brought them unto Adam to see what he would call them : and whatsoever Adam called every living creature, that was the name thereof.

20 And Adam gave names to all cattle, and to the fowl of the air, and to every beast of the field ; but for Adam there was not found a help meet for him.

21 And the LORD God caused a deep sleep to fall upon Adam, and he slept ; and he took one of his ribs, and closed up the flesh instead thereof.

22 And the rib, which the LORD God had taken from man, made he a woman, and brought her unto the man.

23 And Adam said, This is now bone of my bones and flesh of my flesh : she shall be called Woman, because she was taken out of man.

24 Therefore shall a man leave his father and his mother, and shall cleave unto his wife : and they shall be one person.

25 And they were both naked, the man and his wife, and were not ashamed.

CHAPTER III.

NOW the serpent was more subtile than any beast of the field which the LORD God had made. And he said unto the woman, Yea, hath God said, Ye shall not eat of every tree of the garden ?

2 And the woman said unto the serpent, We may eat of the fruit of the trees of the garden :

3 But of the fruit of the tree which is in the midst of the garden, God hath said, Ye shall not eat of it, neither shall ye touch it, lest ye die.

4 And the serpent said unto the woman, Ye shall not die :

5 For God doth know that in the day ye eat thereof, then your eyes

shall be opened, and ye ·shall be as gods, knowing good and evil.

6 And when the woman saw that the tree was good for food, and that it was pleasant to the eyes, and a tree to be desired to make one wise, she took of the fruit thereof, and did eat, and gave also unto her husband with her; and he did eat.

7 And the eyes of them both were opened, and they knew that they were naked; and they sewed fig leaves together, and made themselves aprons.

8 And they heard the voice of the LORD God walking in the garden in the cool of the day: and Adam and his wife hid themselves from the presence of the LORD God amongst the trees of the garden.

9 And the LORD God called unto Adam, and said unto him, Where art thou?

10 And he said, I heard thy voice in the garden, and I was afraid, because I was naked; and I hid myself.

11 And he said, Who told thee that thou wast naked? Hast thou eaten of the tree, whereof I commanded thee that thou shouldest not eat?

12 And the man said, The woman whom thou gavest to be with me, she gave me of the tree, and I did eat.

13 And the LORD God said unto the woman, What is this that thou hast done? And the woman said, The serpent beguiled me, and I did eat.

14 And the LORD God said unto the serpent, Because thou hast done this, thou art cursed above all cattle, and above every beast of the field.

15 Unto the woman he said, I will greatly multiply thy sorrow; in sorrow shalt thou bring up children.

16 And unto Adam he said, Because thou has hearkened unto the voice of thy wife, and hast eaten of the tree, of which I commanded thee, saying, Thou shalt not eat of it: cursed is the ground for thy sake; in sorrow shalt thou eat of it all the days of thy life;

17 Thorns also and thistles shall it bring forth to thee; and thou shalt eat the herb of the field:

18 In the sweat of thy face shalt thou eat bread, till thou return unto the ground; for out of it wast thou taken: for dust thou art, and unto dust shalt thou return.

19 And Adam called his wife's name Eve; because she was the mother of all living.

20 Unto Adam also and to his wife did the LORD God show how to make coats of skins, and clothed them.

21 And the LORD God said, Behold, the man is become as one of us, to know good and evil: and now, lest he put forth his hand, and take also of the tree of life, and eat, and live for ever:

22 Therefore the LORD God sent him forth from the garden of Eden, to till the ground from whence he was taken.

23 So he drove out the man: and he placed at the east of the garden of Eden cherubim, and a flaming sword which turned every way, to guard the way to the tree of life.

CHAPTER IV.

AND Eve bare a son and she called him Cain, and then she again bare his brother Abel. And Abel was a keeper of sheep, but Cain was a tiller of the ground.

2 And in process of time it came to pass, that Cain brought of the fruit of the ground an offering unto the LORD.

3 And Abel, he also brought of the firstlings of his flock and of the fat thereof. And the LORD had respect unto Abel and to his offering:

4 But unto Cain and to his offering he had not respect. And Cain was very wroth, and his countenance fell.

5 And the LORD said unto Cain, Why art thou wroth? and why is thy countenance fallen?

6 If thou doest well, shalt thou not be accepted? and if thou doest not well, sin lieth at the door: and unto thee is its desire, and thou shalt rule over it.

7 And Cain talked with Abel his brother: and it came to pass, when they were in the field, that Cain rose up against Abel his brother, and slew him.

8 And the LORD said unto Cain, Where is Abel thy brother? And he said, I know not: Am I my brother's keeper?

9 And he said, What hast thou done? the voice of thy brother's blood crieth unto me from the ground.

10 And now art thou cursed from the earth, which hath opened her mouth to receive thy brother's blood from thy hand.

11 When thou tillest the ground, it shall not henceforth yield unto thee her strength; a fugitive and a wanderer shalt thou be in the earth.

12 And Cain said unto the LORD, My punishment is greater than I can bear.

.13 Behold, thou hast driven me out this day from the face of the earth; and from thy face shall I be hid; and I shall be a fugitive and a wanderer in the earth; and it shall come to pass, that every one that findeth me shall slay me.

14 And the LORD said unto him, Therefore whosoever slayeth Cain, vengeance shall be taken on him twice sevenfold. And the LORD set a mark upon Cain, lest any finding him should kill him.

CHAPTER V.

AND Cain went out from the presence of the LORD, and dwelt in the land of Nod, on the east of Eden.

2 And Cain had a son, Enoch: and he built a city, and called the name of the city after the name of his son Enoch.

3 And unto Enoch was born Irad: and unto Irad Mehujael: and unto Mehujael Methusael: and Methusael's son was Lamech.

4 And Lamech took unto him two wives: the name of the one was Adah, and the name of the other Zillah.

5 And Adah bare Jabel: he was the father of such as dwell in tents, and of such as have cattle.

6 And his brother's name was Jubal: he was the father of all such as handle the harp and organ.

7 And Zillah, she also bare Tubal-cain, an instructor of every artificer in brass and iron: and the sister of Tubal-cain was Naamah.

8 And Lamech said unto his wives:
Adah and Zillah, hear my voice;
wives of Lamech, listen to my speech;
I slay a man for wounding me,
a youth for inflicting a stripe.
Lo, Cain would be avenged twice sevenfold,
but Lamech seventy-sevenfold.

9 And to Adam another son was born, and Eve called his name Seth: For God, said she, hath appointed me another child instead of Abel, whom Cain slew.

10 And to Seth also was born a son; and he called his name Enosh; then began men to call upon the name of the LORD.

11 This is the Book of the generations of Adam. In the day that God created man, in the likeness of God made he him;

12 Male and female created he them; and blessed them, and called their name Adam, in the day when they were created.

13 And these are the generations of Adam: Adam, Seth, Enosh, Kenan, Mahalaleel, Jared, Enoch, Methuselah, Lamech.

14 And Enoch walked with God: and he was no more, for God took him.

15 And Lamech had a son, and he called his name Noah, saying, This same shall comfort us concerning our work and toil of our hands, because of the ground which the LORD hath cursed.

CHAPTER VI.

THESE are the generations of Noah: Noah was a just man and perfect in his generations, and Noah walked with God.

2 And Noah had three sons, Shem, Ham and Japheth.

3 And God saw that the wickedness of man was great in the earth, and that every imagination of the thoughts of his heart was only evil continually.

4 The earth also was corrupt before God; and the earth was filled with violence.

5 And God looked upon the earth, and behold, it was corrupt; for all flesh had corrupted his way upon the earth.

6 And God said, I will destroy man, whom I have created, from the face of the earth; both man, and beast, and the creeping things, and the fowls of the air; for it repenteth me that I have made them.

7 But Noah found grace in the eyes of the LORD.

8 And God said unto Noah, The end of all flesh is come before me; for the earth is filled with violence through them; and, behold, I will destroy them from the earth.

9 Make thee an ark of gopher wood; rooms shalt thou make in the ark, and shalt pitch it within and without with pitch.

10 And this is the fashion in which thou shalt make it: The length of the ark shall be three hundred cubits, the breadth of it fifty cubits, and the height of it thirty cubits.

11 A window shalt thou make to the ark, and in a cubit shalt thou finish it above; and the door of the ark shalt thou set in the side thereof; with lower, second and third stories shalt thou make it.

12 And behold, I, even I, do bring a flood of waters upon the earth, to destroy all flesh, wherein is the breath of life, from under heaven; and every thing that is in the earth shall die.

13 But with thee will I establish my covenant; and thou shalt come into the ark, thou, and thy sons, and thy sons' wives with thee.

14 And of every living thing of all flesh, two of every sort shalt thou bring into the ark, to keep them alive with thee; they shall be male and female.

15 Of fowls after their kind, and of cattle after their kind, of every creeping thing of the earth after his kind; two of every sort shall come unto thee, to keep them alive.

16 And take thou unto thee of all food that is eaten, and thou shalt

gather it to thee; and it shall be for food for thee, and for them.

17 Thus did Noah; according to all that God commanded him, so did he.

CHAPTER VII.

AND the LORD said unto Noah, Come thou and all thy house into the ark; for thee have I seen righteous before me in this generation.

2 For yet seven days, and I will cause it to rain upon the earth forty days and forty nights; and every living substance that I have made will I destroy from off the face of the earth.

3 And Noah did according unto all that the LORD commanded him.

4 And Noah was six hundred years old when the flood of waters was upon the earth:

5 And Noah went in, and his sons, and his wife, and his sons' wives with him, into the ark, because of the waters of the flood.

6 Of clean beasts, and of beasts that are not clean, and of fowls, and of every thing that creepeth upon the earth.

7 There went in two and two unto Noah into the ark, the male and the female, as God had commanded Noah.

8 And it came to pass after seven days, that the waters of the flood were upon the earth.

9 In the six hundredth year of Noah's life, in the second month, the seventeenth day of the month, the same day were all the fountains of the great deep broken up, and the windows of heaven were opened.

10 And the rain was upon the earth forty days and forty nights.

11 In the selfsame day entered Noah, and Shem, and Ham, and Japhet, the sons of Noah, and Noah's wife, and the three wives of his sons with them, into the ark;

12 They, and every beast after his kind, and all the cattle after their kind, and every creeping thing that creepeth upon the earth after his kind, and every fowl after his kind, every bird of every sort.

13 And they went in unto Noah into the ark, two and two of all flesh, wherein is the breath of life.

14 And they that went in, went in male and female of all flesh, as God had commanded him: and the LORD shut him in.

15 And the flood was forty days upon the earth; and the waters increased, and bore up the ark, and it was lifted up above the earth.

16 And the waters prevailed, and were increased greatly upon the earth; and the ark went upon the face of the waters.

17 And the waters prevailed exceedingly upon the earth; and all the high hills, that were under the whole heaven, were covered.

18 Fifteen cubits upward did the waters prevail; and the mountains were covered.

19 And all flesh died that moved upon the earth, both of fowl, and of cattle, and of beast, and of every creeping thing that creepeth upon the earth, and every man:

20 All in whom was the breath of life, of all that was in the dry land, died.

21 And every living substance was destroyed which was upon the face of the ground, both man, and cattle, and the creeping things, and the fowl of the heaven; and they were destroyed from the earth: and Noah only remained alive, and they that were with him in the ark.

22 And the waters prevailed upon the earth a hundred and fifty days.

CHAPTER VIII.

AND God remembered Noah, and every living thing, and all the cattle that was with him in the ark: and God made a wind to pass over the earth, and the waters assuaged;

2 The fountains also of the deep and the windows of heaven were stopped, and the rain from heaven was restrained.

3 And the waters returned from off the earth continually, and the ark rested in the seventh month, on the seventeenth day of the month, upon the mountains of Ararat.

4 And the waters decreased continually until the tenth month: in the tenth month, on the first day of the month, were the tops of the mountains seen.

5 And it came to pass at the end of forty days, that Noah opened the window of the ark which he had made:

6 And he sent forth a raven, which went forth to and fro, until the waters were dried up from off the earth.

7 Also he sent forth a dove from him, to see if the waters were abated from off the face of the ground.

8 But the dove found no rest for the sole of her foot, and she returned unto him into the ark; for the waters were on the face of the whole earth. Then he put forth his hand, and took her, and brought her in unto him into the ark.

9 And he stayed yet other seven days; and again he sent forth the dove out of the ark.

10 And the dove came in to him in the evening, and, lo, in her mouth was an olive leaf plucked off: so Noah knew that the waters were abated from off the earth.

11 And he stayed yet other seven days, and sent forth the dove; which returned not again unto him any more.

12 And it came to pass in the six hundredth and first year, in the first month, the first day of the month, the waters were dried up from off the earth, and Noah removed the covering of the ark, and looked, and, behold, the face of the ground was dry.

13 And in the second month, on the seven and twentieth day of the month, was the earth dried.

14 And God spake unto Noah, saying,

15 Go forth of the ark, thou, and thy wife, and thy sons, and thy sons' wives with thee.

16 Bring forth with thee every living thing that is with thee, of all flesh, both of fowl, and of cattle, and of every creeping thing that creepeth upon the earth; that they may grow abundantly in the earth, and be fruitful, and multiply upon the earth.

17 And Noah went forth, and his sons, and his wife, and his sons' wives with him:

18 Every beast, every creeping thing, and every fowl, and whatsoever creepeth upon the earth, after their kinds, went forth out of the ark.

19 And Noah builded an altar unto the LORD; and took of every clean beast, and of every clean fowl, and offered burnt offerings on the altar.

20 And the LORD was pleased, and said, I will not again curse the ground any more for man's sake; for the imagination of man's heart is evil from his youth; neither will I again smite any more every thing living, as I have done.

21 While the earth remaineth, seed-

time and harvest, and cold and heat, and summer and winter, and day and night shall not cease.

CHAPTER IX.

AND God blessed Noah and his sons, and said unto them, Be fruitful, and multiply, and replenish the earth.

2 And the fear of you and the dread of you shall be upon every beast of the earth, and upon every fowl of the air, upon all that moveth upon the earth, and upon all the fishes of the sea; into your hand are they delivered.

3 Every moving thing that liveth shall be meat for you: even as the green herb have I given you all things.

4 But flesh with the life thereof, which is the blood thereof, shall ye not eat.

5 And surely your blood of your lives will I require: at the hand of every beast will I require it, and at the hand of man; at the hand of every man's brother will I require the life of man.

6 Whoso sheddeth man's blood, by man shall his blood be shed: for in the image of God made he man, ·

7 And I, behold, I establish my covenant with you, and with your children after you;

8 And with every living creature that is with you, of the fowl, of the cattle, and of every beast of the earth with you; from all that go out of the ark, to every beast of the earth.

9 And I will establish my covenant with you; neither shall all flesh be cut off any more by the waters of a flood; neither shall there any more be a flood to destroy the earth.

10 And God said, This is the token of the covenant which I make between me and you, and every living creature that is with you, for perpetual generations:

11 I do set my bow in the cloud, and it shall be for a token of a covenant between me and the earth.

12 And it shall come to pass, when I bring a cloud over the earth, that the bow shall be seen in the cloud:

13 And I will remember my covenant, which is between me and you and every living creature of all flesh; and the waters shall no more become a flood to destroy all flesh.

14 And Noah began to be a husbandman, and he planted a vineyard:

15 And he drank of the wine, and was drunken; and he lay unconscious within his tent.

16 And Ham, the father of Canaan, saw his father in that state, and told his two brethren without.

17 And Shem and Japheth took a garment, and laid it upon both their shoulders, and went backward, and covered their father; and their faces were backward, and they saw not their father's disgrace.

17 And Noah awoke from his wine, and knew what his younger son had done unto him.

19 And he said, Blessed be the LORD God of Shem; and Canaan shall be his servant.

20 God shall enlarge Japheth, and he shall dwell in the tents of Shem; and Canaan shall be his servant.

CHAPTER X.

AND the whole earth was of one language, and of one speech.

2 And it came to pass, as they journeyed from the east, that they found a plain in the land of Shinar: and they dwelt there.

3 And they said one to another, Go to, let us make brick, and burn them thoroughly. And they had brick for stone, and slime had they for mortar.

4 And they said, Go to, let us build us a city, and a tower, whose top may reach unto heaven; and let us make us a name, lest we be scattered abroad upon the face of the whole earth.

5 And the LORD saw the city and the tower, which the children of men had built.

6 And the LORD said, Behold, the people is one, and they have all one language; and this they begin to do: and now nothing will be restrained from them, which they have imagined to do.

7 Go to, let us confound their language, that they may not understand one anothers's speech.

8 So the LORD scattered them abroad from thence upon the face of all the earth: and they left off to build the city.

9 Therefore is the name of it called Babel: because the LORD did there confound the language of all the earth: and from thence did the LORD scatter them abroad upon the face of all the earth.

CHAPTER XI.

THESE are the generations of Shem: Shem, Arphaxad, Selah, Eber, Peleg, Reu, Serug, Nahor; and Nahor's son was Terah.

2 And Terah had three sons: Abram, Nahor, and Haran; and the son of Haran was Lot.

3 And Haran died before his father Terah in the land of his nativity, in Ur of the Chaldees.

4 And Abram and Nahor took them wives: the name of Abram's wife was Sarai; and the name of Nahor's wife, Milcah, the daughter of Haran, the father of Milcah, and the father of Iscah. But Sarai had no child.

5 And Terah took Abram his son, and Lot, the son of Haran, his son's son, and Sarai his daughter in law, his son Abram's wife; and they went forth with them from Ur of the Chaldees, to go into the land of Canaan; and they came unto Haran, and dwelt there, and Terah died in Haran.

CHAPTER XII.

AND the LORD said unto Abram, Get thee out of thy country, and from thy kindred, and from thy father's house, unto a land that I will shew thee:

2 And I will make of thee a great nation, and I will bless thee, and make thy name great; and thou shalt be a blessing:

3 And I will bless them that bless thee, and curse him that curseth thee: and in thee shall all families of the earth be blessed.

4 So Abram departed, as the LORD had spoken unto him; and Lot went with him: and Abram was seventy and five years old when he departed out of Haran.

5 And Abram took Sarai his wife, and Lot his brother's son, and all their substance that they had gathered, and the souls that they had gotten in Haran; and they went forth to go into the land of Canaan; and into the land of Canaan they came.

6 And Abram passed through the land unto the place of Shechem, unto the oak of Moreh. And the Canaanite was then in the land.

7 And the LORD appeared unto Abram, and said, Unto thy children

will I give this land: and there he builded an altar unto the LORD, who appeared unto him.

8 And he removed from thence unto a mountain on the east of Beth-el, and pitched his tent, having Beth-el on the west, and Ai on the east: and there he builded an altar unto the LORD, and called upon the name of the LORD.

9 And Abram journeyed, going on still toward the south.

10 And there was a famine in the land: and Abram went down into Egypt to sojourn there; for the famine was grievous in the land.

CHAPTER XIII.

AND Abram went up out of Egypt, he, and his wife, and all that he had, and Lot with him, into the south.

2 And Abram was very rich in cattle, in silver, and in gold.

3 And he went on his journeys from the south even to Beth-el, unto the place where his tent had been at the beginning, between Beth-el and Ai;

4 Unto the place of the altar, which he had made there at the first: and there Abram called on the name of the LORD.

5 And Lot also, which went with Abram, had flocks, and herds, and tents.

6 And the land was not able to bear them, that they might dwell together: for their substance was great, so that they could not dwell together.

7 Aud there was a strife between the herdmen of Abram's cattle and the herdmen of Lot's cattle: and the Canaanite and the Perizzite dwelt then in the land.

8 And Abram said unto Lot, Let there be no strife, I pray thee, between me and thee, and between my herdmen and thy herdmen; for we be brethren.

9 Is not the whole land before thee; separate thyself, I pray thee, from me: if thou wilt take the left hand, then I will go to the right; or if thou depart to the right, then I will go to the left.

10 And Lot lifted up his eyes, and beheld all the plain of Jordan, that it was well watered every where, before the LORD destroyed Sodom and Gomorrah, even as the garden of the LORD, like the land of Egypt, as thou comest unto Zoar.

11 Then Lot chose him all the plain of Jordan ; and Lot journeyed east : and they separated themselves the one from the other.

12 Abram dwelt in the land of Canaan, and Lot dwelt in the cities of the plain, and pitched his tent toward Sodom.

13 But the men of Sodom were wicked and sinners before the LORD exceedingly.

14 And the LORD said unto Abram, after that Lot was separated from him, Lift up now thine eyes, and look from the place where thou art northward, and southward, and eastward, and westward :

15 For all the land which thou seest, to thee will I give it, and to thy children for ever.

16 And I will make thy children as the dust of the earth : so that if a man can number the dust of the earth, then shall they also be numbered.

17 Arise, walk through the land in the length of it and in the breadth of it ; for I will give it unto thee.

18 Then Abram removed his tent, and came and dwelt in the grove of Mamre, which is in Hebron, and built there an altar unto the LORD.

CHAPTER XIV.

AND it came to pass that Kedor-Laomer, king of Elam, made war with Bera, king of Sodom.

2 And there went out the king of Sodom, and the king of Gomorrah, and the king of Admah, and the king of Zeboiim, and the king of Bela, (the same is Zoar:) and they joined the battle with them in the vale of Siddim, which is now the Salt Sea.

3 And the vale of Siddim was full of slimepits; and the king of Sodom and Gomorrah fled, and fell there; and they that remained fled to the mountain.

4 And the enemy took all the goods of Sodom and Gomorrah, and all their victuals, and went their way.

5 And they took Lot, Abram's brother's son, who dwelt in Sodom, and his goods and departed.

6 And there came one that had escaped, and told Abram the Hebrew; for he dwelt in the plain of Mamre the Amorite, brother of Eshcol, and brother of Aner: and these were confederate with Abram.

7 And when Abram heard that his brother was taken captive, he armed his trained servants, born in his own house, three hundred and eighteen, and pursued them unto Dan.

8 And he divided himself against them, he and his servants, by night, and smote them, and pursued them, unto Hobah, which is on the left hand of Damascus.

9 And he brought back all the goods, and also brought again his brother Lot, and his goods, and the women also, and the people.

10 And the king of Sodom went out to meet him, after his return from the slaughter of Kedor-Laomer and of the kings that were with him, at the valley of Shaveh, which is the king's dale.

11 And Melchizedek king of Salem brought forth bread and wine: and he was the priest of the Most High God.

12 And he blessed him, and said, Blessed be Abram of the Most High God, possessor of heaven and earth:

13 And blessed be the Most High God, which hath delivered thine enemies into thy hand. And he gave him tithes of all.

14 And the king of Sodom said unto Abram, Give me the persons, and take the goods to thyself.

15 And Abram said to the king of Sodom, I have lifted up mine hand unto the LORD, the Most High God, the possessor of heaven and earth,

16 That I will not take from a thread even to a shoelatchet, and that I will not take any thing that is thine, lest thou shouldest say, I have made Abram rich:

17 Save only that which the young men have eaten, and the portion of the men which went with me, Aner, Eshcol, and Mamre; let them take their portion.

CHAPTER XV.

AFTER these things the word of the LORD came unto Abram in a vision, saying, Fear not, Abram: I am thy shield, thy reward shall be exceedingly great.

2 And Abram said, LORD GOD, what wilt thou give me, seeing I go childless, and the steward of my house is this Eliezer of Damascus?

3 And Abram said, Behold, to me thou hast given no child: and, lo, one born in my house is mine heir.

4 And, behold, the word of the LORD

came unto him, saying, This one shall not be thine heir; but thine own child shall be thine heir.

5 And he brought him forth abroad, and said, Look now toward heaven, and count the stars, if thou be able to number them: and he said unto him, So shall thy offspring be.

6 And he believed in the LORD; and he counted it to him for righteousness.

7 And he said unto him, I am the LORD that brought thee out of Ur of the Chaldees, to give thee this land to inherit it.

8 And he said, LORD GOD, whereby shall I know that I shall inherit it?

9 And when the sun was going down, a deep sleep fell upon Abram; and, lo, a horror of great darkness fell upon him.

10 And the LORD said unto Abram, Know of a surety that thy children shall be strangers in a land that is not theirs, and shall serve them; and they shall afflict them four hundred years;

11 And also that nation, whom they shall serve, will I judge: and afterward shall they come out with great substance.

12 And thou shalt go to thy fathers in peace; thou shalt be buried in a good old age.

13 But in the fourth generation they shall come hither again: for the iniquity of the Amorites is not yet full.

14 In that same day the LORD made a covenant with Abram, saying, Unto thy children have I given this land, from the river of Egypt unto the great river, the river Euphrates.

CHAPTER XVI.

NOW Sarai, Abram's wife, bare him no children: and she had a handmaid, an Egyptian, whose name was Hagar.

2 And Sarai, Abram's wife, took Hagar her maid the Egyptian, after Abram had dwelt ten years in the land of Canaan, and gave her to her husband Abram to be his wife.

3 And it came to pass that Hagar behaved haughtily toward Sarai. And when Sarai dealt hardly with her, she fled from her face.

4 And the angel of the LORD found her by a fountain of water in the wilderness, by the fountain in the way to Shur.

5 And he said, Hagar, Sarai's maid, whence camest thou? and whither wilt thou go? And she said, I flee from the face of my mistress Sarai.

6 And the angel of the LORD said unto her, Return to thy mistress, and submit thyself under her hands.

7 And the angel of the LORD said unto her, Behold, thou shalt have a son, and shalt call his name Ishmael; because the LORD hath heard thy affliction.

8 And he will be a wild man; his hand will be against every man, and every man's hand against him: and he shall dwell in the presence of all his brethren.

9 And she called the name of the LORD that spoke unto her, Thou God seest me: for she said, Have I also here looked after him that seeth me?

10 Wherefore the well was called Beer-lahai-roi: behold, it is between Kadesh and Bared.

11 And Hagar bare Abram a son: and Abram called his son's name, which Hagar bare, Ishmael.

12 And Abram was fourscore and six years old, when Hagar bare Ishmael to Abram.

CHAPTER XVII.

AND when Abram was ninety years old and nine, the LORD appeared to Abram, and said unto him, I am the Almighty God; walk before me, and be thou perfect.

2 And I will make my covenant between me and thee, and will multiply thee exceedingly.

3 And Abram fell on his face: and God spake with him, saying,

4 As for me, behold, my covenant is with thee, and thou shalt be a father of many nations.

5 Neither shall thy name any more be called Abram, but thy name shall be Abraham; for a father of many nations have I made thee.

6 And I will make thee exceedingly fruitful, and I will make nations of thee, and kings shall come of thee.

7 And I will establish my covenant between me and thee and thy children after thee in their generations, for an everlasting covenant, to be a God unto thee and to thy children after thee.

8 And I will give unto thee, and to thy children after thee, the land wherein thou art a stranger, all the land of Canaan, for an everlasting possession; and I will be their God.

9 And God said unto Abraham, Thou shalt keep my covenant therefore, thou, and thy children after thee in their generations.

10 This is my covenant, which ye shall keep, between me and you and thy children after thee; Every man child among you shall be circumcised.

11 And God said unto Abraham, As for Sarai thy wife, thou shalt not call her name Sarai, but Sarah shall her name be.

12 And I will bless her, and give thee a son also of her: yea, I will bless her, and she shall be a mother of nations; kings of people shall be of her.

13 And Abraham said unto God, O that Ishmael might live before thee!

14 And God said, Sarah thy wife shall bare thee a son indeed; and thou shalt call his name Isaac: and I will establish my covenant with him for an everlasting covenant, and with his children after him.

15 And as for Ishmael, I have heard thee: Behold, I have blessed him, and will make him fruitful, and will multiply him exceedingly; the father of twelve princes shall he be, and I will make him a great nation.

16 But my covenant will I establish with Isaac, which Sarah shall bear unto thee at this set time in the next year.

17 And he left off speaking with him, and God went up from Abraham.

CHAPTER XVIII.

AND God appeared unto him in the grove of Mamre: and he sat in the tent door in the heat of the day;

2 And he lifted up his eyes and looked, and, lo, three men stood by him: and when he saw them, he ran to meet them from the tent door, and bowed himself toward the ground,

3 And said, My Lord, if now I have found favour in thy sight, pass not away, I pray thee, from thy servant:

4 Let a little water, I pray you, be fetched, and wash your feet, and rest yourselves under the tree:

5 And I will fetch a morsel of bread, and comfort ye your hearts; after that ye shall pass on: for therefore are ye come to your servant. And they said, Do so, as thou hast said.

6 And Abraham hastened into the

tent unto Sarah, and said, Make ready quickly three measures of fine meal, knead it, and make cakes upon the hearth.

7 And Abraham ran unto the herd, and fetched a calf tender and good, and gave it unto a young man; and he hasted to dress it.

8 And he took butter, and milk, and the calf which he had dressed, and set it before them; and he stood by them under the tree, and they did eat.

9 And they said unto him, Where is Sarah thy wife? And he said, Behold, in the tent.

10 And he said, I will certainly return unto thee according to the time of life; and, lo, Sarah thy wife shall have a son. And Sarah heard it in the tent door, which was behind him.

11 Now Abraham and Sarah were old and well stricken in age.

12 Therefore Sarah laughed within herself, saying, After I am waxed old shall I have children?

13 And the LORD said unto Abraham, Wherefore did Sarah laugh, saying, Shall I of a surety bear a child, being so old?

14 Is any thing too hard for the LORD? At the time appointed I will return unto thee, according to the time of life, and Sarah shall have a son.

15 Then Sarah denied, saying, I laughed not; for she was afraid. And he said, Nay; but thou didst laugh.

16 And the men rose up from thence, and looked toward Sodom: and Abraham went with them to bring them on the way.

17 And the LORD said, Shall I hide from Abraham that thing which I do;

18 Seeing that Abraham shall surely become a great and mighty nation, and all the nations of the earth shall be blessed in him?

19 For I know him, that he will command his children and his household after him, and they shall keep the way of the LORD, to do justice and judgment; that the LORD may bring upon Abraham that which he hath spoken of him.

20 And the LORD said, Because the cry of Sodom and Gomorrah is great, and because their sin is very grievous,

21 I will go down now, and see whether they have done altogether according to the cry of it, which is come unto me; and if not, I will know.

22 And the men turned their faces from thence, and went toward Sodom: but Abraham stood yet before the LORD.

23 And Abraham drew near, and said, Wilt thou also destroy the righteous with the wicked?

24 Peradventure there be fifty righteous within the city: wilt thou also destroy and not spare the place for the fifty righteous that are therein?

25 That be far from thee to do after this manner, to slay the righteous with the wicked; and that the righteous should be as the wicked, that be far from thee: Shall not the Judge of all the earth do right?

26 And the LORD said, If I find in Sodom fifty righteous within the city, then I will spare all the place for their sakes.

27 And Abraham answered and said, Behold now, I have taken upon me to speak unto the Lord, and I am but dust and ashes:

28 Peradventure there shall lack five of the fifty righteous: wilt thou destroy all the city for lack of five? And he

said, If I find there forty and five, I will not destroy it.

29 And he spake unto him yet again, and said, Peradventure there shall be forty found there. And he said, I will not do it for forty's sake.

30 And he said unto him, Oh let not the Lord be angry, and I will speak: Peradventure there shall thirty be found there. And he said, I will not do it, if I find thirty there.

31. And he said, Behold now, I have taken upon me to speak unto the Lord: Peradventure there shall be twenty found there. And he said, I will not destroy it for twenty's sake.

32 And he said, Oh let not the Lord be angry, and I will speak yet but this once: Peradventure ten shall be found there. And he said, I will not destroy it for ten's sake.

33 And the LORD went his way, as soon as he had left communing with Abraham: and Abraham returned unto his place.

CHAPTER XIX.

AND there came two angels to Sodom at evening; and Lot sat in the gate of Sodom: and Lot seeing them rose up to meet them; and he bowed himself with his face toward the ground;

2 And he said, Behold now, my lords, turn in, I pray you, into your servant's house, and tarry all night, and wash your feet, and ye shall rise up early, and go on your ways. And they said, Nay; but we will abide in the street all night.

3 And he pressed upon them greatly; and they turned in unto him and entered into his house: and he made them a feast, and did bake unleavened bread, and they did eat.

4 But before they lay down, the men of the city, even the men of Sodom, compassed the house round, both old and young, all the people from every quarter:

5 And they called unto Lot, and said unto him, Where are the men which came in to thee this night? bring them out unto us, that we may know them.

6 And Lot went out at the door unto them, and shut the door after him,

7 And said, I pray you, brethren, do not so wickedly: unto these men do no harm; for therefore came they under the shadow of my roof.

8 And they said, Stand back. And they said again, This one fellow came in to sojourn, and he will needs be a judge: now will we deal worse with thee than with them. And they pressed sore upon the man, even Lot, and came near to break the door.

9 But the men put forth their hand, and pulled Lot into the house to them, and shut the door.

10 And they smote the men that were at the door of the house with blindness, both small and great: so that they wearied themselves to find the door.

11 And the men said unto Lot, Hast thou here any besides? son in law, and thy sons, and thy daughters, and whomsoever thou hast in the city, bring them out of this place:

12 For we will destroy this place, because the cry of them is waxen great before the face of the LORD; and the LORD hath sent us to destroy it.

13 And Lot went out, and spoke unto his sons in law, which married his daughters, and said, Up, get out of this place; for the LORD will destroy this city. But he seemed as one that mocked unto his sons in law.

14 And when the morning arose,

then the angels hastened Lot, saying, Arise, take thy wife,˙ and thy two daughters, which are here; lest thou be consumed in the iniquity of the city.

15 And while he lingered, the men laid hold upon his hand, and upon the hand of his wife, and upon the hand of his two daughters, — out of God's mercy unto him: and they brought him forth, and set him without the city.

16 And it came to pass, when they had brought them forth abroad, that he said, Escape for thy life; look not behind thee, neither stay thou in all the plain: escape to the mountain, lest thou be consumed.

17 And Lot said unto them, Oh, not so, my Lord:

18 Behold now, thy servant hath found grace in thy sight, and thou hast magnified thy mercy, which thou hast shewed unto me in saving my life; and I cannot escape to the mountain, lest some evil overtake me, and I die:

19 Behold now, this city is near to flee unto, and it is a little one: O, let me escape thither, and my soul shall live.

20 And he said unto him, See, I have accepted thee concerning this thing also, that I will not overthrow this city, for which thou hast spoken.

21 Haste thee, escape thither; for I cannot do any thing till thou be come thither. Therefore the name of the city was called Zoar.

22 The sun was risen upon the earth when Lot entered into Zoar.

23 Then the LORD rained upon Sodom and upon Gomorrah brimstone and fire from out of heaven;

24 And he overthrew those cities, and all the plain, and all the inhabitants of the cities, and that which grew upon the ground.

25 But Lot's wife looked back from behind him, and she became a pillar of salt.

26 And Abraham got up early in the morning to the place where he stood before the LORD:

27 And he looked toward Sodom and Gomorrah, and toward all the land of the plain, and he saw, and, lo, the smoke of the country went up as the smoke of a furnace.

28 And it came to pass, when God destroyed the cities of the plain, that God remembered Abraham, and sent Lot out of the midst of the overthrow, when he overthrew the cities in which Lot dwelt.

CHAPTER XX.

AND the LORD visited Sarah as he had said, and the LORD remembered Sarah as he had spoken.

2 And Sarah bare Abraham a son in his old age, at the set time of which God had spoken to him.

3 And Abraham called the name of his son that was born unto him, Isaac.

4 And Abraham circumcised his son Isaac when eight days old, as God had commanded him.

5 And Abraham was a hundred years old, when his son Isaac was born unto him.

6 And the child grew, and was weaned: and Abraham made a great feast the same day that Isaac was weaned.

7 And Sarah saw the son of Hagar the Egyptian, which she had borne unto Abraham, mocking.

8 Wherefore she said unto Abraham, Cast out this bondwoman and her son: for the son of this bondwoman shall not be heir with my son, even with Isaac.

9 And the thing was very grievous in Abraham's sight because of his son.

10 And God said unto Abraham, Let it not be grievous in thy sight because of the lad, and because of thy bondwoman; in all that Sarah hath said unto thee, hearken unto her voice; for in Isaac shall thy name be called.

11 And also of the son of the bondwoman will I make a nation, because he is thy child.

12 And Abraham rose up early in the morning, and took bread, and a bottle of water, and gave it unto Hagar, putting it on her shoulder, and the child, and sent her away: and she departed, and wandered in the wilderness of Beer-sheba.

13 And the water was spent in the bottle, and she cast the child under one of the shrubs.

14 And she went, and sat her down over against him a good way off, as it were, a bowshot: for she said, Let me not see the death of the child. And she sat over against him, and lifted up her voice, and wept.

15 And God heard the voice of the lad; and the angel of God called to Hagar out of heaven, and said unto her, What aileth thee, Hagar? fear not; for God hath heard the voice of the lad where he is.

16 Arise, lift up the lad, and hold him in thine hand; for I will make him a great nation.

17 And God opened her eyes, and she saw a well of water; and she went, and filled the bottle with water, and gave the lad drink.

18 And God was with the lad; and he grew, and dwelt in the wilderness, and became an archer.

19 And he dwelt in the wilderness of Paran: and his mother took him a wife out of the land of Egypt.

CHAPTER XXI.

AND it came to pass at that time, that Abimelech and Phichol the chief captain of his host spoke unto Abraham, saying, God is with thee in all that thou doest:

2 Now therefore swear unto me here by God, that thou wilt not deal falsely with me, nor with my son, nor with my son's son: but according to the kindness that I have done unto thee, thou shalt do unto me, and to the land wherein thou hast sojourned.

3 And Abraham said, I will swear.

4 And Abraham reproved Abimelech because of a well of water, which Abimelech's servants had violently taken away.

5 And Abimelech said, I know not who hath done this thing: neither didst thou tell me, neither yet heard I of it, but to day.

6 And Abraham took sheep and oxen, and gave them unto Abimelech; and both of them made a covenant.

7 Wherefore he called that place Beer-sheba; because there they swore peace both of them.

8 Thus they made a covenant at Beer-sheba: then Abimelech rose up, and Phichol the chief captain of his host, and they returned into the land of the Philistines.

9 And Abraham planted a grove in Beer-sheba, and called there on the name of the Lord, the everlasting God.

10 And Abraham sojourned in the Philistines' land many days.

CHAPTER XXII.

AND it came to pass after these things, that God tried Abraham, and said unto him, Abraham: and he said, Behold, here I am.

2 And he said, Take now thy son, thine only son Isaac, whom thou lovest, and get thee into the land of Moriah; and offer him there for a burnt offering upon one of the mountains which I will tell thee of.

3 And Abraham rose up early in the morning, and saddled his ass, and took two of his young men with him, and Isaac his son, and clave the wood for the burnt offering, and rose up, and went unto the place of which God had told him.

4 Then on the third day Abraham lifted up his eyes, and saw the place afar off.

5 And Abraham said unto his young men, Abide ye here with the ass; and I and the lad will go yonder and worship, and come again to you.

6 And Abraham took the wood of the burnt offering, and laid it upon Isaac his son; and he took the fire in his hand, and a knife; and they went both of them together.

7 And Isaac spake unto Abraham his father, and said, My Father; and he said, Here am I, my son. And he said, Behold the fire and the wood: but where is the lamb for a burnt offering?

8 And Abraham said, My son, God will provide himself a lamb for a burnt offering: so they went both of them together.

9 And they came to the place which God had told him of; and Abraham built an altar there, and laid the wood in order, and bound Isaac his son, and laid him on the altar upon the wood.

10 And Abraham stretched forth his hand, and took the knife to slay his son.

11 And the angel of the LORD called unto him out of heaven, and said, Abraham, Abraham: and he said, Here am I.

12 And he said, Lay not thine hand upon the lad, neither do thou any thing unto him: for now I know that thou fearest God, seeing thou hast not withheld thy son, thine only son, from me.

13 And Abraham lifted up his eyes, and looked, and behold, a ram caught in a thicket by his horns: and Abraham went and took the ram, and offered him up for a burnt offering in the stead of his son.

14 And Abraham called the name of that place Adonai-jireh, (God seeth): as it is said to this day, In the mount of the LORD it shall be seen.

15 And the angel of the LORD called unto Abraham out of heaven the second time,

16 And said, By myself have I sworn, saith the LORD, for because thou hast done this thing, and hast not withheld thy son, thine only son,

17 That I will bless thee, and I will multiply thy offspring as the stars of the heaven, and as the sand which is upon the sea shore; and thy offspring shall possess the gate of his enemies;

18 And in thy children shall all the nations of the earth be blessed; because thou hast obeyed my voice.

19 So Abraham returned unto his young men, and they rose up and went together to Beer-sheba; and Abraham dwelt at Beer-sheba.

CHAPTER XXIII.

AND Sarah lived a hundred and seven and twenty years: these were the years of the life of Sarah.

2 And Sarah died in Kirjath-arba; the same is Hebron in the land of

Canaan: and Abraham came to mourn for Sarah, and to weep for her.

3 And Abraham stood up from before his dead, and spoke unto the sons of Heth, saying,

4 I am a stranger and a sojourner with you: give me a possession of a burying-place with you, that I may bury my dead out of my sight.

5 And the children of Heth answered Abraham. saying unto him,

6 Hear us, my lord: thou art a mighty prince among us: in the choice of our sepulchres bury thy dead; none of us shall withhold from thee his sepulchre, but that thou mayest bury thy dead.

7 And Abraham stood up, and bowed himself to the people of the land, even to the children of Heth.

8 And he communed with them, saying, If it be your mind that I should bury my dead out of my sight, hear me, and entreat for me to Ephron the son of Zohar.

9 That he may give me the cave of Machpelah, which he hath, which is in the end of his field; for as much money as it is worth he shall give it me for a possession of a buryingplace amongst you.

10 And Ephron was present among the children of Heth: and Ephron the Hittite answered Abraham in the audience of the children of Heth, even of all that went in at the gate of his city, saying,

11 Nay, my lord, hear me: the field I give thee, and the cave that is therein, I give it thee ; in the presence of the sons of my people give I it thee: bury thy dead.

12 And Abraham bowed down himself before the people of the land.

13 And he spoke unto Ephron in the audience of the people of the land,

saying, But if thou wilt give it, I pray thee, hear me: I will give thee money for the field; take it of me, and I will bury my dead there. ·

14 And Ephron answered Abraham, saying unto him,

15 My lord, hearken unto me: the land is worth four hundred shekels of silver; what is that betwixt me and thee ? bury therefore thy dead.

16 And Abraham hearkened unto Ephron; and Abraham weighed to Ephron the silver, which he had named in the audience of the sons of Heth, four hundred shekels of silver, current money with the merchant.

17 And the field of Ephron, which was in Machpelah, which was before Mamre, the field, and the cave which was therein, and all the trees that were in the field, that were in all the borders round about, were made sure

18 Unto Abraham for a possession, in the presence of the children of Heth, before all that went in at the gate of his city.

19 And after this, Abraham buried Sarah his wife in the cave of the field of Machpelah before Mamre: the same is Hebron in the land of Canaan.

20 And the field, and the cave that is therein, were made sure unto Abraham for a possession of a buryingplace by the sons of Heth.

CHAPTER XXIV. .

AND Abraham was old, and well. stricken in age: and the LORD had blessed Abraham in all things.

2 And Abraham said unto the eldest servant of his house, that ruled over. all that he had, Put, I pray thee, thy hand into mine.

3 And I will make thee swear by the LORD, the God of heaven, and the

God of the earth, that thou shalt not take a wife unto my son of the daughters of the Canaanites, among whom I dwell:

4 But thou shalt go unto my country, and to my kindred, and take a wife unto my son Isaac.

5 And the servant said unto him, Peradventure the woman will not be willing to follow me unto this land: must I needs bring thy son again unto the land from whence thou camest?

6 And Abraham said unto him, Beware thou that thou bring not my son thither again.

7 The LORD God of heaven, which took me from my father's house, and from the land of my kindred, and which spoke unto me, and that sware unto me, saying, Unto thy children will I give this land; he shall send his angel before thee, and thou shalt take a wife unto my son from thence.

8 And if the woman will not be willing to follow thee, then thou shalt be clear from this my oath: only bring not my son thither again.

9 And the servant swore to him concerning that matter.

10 And the servant took ten camels of the camels of his master, and departed; for all the goods of his master were in his hand: and he arose, and went to Mesopotamia, unto the city of Nahor.

11 And he made his camels to kneel down without the city by a well of water at the time of the evening, even the time that women go out to draw water.

12 And he said, O LORD God of my master Abraham, I pray thee, send me good speed this day, and shew kindness unto my master Abraham.

13 Behold, I stand here by the well of water; and the daughters of the men of the city come out to draw water:

14 And let it come to pass, that the damsel to whom I shall say, Let down thy pitcher, I pray thee, that I may drink; and she shall say, Drink, and I will give thy camels drink also: let the same be she that thou hast appointed for thy servant Isaac; and thereby shall I know that thou hast shewed kindness unto my master.

15 And it came to pass, before he had done speaking, that, behold, Rebekah came out, who was born to Bethnel, son of Milcah, the wife of Nahor, Abraham's brother, with her pitcher upon her shoulder.

16 And the damsel was very fair to look upon, and she went down to the well, and filled her pitcher, and came up.

17 And the servant ran to meet her, and said, Let me, I pray thee, drink a little water of thy pitcher.

18 And she said, Drink, my lord: and she hasted, and let down her pitcher upon her hand, and gave him drink.

19 And when she had done giving him drink, she said, I will draw water for thy camels also, until they have done drinking.

20 And she hasted, and emptied her pitcher into the trough, and ran again unto the well to draw water, and drew for all his camels.

21 And the man, wondering at her, held his peace, to wit whether the LORD had made his journey prosperous or not.

22 And it came to pass, as the camels had done drinking, that the man took a golden earring of half a shekel weight, and two bracelets for her hands of ten shekels weight of gold;

23 And said, Whose daughter art

thou? tell me, I pray thee: is there room in thy father's house for us to lodge in?

24 And she said unto him, I am the daughter of Bethuel the son of Milcah, which she bare unto Nahor.

25 She said moreover unto him, We have both straw and provender enough, and room to lodge in.

26 And the man bowed down his head, and worshipped the LORD.

27 And he said, Blessed be the LORD God of my master Abraham, who hath not left destitute my master of his mercy and his truth: I being in the way, the LORD led me to the house of my master's brethren.

28 And the damsel ran, and told them of her mother's house these things.

29 And Rebekah had a brother, and his name was Laban: and Laban ran out unto the man, unto the well.

30 And it came to pass, when he saw the earring, and bracelets upon his sister's hands, and when he heard the words of Rebekah his sister, saying, Thus spoke the man unto me: he came unto the man; and, behold, he stood by the camels at the well.

31 And he said, Come in, thou blessed of the LORD; wherefore standest thou without? for I have prepared the house, and room for the camels.

32 And the man came into the house: and he ungirded his camels, and gave straw and provender for the camels, and water to wash his feet, and the men's feet that were with him.

33 And there was set meat before him to eat: but he said, I will not eat, until I have told mine errand. And he said, Speak on.

34 And he said, I am Abraham's servant.

35 And the LORD hath blessed my master greatly, and he is become great: and he hath given him flocks, and herds, and silver, and gold, and menservants, and maidservants, and camels, and asses.

36 And Sarah my master's wife bare a son to my master when she was old: and unto him hath he given all that he hath.

37 And my master made me swear, saying, Thou shalt not take a wife to my son of the daughters of the Canaanites, in whose land I dwell:

38 But thou shalt go unto my father's house, and to my kindred, and take a wife unto my son.

39 And I said unto my master, Peradventure the woman will not follow me.

40 And he said unto me, The LORD, before whom I walk, will send his angel with thee, and prosper thy way; and thou shalt take a wife for my son of my kindred, and of my father's house:

41 Then shalt thou be clear from this my oath, when thou comest to my kindred; and if they give not thee one, thou shalt be clear from my oath.

42 And I came this day unto the well, and said, O LORD God of my master Abraham, if now thou do prosper my way which I go:

43 Behold, I stand by the well of water: and it shall come to pass, that when the damsel cometh forth to draw water, and I say to her, Give me, I pray thee, a little water of thy pitcher to drink;

44 And she say to me, Both drink thou, and I will also draw for thy camels: let the same be the woman whom the LORD hath appointed for my master's son.

45 And before I had done speaking

in mine heart, behold, Rebekah came forth with her pitcher on her shoulder; and she went down unto the well, and drew water: and I said unto her, Let me drink, I pray thee.

46 And she made haste, and let down her pitcher from her shoulder, and said, Drink, and I will give thy camels drink also: so I drank, and she made the camels drink also.

47 And I asked her, and said, Whose daughter art thou? And she said, The daughter of Bethuel, Nahor's son, whom Milcah bare unto him: and I put the earring upon her face, and the bracelets upon her hands.

48 And I bowed down my head, and worshipped the LORD, and blessed the LORD God of my master Abraham, which had led me in the right way to take my master's brother's daughter unto his son.

49 And now, if ye will deal kindly and truly with my master, tell me: and if not, tell me; that I may turn to the right hand, or to the left.

50 Then Laban and Bethuel answered and said, The thing proceedeth from the LORD: we cannot speak unto thee bad or good.

51 Behold, Rebekah is before thee; take her, and go, and let her be thy master's son's wife, as the LORD hath spoken.

52 And it came to pass, that, when Abraham's servant heard their words, he worshipped the LORD, bowing himself to the earth.

53 And the servant brought forth jewels of silver, and jewels of gold, and raiment, and gave them to Rebekah: he gave also to her brother and to her mother precious things.

54 And they did eat and drink, he and the men that were with him, and tarried all night; and then rose up in the morning, and he said, Send me away unto my master.

55 And her brother and her mother said, Let the damsel abide with us a few days, at the least ten; after that she shall go.

56 And he said unto them, Hinder me not, seeing the LORD hath prospered my way; send me away that I may go to my master.

57 And they said, We will call the damsel, and inquire at her mouth.

58 And they called Rebekah, and said unto her, Wilt thou go with this man? And she said, I will go.

59 And they sent away Rebekah their sister, and her nurse, and Abraham's servant, and his men.

60 And they blessed Rebekah, and said unto her, Thou, O our sister, be thou the mother of thousands, of millions, and let thy children possess the gate of those which hate them.

61 And Rebekah arose, and her damsels and they rode upon the camels, and followed the man: and the servant took Rebekah, and went his way.

62 And Isaac came from the way of the well Lahai-roi; for he dwelt in the south country.

63 And Isaac went out to meditate in the field at the eventide: and he lifted up his eyes, and saw, and behold, the camels were coming.

64 And Rebekah lifted up her eyes, and when she saw Isaac, she lighted off the camel.

65 For she had said unto the servant, What man is this that walketh in the field to meet us? And the servant had said, It is my master: therefore she took a veil, and covered herself.

66 And the servant told Isaac all things that he had done.

67 And Isaac brought her into his mother Sarah's tent, and took Rebekah, and she beame his wife; and he loved her: and Isaac was comforted after his mother's death.

CHAPTER XXV.

THESE are the days of the years of Abraham's life which he lived, a hundred threescore and fifteen years.

2 Then Abraham gave up the ghost, and died in a good old age, an old man, and full of years; and was gathered to his people.

3 And his sons Isaac and Ishmael buried him in the cave of Machpelah, in the field of Ephron the son of Zohar the Hittite, which is before Mamre;

4 The field which Abraham purchasèd of the sons of Heth: there was Abraham buried, and Sarah his wife.

5 And it came to pass after the death of Abraham, that God blessed his son Isaac; and Isaac dwelt by the well Lahai-roi.

6 Now these are the generations of Isaac, Abraham's son.

7 Isaac was forty years old when he took Rebekah to wife, the daughter of Bethuel the Syrian of Padan-aram, the sister to Laban the Syrian.

8 And Isaac entreated the LORD for his wife: and the LORD was entreated of him, and Rebekah his wife bore him twins.

9 And the first one was red, all over like a hairy garment; and they called his name Esau.

10 And after that came his brother, and his hand took hold on Esau's heel; and his name was called Jacob: and Isaac was threescore years old when she bare them.

11 And the boys grew up: and Esau was a cunning hunter, a man of the field; and Jacob was a plain man, dwelling in tents.

12 And Isaac loved Esau, because he did eat of his venison: but Rebekah loved Jacob.

13 And Jacob sod pottage: and Esau came home from the field, and he was faint:

14 And Esau said to Jacob, Feed me, I pray thee, with that same red pottage; for I am faint: therefore was his name called Edom.

15 And Jacob said, Sell me this day thy birthright.

16 And Esau said, Behold, I am at the point to die: and what profit shall this birthright do to me?

17 And Jacob said, Swear to me this day; and he sware unto him: and he sold his birthright unto Jacob.

18 Then Jacob gave Esau bread and pottage of lentiles; and he did eat and drink, and rose up, and went his way. Thus Esau despised his birthright.

CHAPTER XXVI.

AND there was a famine in the land, besides the first famine that was in the days of Abraham. And Isaac went unto Abimelech king of the Philistines unto Gerar.

2 And the LORD appeared unto him, and said, Go not down into Egypt; dwell in the land which I shall tell thee of.

3 Sojourn in this land, and I will be with thee, and will bless thee; for unto thee, and unto thy children, I will give all these countries, and I will perform the oath which I swore unto Abraham thy father;

4 And I will make thy offspring to multiply as the stars of heaven, and will give unto thy children all these

countries; and in thy children shall all the nations of the earth be blessed:

5 Because that Abraham obeyed my voice, and kept my charge, my commandments, my statutes, and my laws.

6 And Isaac dwelt in Gerar.

7 Then Isaac sowed in that land, and received in the same year a hundredfold: and the LORD blessed him.

8 And the man waxed great, and went forward, and grew until he became very rich:

9 For he had possession of flocks, and possession of herds, and great store of servants: and the Philistines envied him.

10 And all the wells which his father's servants had digged in the days of Abraham his father, the Philistines stopped them, and filled them with earth.

11 And Abimelech said unto Isaac, Go from us; for thou art much mightier than we.

12 And Isaac departed thence, and pitched his tent in the valley of Gerar, and dwelt there.

13 And Isaac digged again the wells of water, which they had digged in the days of Abraham his father; for the Philistines had stopped them after the death of Abraham: and he called their names after the names by which his father had called them.

14 And Isaac's servants digged in the valley, and found there a well of springing water.

15 And the herdmen of Gerar did strive with Isaac's herdmen, saying, The water is ours: and he called the name of the well Esek (Strife); because they strove with him.

16 And they digged another well, and strove for that also: and he called the name of it Sitnah (Quarrel).

17 And he removed from thence, and digged another well; and for that they strove not: and he called the name of it Rehoboth (Enlargement); and he said, For now the LORD hath made room for us, and we shall be fruitful in the land.

18 And he went up from thence to Beer-sheba.

19 And the LORD appeared unto him the same. night, and said, I am the God of Abraham thy father: fear not, for I am with thee, and will bless thee, and multiply thee for my servant Abraham's sake.

20 And he builded an altar there, and called upon the name of the LORD, and pitched his tent there: and there Isaac's servants digged a well.

21 Then Abimelech went to him from Gerar, and Ahuzzath one of his friends, and Phichol the chief captain of his army.

22 And Isaac said unto them, Wherefore come ye to me, seeing ye hate me, and have sent me away from you?

23 And they said, We saw certainly that the LORD was with thee: and we said, Let there be now an oath betwixt us, even between us and thee, and let us make a covenant with thee;

24 That thou wilt do us no hurt, as we have not touched thee, and as we have done unto thee nothing but good, and have sent thee away in peace: thou art now the blessed of the LORD.

25 And he made them a feast, and they did eat and drink.

26 And they rose up betimes in the morning, and swore peace one to another: and Isaac sent them away, and they departed from him in peace.

27 And it came to pass the same day, that Isaac's servants came, and told him concerning the well which

they had digged, and said unto him, We have found water.

28 And he called it Shebah (Swearing): therefore the name of the city is Beer-sheba unto this day.

29 And Esau took to wife Judith the daughter of Beeri the Hittite, and Bassemath the daughter of Elon the Hittite:

30 Which were a grief of mind unto Isaac and to Rebekah. .

CHAPTER XXVII.

AND it came to pass, that when Isaac was old, and his eyes were dim, so that he could not see, he called Esau his eldest son, and said unto him, My son: and he said unto him, Behold, here am I.

2 And he said, Behold now, I am old, I know not the day of my death:

3 Now therefore take, I pray thee, thy weapons, thy quiver and thy bow, and go out to the field, and take me some venison;

4 And make me savoury meat, such as I love, and bring it to me, that I may eat; that my soul may bless thee before I die.

5 And Rebekah heard when Isaac spake to Esau his son. And Esau went to the field to hunt for venison, and to bring it.

6 And Rebekah spoke unto Jacob her son, saying, Behold, I heard thy father speak unto Esau thy brother, saying,

7 Bring me venison, and make me savoury meat, that I may eat, and bless thee before the LORD before my death.

8 Now therefore, my son, obey my voice according to that which I command thee.

9 Go now to the flock, and fetch me from thence two good kids of the goats; and I will make them savoury meat for thy father, such as he loveth:

10 And thou shalt bring it to thy father, that he may eat, and that he may bless thee before his death.

11 And Jacob said to Rebekah his mother, Behold, Esau my brother is a hairy man, and I am a smooth man:

12 My father peradventure will feel me, and I shall seem to him as a deceiver; and I shall bring a curse upon me, and not a blessing.

13 And his mother said unto him, Upon me be thy curse, my son: only obey my voice, and go fetch me them.

14 And he went, and fetched, and brought them to his mother: and his mother made savoury meat, such as his father loved.

15 And Rebekah took the goodly raiment of her eldest son Esau, which were with her in the house, and put them upon Jacob her younger son:

16 And she put the skins of the kids of the goats upon his hands, and upon the smooth of his neck:

17 And she gave the savoury meat and the bread, which she had prepared, into the hand of her son Jacob.

18 And he came unto his father, and said, My father: and he said, Here am I; who art thou my son?

19 And Jacob said unto his father, I am Esau thy firstborn; I have done according as thou badest me: arise, I pray thee, sit and eat of my venison, that thy soul may bless me.

20 And Isaac said unto his son, How is it that thou hast found it so quickly, my son? And he said, Because the LORD thy God brought it to me.

21 And Isaac said unto Jacob, Come near, I pray thee, that I may feel

thee, my son, whether thou be my son Esau or not.

22 And Jacob went near unto Isaac his father; and he felt him, and said, The voice is Jacob's voice, but the hands are the hands of Esau.

23 And he discerned him not, because his hands were hairy, as his brother Esau's hands: so he blessed him.

24 And he said, Art thou my very son Esau? And he said, I am.

25 And he said, Bring it near to me, and I will eat of my son's venison, that my soul may bless thee. And he brought it near to him, and he did eat: and he brought him wine, and he drank.

26 And his father Isaac said unto him, Come near now, and kiss me, my son.

27 And he came near, and kissed him: and he smelled the smell of his raiment, and blessed him, and said, See, the smell of my son is as the smell of the field which the LORD hath blessed:

28 Therefore God give thee of the dew of heaven, and the fatness of the earth, and plenty of corn and wine:

29 Let people serve thee, and nations bow down to thee: be lord over thy brethren, and let thy mother's sons bow down to thee: cursed be every one that curseth thee, and blessed be he that blesseth thee.

30 And it came to pass, as soon as Isaac had made an end of blessing Jacob, and Jacob was yet scarce gone out from the presence of Isaac his father, that Esau his brother came in from his hunting.

31 And he also had made savoury meat, and brought it unto his father, and said unto his father, Let my father arise, and eat of his son's venison, that thy soul may bless me.

32 And Isaac his father said unto him, Who art thou? And he said, I am thy son, thy firstborn, Esau.

33 And Isaac trembled very exceedingly, and said, Who? where is he that hath taken venison, and brought it me, and I have eaten of all before thou camest, and have blessed him? yea, and he shall be blessed.

34 And when Esau heard the words of his father, he cried with a great and exceeding bitter cry, and said unto his father, Bless me, even me also, O my father.

35 And he said, Thy brother came with subtilty, and hath taken away thy blessing.

36 And he said, Is not he rightly named Jacob? for he hath supplanted me these two times: he took away my birthright; and, behold, now he hath taken away my blessing. And he said, Hast thou not reserved a blessing for me?

37 And Isaac answered and said unto Esau, Behold, I have made him thy lord, and all his brethren have I given to him for servants; and with corn and wine have I sustained him: and what shall I do now unto thee, my son?

38 And Esau said unto his father, Hast thou but one blessing, my father? bless me, even me also, O my father. And Esau lifted up his voice, and wept.

39 And Isaac his father answered and said unto him, Behold, thy dwelling shall be the fatness of the earth, and of the dew of heaven from above;

40 And by the sword shalt thou live, and shalt serve thy brother: and it shall come to pass when thou shalt

have the dominion, that thou shalt break his yoke from off thy neck.

41 And Esau hated Jacob because of the blessing wherewith his father blessed him: and Esau said in his heart, The days of mourning for my father are at hand; then will I slay my brother Jacob.

42 And these words of Esau her elder son were told to Rebekah: and she sent and called Jacob her younger son, and said unto him, Behold, thy brother Esau doth intend to kill thee.

43 Now therefore, my son, obey my voice; and arise, flee thou to Laban my brother to Haran;

44 And tarry with him a few days, until thy brother's fury turn away;

45 Until thy brother's anger turn away from thee, and he forget that which thou hast done to him: then I will send, and fetch thee from thence: why should I be deprived also of you both in one day? .

46 And Rebekah said to Isaac, I am weary of my life because of the daughters of Heth, such as these which are of the daughters of the land, what good shall my life do me?

CHAPTER XXVIII.

A^ND Isaac called Jacob, and blessed him, and charged him, and said unto him, Thou shalt not take a wife of the daughters of Canaan.

2 Arise, go to Padan-aram, to the house of Bethuel thy mother's father; and take thee a wife from thence of the daughters of Laban thy mother's brother.

3 And God Almighty bless thee, and make thee fruitful, and multiply thee, that thou mayest be a multitude of people;

4 And give thee the blessing of Abraham, to thee, and to thy children with the; that thou mayest inherit the land wherein thou art a stranger, which God gave unto Abraham.

5 And Isaac sent away Jacob: and he went to Padan-aram unto Laban, son of Bethuel the Syrian, the brother of Rebekah, Jacob's and Esau's mother.

6 And Jacob went out from Beersheba, and went toward Haran.

7 And he lighted upon a certain place, and tarried there all night, because the sun had set; and he took of the stones of that place, and put them for his pillows, and lay down in that place to sleep.

8 And he dreamed, and behold a ladder set up on the earth, and the top of it reached to heaven: and behold the angels of God ascending and descending on it.

9 And, behold, the LORD stood above him, and said, I am the LORD God of Abraham thy father, and the God of Isaac: the land whereon thou liest, to thee will I give it, and to thy children;

10 And thy children shall be as the dust of the earth; and thou shalt spread abroad to the west, and to the east, and to the north, and to the south: and in thee and in thy children shall all the families of the earth be blessed.

11 And, behold, I am with thee, and will keep thee in all places whither thou goest, and will bring thee again into this land; for I will not leave thee, until I have done that which I have spoken to thee of.

12 And Jacob awaked out of his sleep, and he said, Surely the LORD is in this place; and I knew it not.

13 And he was afraid, and said, How sublime is this place! this is

none other but the house of God, and this is the gate of heaven.

14 And Jacob rose up early in the morning, and took the stone that he had put for his pillows, and set it up for a pillar, and poured oil upon the top of it.

15 And he called the name of that place Beth-el: but the name of that city was called Luz at the first.

16 And Jacob vowed a vow, saying, If God will be with me, and will keep me in this way that I go, and will give me bread to eat, and raiment to put on,

17 So that I come again to my father's house in peace; then shall the LORD be my God:

18 And this stone, which I have set for a pillar, shall be God's house: and of all that thou shalt give me I will surely give the tenth unto thee.

CHAPTER XXIX.

THEN Jacob went on his journey, and came into the land of the people of the east.

2 And he looked, and behold a well in the field, and, lo, there were three flocks of sheep lying by it; for out of that well they watered the flocks: and a great stone was upon the well's mouth.

3 And thither were all the flocks gathered: and they rolled the stone from the well's mouth, and watered the sheep, and put the stone again upon the well's mouth in his place.

4 And Jacob said unto them, My brethren, whence be ye? And they said, Of Haran are we.

5 And he said unto them, Know ye Laban the son of Nahor? And they said, We know him.

6 And he said unto them, Is he well? And they said, He is well: and,

behold, Rachel his daughter cometh with the sheep.

7 And he said, Lo, it is yet high day, neither is it time that the cattle should be gathered together: water ye the sheep, and go and feed them.

8 And they said, We cannot, until all the flocks be gathered together, and till they roll the stone from the well's mouth; then we water the sheep.

9 And while he yet spoke with them, Rachel came with her father's sheep: for she kept them.

10 And it came to pass, when Jacob saw Rachel the daughter of Laban his mother's brother, and the sheep of Laban his mother's brother, that Jacob went near, and rolled the stone from the well's mouth, and watered the flock of Laban his mother's brother.

11 And Jacob kissed Rachel, and lifted up his voice, and wept.

12 And Jacob told Rachel that he was her father's brother, and that he was Rebekah's son: and she ran and told her father.

13 And it came to pass, when Laban heard the tidings of Jacob his sister's son, that he ran to meet him, and embraced him, and kissed him, and brought him to his house. And he told Laban all these things.

14 And Laban said to him, Surely thou art my bone and my flesh. And he abode with him the space of a month.

15 And Laban said unto Jacob, Because thou art my brother, shouldest thou therefore serve me for nought? tell me, what shall thy wages be?

16 And Laban had two daughters: the name of the elder was Leah, and and the name of the younger was Rachel.

17 Leah was weak-eyed; but Rachel was beautiful and well favoured.

18 And Jacob loved Rachel; and said, I will serve thee seven years for Rachel thy younger daughter.

19 And Laban said, It is better that I give her to thee, than that I should give her to another man: abide with me.

20 And Jacob served seven years for Rachel; and they seemed unto him but a few days, for the love he had to her.

21 And Jacob said unto Laban, Give me my wife, for my days are fulfilled.

22 And Laban gathered together all the men of the place, and made a feast.

23 And it came to pass when the wedding-hour arrived, that he took Leah his daughter, and brought her to him.

24 And Laban gave unto his daughter Leah Zilpah his maid for a handmaid.

25 And Jacob said to Laban, What is this thou hast done unto me? did not I serve with thee for Rachel? wherefore then hast thou beguiled me?

26 And Laban said, It must not be so done in our country, to give the younger before the firstborn.

27 Fulfil her week, and we will give thee this also for the service which thou shalt serve with me yet seven other years.

28 And Jacob did so, and fulfilled her week: and he gave him Rachel his daughter to wife also.

29 And Laban gave to Rachel his daughter Bilhah his handmaid to be her maid.

30 And he loved Rachel more than Leah, and served with him yet seven other years.

31 And there were born unto Jacob twelve sons and one daughter.

32 Leah bare unto him: Reuben, Simeon, Levi, Judah, Issachar and Zebulun, and one daughter, Dinah;

33 Zilpah, Leah's maid, bare him two sons: Gad and Asher;

34 Bilhah Rachel's maid bare him two sons: Dan and Naphtali.

35 And Rachel had two sons: Joseph and Benjamin.

CHAPTER XXX.

AND it came to pass, when Rachel had born Joseph, that Jacob said unto Laban, Send me away, that I may go unto mine own place, and to my country.

2 Give me my wives and my children, for whom I have served thee, and let me go: for thou knowest my service which I have done thee.

3 And Laban said unto him, I pray thee, if I have found favour in thine eyes, tarry: for I have learned by divination that the LORD hath blessed me for thy sake.

4 And he said, Appoint me thy wages, and I will give it.

5 And he said unto him, Thou knowest how I have served thee, and how thy cattle was with me.

6 For it was little which thou hadst before I came, and it is now increased unto a multitude; and the LORD hath blessed thee since my coming: and, now, when shall I provide for mine own house also?

7 And he said, What shall I give thee? And Jacob said, Thou shalt not give me any thing: if thou wilt do this thing for me, I will again feed and keep thy flock.

8 I will pass through all thy flock to day, removing from thence all the speckled and spotted cattle, and all the brown cattle among the sheep, and the

spotted and speckled among the goats: and of such shall be my hire.

9 So shall my righteousness answer for me in time to come, when it shall come for my hire before thy face: every one that is not speckled and spotted among the goats, and brown among the sheep, that shall be counted stolen with me.

10 And Laban said, Behold, I would it might be according to thy word.

11 And the man increased exceedingly, and had much cattle, and maidservants, and menservants, and camels, and asses.

CHAPTER XXXI.

AND Jacob heard the words of Laban's sons, saying, Jacob hath taken away all that was our father's; and of that which was our father's hath he gotten all this glory.

2 And Jacob beheld the countenance of Laban, and, behold, it was not toward him as before.

3 And the LORD said unto Jacob, Return unto the land of thy fathers, and to thy kindred; and I will be with thee.

4 And Jacob sent and called Rachel and Leah to the field unto his flock,

5 And said unto them, I see your father's countenance, that it is not toward me as before; but the God of my father hath been with me.

6 And ye know that with all my power I have served your father.

7 And the angel of God spake unto me in a dream, saying, Jacob: and I said, Here am I.

8 And he said, I am the God of Beth-el, where thou anointedst the pillar, and where thou vowedst a vow unto me: now arise, get thee out from this land, and return unto the land of thy kindred.

9 And Rachel and Leah answered and said unto him, Is there yet any portion or inheritance for us in our father's house?

10 Are we not counted of him as strangers? Now then, whatsoever God hath said unto thee, do.

11 Then Jacob rose up, and set his sons and his wives upon camels;

12 And he carried away all his cattle, and all his goods which he had gotten in Padan-aram, to go to Isaac his father in the land of Canaan.

13 And Laban went to shear his sheep: and Rachel had stolen the images that were her father's.

14 And Jacob stole away unawares to Laban the Syrian, in that he told him not that he fled.

15 So he fled with all that he had; and he rose up, and passed over the river, and set his face toward the mount Gilead.

16 And it was told Laban on the third day, that Jacob was fled.

17 And he took his brethren with him, and pursued after him seven days' journey; and they overtook him in the mount Gilead.

18 And God came to Laban the Syrian in a dream by night, and said unto him, Take heed, that thou speak not to Jacob either good or bad.

19 Then Laban overtook Jacob. Now Jacob had pitched his tent in the mount: and Laban with his brethren pitched in the mount of Gilead.

20 And Laban said to Jacob, What hast thou done, that thou hast stolen away unawares to me, and carried away my daughters, as captives taken with the sword?

21 Wherefore didst thou flee away

secretly, and steal away from me; and didst not tell me, that I might have sent thee away with mirth, and with songs, with tabret, and with harp?

22 And hast not suffered me to kiss my sons and my daughters? thou hast now done foolishly in so doing. ·

23 It is in the power of my hand to do you hurt: but the God of your father spake unto me yesternight, saying, Take thou heed that thou speak not to Jacob either good or bad.

24 And now, though thou wouldest needs be gone, because thou sore longedst after thy father's house, yet wherefore hast thou stolen my gods?

25 And Jacob answered and said to Laban, Because I was afraid: for I said, Peradventure thou wouldest take by force thy daughters from me.

26 With whomsoever thou findest thy gods, let him not live: before our brethen discern thou what is thine with me, and take it to thee. But Jacob knew not that Rachel had stolen them.

27 And Laban went into Jacob's tent, and into Leah's tent, and into the two maidservants' tents; but he found them not. Then went he out of Leah's tent, and entered into Rachel's tent.

28 Now Rachel had taken the images, and put them in the camel's furniture, and sat upon them. And Laban searched all the tent, but found them not.

29 And she said to her father, Let it not displease my lord that I cannot rise up before thee; for I am not well. And he searched, but found not the images.

30 And Jacob was wroth, and chode with Laban: and Jacob answered and said to Laban, What is my trespass?

what is my sin, that thou hast so hotly pursued after me?

31 Whereas thou hast searched all my stuff, what hast thou found of all thy household stuff? set it here before my brethren and thy brethren, that they may judge between us both.

32 These twenty years have I been with thee; thy ewes and thy goats have not suffered, and the rams of thy flock have I not eaten.

33 That which was torn of beasts. I brought not unto thee; I bare the loss of it; of my hand didst thou require it, whether stolen by day, or stolen by night.

34 Thus was I treated; in the day the drought consumed me, and the frost by night; and my sleep departed from mine eyes.

35 Thus have I been twenty years in thy house: I served thee fourteen years for thy two daughters, and six years for thy cattle; and thou hast changed my wages ten times.

36 Except the God of my father, the God of Abraham, and the fear of Isaac, had been with me, surely thou hadst sent me away now empty. God hath seen mine affliction and the labour of my hands, and rebuked thee yesternight.

37 And Laban answered and said unto Jacob, These daughters are my daughters, and these children are my children, and these cattle are my cattle, and all that thou seest is mine: and what can I do this day unto these my daughters, or unto their children which they have born?

38 Now therefore come thou, let us make a covenant, I and thou; and let it be for a witness between me and thee.

39 And Jacob took a stone, and set it up for a pillar.

40 And Jacob said unto his brethren, Gather stones; and they took stones, and made a heap: and they did eat there upon the heap.

41 And Laban called it Jegar-sahadutha: but Jacob called it Galeed.

42 And Laban said, This heap is a witness between me and thee this day. Therefore was the name of it called Galeed,

43 And Mizpah; for he said, The LORD watch between me and thee, when we are absent one from another.

44 If thou shalt afflict my daughters, or if thou shalt take other wives beside my daughters, no man is with us: see, God is witness between me and thee.

45 And Laban said to Jacob, Behold this heap, and behold this pillar, which I have cast between me and thee;

46 This heap be witness, and this pillar be witness, that I will not pass over this heap to thee, and that thou shalt not pass over this heap and this pillar unto me, for harm.

47 The God of Abraham, and the God of Nahor, the God of their father, judge between us. And Jacob sware by the fear of his father Isaac.

48 Then Jacob offered sacrifice upon the mount, and called his brethren to eat bread: and they did eat bread, and tarried all night on the mount.

49 And early in the morning Laban rose up, and kissed his sons and his daughters, and blessed them: and Laban departed, and returned unto his place.

CHAPTER XXXII.

AND Jacob went on his way, and the angels of God met him.

2 And when Jacob saw them, he said, This is God's host: and he called the name of that place Mahanaim.

3 And Jacob sent messengers before him to Esau his brother unto the land of Seir, the country of Edom.

4 And he commanded them, saying, Thus shall ye speak unto my lord Esau; Thy servant Jacob saith thus, I have sojourned with Laban, and stayed there until now:

5 And I have oxen, and asses, flocks, and men-servants, and maid-servants: and I have sent to tell my lord, that I may find grace in thy sight.

6 And the messengers returned to Jacob, saying, We came to thy brother Esau, and also he cometh to meet thee, and four hundred men with him.

7 Then Jacob was greatly afraid and distressed: and he divided the people that was with him, and the flocks, and herds, and the camels, into two bands;

8 And said, If Esau come to the one company, and smite it, then the other company which is left shall escape.

9 And Jacob said, O God of my father Abraham, and God of my father Isaac, the LORD which saidst unto me, Return unto thy country, and to thy kindred, and I will deal well with thee:

10 I am not worthy of the least of all the mercies, and of all the truth, which thou hast shewed unto thy servant; for with my staff I passed over this Jordan; and now I am become two camps.

11 Deliver me, I pray thee, from the hand of my brother, from the hand of Esau: for I fear him, lest he will come and smite me, both, the mother with the children.

12 And thou saidst, I will surely do thee good, and make thy offspring as the sand of the sea, which cannot be numbered for multitude.

13 And he lodged there that same

night; and took of that which came to his hand a present for Esau his brother;

14 Two hundred she-goats and twenty he-goats, two hundred ewes and twenty rams,

15 Thirty milch camels with their colts, forty kine and ten bulls, twenty asses and ten foals.

16 And he delivered them into the hand of his servants, every drove by themselves; and said unto his servants, Pass over before me, and put a space between drove and drove.

17 And he commanded the foremost, saying, When Esau my brother meeteth thee, and asketh thee, saying, Whose art thou? and whither goest thou? and whose are these before thee?

18 Then thou shalt say, They be thy servant Jacob's; it is a present sent unto my lord Esau: and, behold, also he is behind us.

19 And so commanded he the second, and the third, and all that followed the droves, saying, On this manner shall ye speak unto Esau, when ye find him.

20 And say ye moreover, Behold, thy servant Jacob is behind us. For he said, I will appease him with the present that goeth before me, and afterward I will see his face; peradventure he will accept of me.

21 So went the present over before him; and he himself lodged that night in the company.

22 And he rose up that night, and took his two wives, and his two womenservants, and his eleven sons. and passed over the ford Jabbok.

23 And he took them, and sent them over the brook, and sent over all that he had.

24 And Jacob was left alone; and there wrestled a man with him until the breaking of the day.

25. And when he saw that he prevailed not against him, he touched the hollow of his thigh; and the hollow of Jacob's thigh was out of joint, as he wrestled with him.

26 And he said, Let me go, for the day breaketh. And he said, I will not let thee go, except thou wilt bless me.

27 And he said unto him. What is thy name? And he said, Jacob.

28 And he said, Thy name shall be called no more Jacob, but Israel: for as a prince hast thou power with God and with men, and hast prevailed.

29 And Jacob asked him, and said, Tell me, I pray thee, thy name. And he said, Wherefore dost thou ask after my name? And he blessed him there.

30 And Jacob called the name of the place Peniel: for I have seen God face to face, and my life is preserved.

31 And as he passed over Penuel the sun rose upon him, and he halted upon his thigh.

CHAPTER XXXIII.

AND Jacob lifted up his eyes, and looked, and, behold, Esau came, and with him four hundred men. And he divided the children unto Leah, and unto Rachel, and unto the two handmaids.

2 And he put the handmaids and their children foremost, and Leah and her children after, and Rachel and Joseph hindermost.

3 And he passed over before them, and bowed himself to the ground seven times, until he came near to his brother.

4 And Esau ran to meet him, and embraced him, and fell on his neck, and kissed him: and they wept.

5 And he lifted up his eyes, and saw

the women and the children, and said, Who are those with thee? And he said, The children which God hath graciously given thy servant.

6 Then the handmaidens came near, they and their children, and they bowed themselves.

7 And Leah also with with her children came near, and bowed themselves: and after came Joseph near and Rachel, and they bowed themselves.

8 And he said, What meanest thou by all this drove which I met? And he said, These are to find grace in the sight of my lord.

9 And Esau said, I have enough, my brother; keep thou what thou hast unto thyself.

10 And Jacob said, Nay, I pray thee, if now I have found grace in thy sight, then receive my present at my hand: for therefore I have seen thy face, as though I had seen the face of God, and thou wast pleased with me,

11 Take, I pray thee, my blessing that is brought to thee; because God hath dealt graciously with me, and because I have enough. And he urged him, and he took it.

12 And he said, Let us take our journey, and let us go together, and I will go before thee.

13 And he said unto him, My lord knoweth that the children are tender, and the flocks and herds with their young are with me; and if men should overdrive them one day, all the flock will die.

14 Let my lord, I pray thee, pass over before his servant; and I will lead on softly, according as the cattle that goeth before me and the children be able to endure, until I come unto my lord unto Seir.

15 And Esau said, Let me now leave with thee some of the folk that are with me. And he said, What needeth it? let me find grace in the sight of my lord.

16 So Esau returned that day on his way unto Seir.

17 And Jacob journeyed to Succoth, and built him a house, and made booths for his cattle: therefore the name of the place is called Succoth.

18 And Jacob came safely to the city of Shechem, which is in the land of Canaan, when he came from Padan-aram; and pitched his tent before the city.

19 And he bought a parcel of a field, where he had spread his tent, at the hand of the children of Hamor, Sheeb-em's father, for a hundred pieces of money.

20 And he erected there an altar, and called it El-Elohe-Israel, (LORD God of Israel).

CHAPTER XXXIV.

AND Dinah, the daughter of Leah, went out to see the daughters of the land.

2 And when Shechem the son of Hamor the Hivite, prince of the country, saw her, he took her, and brought her to his father's house.

3 And his soul clave unto Dinah the daughter of Jacob, and he loved the damsel, and spoke kindly unto the damsel.

4 And Shechem spoke unto his father Hamor, saying, Get me this damsel to wife.

5 And Jacob heard what befell Dinah his daughter: now his sons were with his cattle in the field: and Jacob held his peace until they were come.

6 And Hamor the father of Shechem

went out unto Jacob to commune with him.

7 And the sons of Jacob came out of the field when they heard it, and the men were grieved, and they were very wroth.

8 And Hamor communed with them, saying, The soul of my son Shechem longeth for your daughter: I pray you give her him to wife.

9 And make ye marriages with us, and give your daughters unto us, and take our daughters unto you.

10 And ye shall dwell with us: and the land shall be before you; dwell and trade ye therein, and get you possessions therein.

11 And Shechem said unto her father and unto her brethren, Let me find grace in your eyes, and what ye shall say unto me I will give.

12 Ask me never so much dowry and gift, and I will give according as ye shall say unto me: but give me the damsel to wife.

13 And the sons of Jacob answered Shechem and Hamor his father deceitfully, and said unto them, We cannot do this thing, to give our sister to one that is not of our own faith; for that were a reproach unto us.:

14 But in this will we consent unto you: If ye will be as we be,

15 Then will we give our daughters unto you, and we will take your daughters to us, and we will dwell with you, and we will become one people.

16 But if ye will not hearken unto us, then will we take our daughter, and we will be gone.

17 And their words pleased Hamor and Shechem Hamor's son.

18 And the young man deferred not to do the thing, because he had delight in Jacob's daughter: and he was more honourable than all the house of his father.

19 And Hamor and Shechem his son came unto the gate of their city, and communed with the men of their city, saying,

20 These men are peaceable with us; therefore let them dwell in the land, and trade therein; for the land, behold, it is large enough for them; let us take their daughters to us for wives, and let us give them our daughters.

21 Only herein will the men consent unto us for to dwell with us, to be one people, if we all be of their faith.

22 Shall not their cattle and their substance and every beast of theirs be ours? only let us consent unto them, and they will dwell with us.

23 And unto Hamor and unto Shechem his son hearkened all that went out of the gate of his city, and did according to their words.

24 And it came to pass when they were unaware, that two of the sons of Jacob, Simeon and Levi, Dinah's brethren, took each man his sword, and came upon the city boldly, and slew all the males.

25 And they slew Hamor and Shechem his son with the edge of the sword, and took Dinah out of Shechem's house, and went out.

26 And Jacob said to Simeon and Levi, Ye have troubled me to make me to be hated among the inhabitants of the land, among the Canaanites and the Perizzites: and I being few in number, they shall gather themselves together against me, and slay me; and I shall be destroyed, I and my house.

27 And they said, Should he deal with our sister in such a manner?

CHAPTER XXXV.

AND God said unto Jacob, Arise, go up to Beth-el, and dwell there; and make there an altar unto God, that appeared unto thee when thou didst flee from the face of Esau thy brother.

2 Then Jacob said unto his household, and to all that were with him, Put away the strange gods that are among you, and be clean, and change your garments :

3 And let us arise, and go up to Beth-el ; and I will make there an altar unto God, who answered me in the day of my distress, and was with me in the way which I went.

4 And they gave unto Jacob all the strange gods which were in their hand, and all their earrings which were in their ears ; and Jacob hid them under the oak which was by Shechem.

5 And they journeyed: and the terror of God was upon the cities that were round about them, and they did not pursue after the sons of Jacob.

6 So Jacob came to Luz, which is in the land of Canaan, that is, Beth-el, he and all the people that were with him.

7 And he built there an altar, and called the place El-beth-el ; because there God appeared unto him, when he fled from the face of his brother.

8 There Deborah Rebekah's nurse died, and she was buried beneath Beth-el under an oak : and the name of it was called Allon-bachuth.

9 And God appeared unto Jacob again, when he came out of Padan-aram, and blessed him.

10 And God said unto him, Thy name is Jacob: thy name shall not be called any more Jacob, but Israel shall be thy name ; and he called his name Israel.

11 And God said unto him, I am God Almighty : be fruitful and multiply; a nation and a company of nations shall be of thee, and thou shalt be the father of kings.

12 And the land which I gave Abraham and Isaac, to thee I will give it, and to thy children after thee will I give the land.

13 And Jacob set up a pillar in the place where he talked with him, even a pillar of stone : and he poured a drink offering thereon, and he poured oil thereon.

14 And Jacob called the name of the place where God spoke with him, Beth-el.

15 And they journeyed from Beth-el; and there was but a little way to come to Ephrath, when Rachel bore a son.

16 And it came to pass, as her soul was in departing, (for she died,) that she called his name Ben-oni : but his father called him Benjamin.

17 And Rachel died, and was buried in the way to Ephrath, which is Beth-lehem.

18 And Jacob set a pillar upon her grave : that is the pillar of Rachel's grave unto this day.

19 And Israel journeyed, and spread his tent beyond the tower of Edar.

20 Now the sons of Jacob were twelve : The sons of Leah ; Reuben, Jacob's firstborn, and Simeon, and Levi, and Judah, and Issachar, and Zebulun :

21 The sons of Rachel; Joseph, and Benjamin :

22 And the sons of Bilhah, Rachel's handmaid ; Dan, and Naphtali :

23 And the sons of Zilpah, Leah's

handmaid ; Gad, and Asher. These are the sons of Jacob, which were born to him in Padan-aram.

24 And Jacob came unto Isaac his father unto Mamre, unto the city of Arba, which is Hebron, where Abraham and Isaac sojourned.

25 And the days of Isaac were a hundred and fourscore years.

26 And Isaac gave up the ghost, and died, and was gathered unto his people, being old and full of days : and his sons Esau and Jacob buried him.

CHAPTER XXXVI.

AND Jacob dwelt in the land wherein his father was a stranger, in the land of Canaan.

2 These are the generations of Jacob. Joseph, being seventeen years old, was feeding the flock with his brethren ; and the lad was with the sons of Bilhah, and with the sons of Zilpah : and Joseph brought unto his father the evil report of his brethern.

3 Now Israel loved Joseph more than all his children, because he was the son of his old age : and he made him a coat of bright colours.

4 And when his brethren saw that their father loved him more than all his brethren, they hated him, and could not speak kindly unto him.

5 And Joseph dreamed a dream, and he told it his brethren : and they hated him yet the more.

6 And he said unto them, Hear, I pray you, this dream which I have dreamed :

7 For, behold, we were binding sheaves in the field, and, lo, my sheaf arose, and also stood upright ; and, behold, your sheaves stood round about, and made obeisance to my sheaf.

8 And his brethren said to him, Shalt thou indeed reign over us ? or shalt thou indeed have dominion over us ? And they hated him yet the more for his dreams, and for his words.

9 And he dreamed yet another dream, and told it his brethren, and said, Behold, I have dreamed a dream more ; and behold, the sun and the moon and the eleven stars made obeisance to me.

10 And he told it to his father, and to his brethren : and his father rebuked him, and said unto him, What is this dream that thou hast dreamed ? Shall I and thy mother and thy brethren indeed come to bow down ourselves to thee to the earth ?

11 And his brethren envied him ; but his father observed the matter.

CHAPTER XXXVII.

ONCE his brethren went to feed their father's flock in Schechem.

2 And Israel said unto Joseph, Do not thy brethren feed the flock in Schechem ? come, and I will send thee unto them. And he said to him, Here am I.

3 And he said to him, Go, I pray thee, see whether it be well with thy brethren, and well with the flocks ; and bring me word again. So he sent him out of the vale of Hebron, and he came to Shechem.

4 And a certain man found him, and, behold, he was wandering in the field : and the man asked him, saying, What seekest thou ?

5 And he said, I seek my brethren : tell me, I pray thee, where they feed their flocks.

6 And the man said, They are departed hence ; for I heard them say, Let us go to Dothan. And Joseph

went after his brethren, and found them in Dothan.

7 And when they saw him afar off, even before he came near unto them, they conspired against him to slay him.

8 And they said one to another, Behold, this dreamer cometh.

9 Come now therefore, and let us slay him, and cast him into some pit, and we will say, Some wild beast hath devoured him: and we shall see what will become of his dreams.

10 And Reuben heard it, and he would deliver him out of their hands; and said, Let us not kill him.

11 And Reuben said unto them, Shed no blood, but cast him into this pit that is in the wilderness, and lay no hand upon him; that he might rid him out of their hands, to deliver him to his father again.

12 And it came to pass, when Joseph was come unto his brethren, that they stripped Joseph out of his coat, his coat of bright colours that was on him;

13 And they took him, and cast him into a pit: but the pit was empty, there was no water in it.

14 And they sat down to eat bread: and they lifted up their eyes and looked, and, behold, a company of Ishmaelites came from Gilead, with their camels bearing spicery and balm and myrrh, going to carry it down to Egypt.

15 And Judah said unto his brethren, What profit is it if we slay our brother, and conceal his blood?

16 Come, and let us sell him to the Ishmaelites, and let not our hand be upon him; for he is our brother and our flesh: and his brethren were content.

17 Then there passed by Midianite merchantmen; and they drew and lifted up Joseph out of the pit, and sold Joseph to the Ishmaelites for twenty pieces of silver: and they brought Joseph into Egypt.

18 And Reuben returned unto the pit; and, behold, Joseph was not in the pit; and he rent his clothes.

19 And he returned unto his brethren, and said, The child is not here; and I, whither shall I go?

20 And they took Joseph's coat, and killed a kid of the goats, and dipped the coat in the blood:

21 And they sent the coat of bright colours, and they brought it to their father; and said, This have we found: know now whether it be thy son's coat or not.

22 And he knew it, and said, It is my son's coat; a wild beast hath devoured him; Joseph is without doubt rent in pieces.

23 And Jacob rent his clothes, and put sackcloth upon his loins, and mourned for his son many days.

24 And all his sons and all his daughters rose up to comfort him; but he refused to be comforted; and he said, For I will go down into the grave unto my son mourning. Thus his father wept for him.

CHAPTER XXXVIII.

AND Joseph was brought down to Egypt; and Potiphar, an officer of Pharaoh, captain of the guard, an Egyptian, bought him of the hands of the Ishmaelites, which had brought him down thither.

2 And the LORD was with Joseph, and he was a prosperous man; and he was in the house of his master the Egyptian.

3 And his master saw that the LORD was with him, and that God made all that he did to prosper in his hand.

4 And Joseph found grace in his sight, and he served him : and he made him overseer over his house, and all that he had he put into his hand.

5 And it came to pass from the time that he had made him overseer in his house, and over all that he had, that the LORD blessed the Egyptian's house for Joseph's sake; and the blessing of God was upon all that he had in the house, and in the field.

6 And he left all that he had in Joseph's hand; and he knew not aught he had, save the bread which he did eat. And Joseph was a fair person, and well favoured.

7 And it came to pass after these things, that without just cause his master's wife hated Joseph and slandered him to his master.

8 And it came to pass, when his master heard the words of his wife, which she spoke unto him, saying, After this manner did thy servant speak to me; that his wrath was kindled.

9 And Joseph's master took him, and put him into the prison, a place where the king's prisoners were bound: and he was there in the prison.

10 But the LORD was with Joseph, and shewed him mercy, and gave him favour in the sight of the keeper of the prison.

11 And the keeper of the prison committed to Joseph's hand all the prisoners that were in the prison ; and whatsoever they did there, he was the doer of it.

12 The keeper of the prison looked not to any thing that was under his hand ; because the LORD was with him, and that which he did, the LORD made it to prosper.

CHAPTER XXXIX.

AND it came to pass after these things, that the butler of the king of Egypt and his baker had offended their lord the king of Egypt.

2 And Pharaoh was wroth against two of his officers, against the chief of the butlers, and against the chief of the bakers.

3 And he put them in ward in the house of the captain of the guard, into the prison, the place where Joseph was bound.

4 And the captain of the guard charged Joseph with them, and he served them : and they continued a season in ward.

5 And they dreamed a dream both of them, each man his dream in one night, each man according to the interpretation of his dream, the butler and the baker of the king of Egypt, which were bound in the prison.

6 And Joseph came in unto them in the morning, and looked upon them, and, behold, they were sad.

7 And he asked Pharaoh's officers that were with him in the ward of his lord's house, saying, Wherefore look ye so sadly to-day?

8 And they said unto him, We have dreamed a dream, and there is no interpreter of it. And Joseph said unto them, Do not interpretations belong to God? tell me them, I pray you.

9 And the chief butler told his dream to Joseph, and said to him, In my dream, behold, a vine was before me ;

10 And in the vine were three branches : and it was as though it budded, and her blossoms shot forth ;

and the clusters thereof brought forth ripe grapes:

11 And Pharaoh's cup was in my hand: and I took the grapes, and pressed them into Pharaoh's cup, and I gave the cup into Pharaoh's hand.

12 And Joseph said unto him, This is the interpretation of it: The three branches are three days:

13 Yet within three days shall Pharaoh lift up thy head, and restore thee unto thy place; and thou shalt deliver Pharaoh's cup into his hand, after the former manner when thou wast his butler.

14 But think of me when it shall be well with thee, and shew kindness, I pray thee, unto me, and make mention of me unto Pharaoh, and bring me out of this house:

15 For indeed I was stolen away out of the land of the Hebrews: and here also have I done nothing, that they should put me into the dungeon.

16 When the chief baker saw that the interpretation was good, he said unto Joseph, I also had a dream, and, behold, I had three white baskets on my head:

17 And in the uppermost basket there was of all manner of bakemeats for Pharaoh; and the birds did eat them out of the basket upon my head.

18 And Joseph answered and said, This is the interpretation thereof: The three baskets are three days:

19 Yet within three days shall Pharaoh lift up thy head from off thee, and shall hang thee on a tree; and the birds shall eat thy flesh from off thee.

20 And it came to pass the third day, which was Pharaoh's birthday, that he made a feast unto all his servants: and he lifted up the head of the chief butler and of the chief baker among his servants.

21 And he restored the chief butler unto his butlership again; and he gave the cup into Pharaoh's hand:

22 But he hanged the chief baker: as Joseph had interpreted to them.

23 Yet did not the chief butler remember Joseph, but forgot him.

CHAPTER XL.

AND it came to pass at the end of two full years, that Pharaoh dreamed: and, behold, he stood by the river.

2 And, behold, there came up out of the river seven well favoured kine and fatfleshed; and they fed in a meadow.

3 And, behold, seven other kine came up after them out of the river, ill favoured and leanfleshed; and stood by the other kine upon the brink of the river.

4 And the ill favoured and leanfleshed kine did eat up the seven well favoured and fat kine. Then Pharaoh awoke.

5 And he slept and dreamed the second time: and, behold, seven ears of corn came up upon one stalk, rank and good.

6 And, behold, seven thin ears and blasted with the east wind sprung up after them.

7 And the seven thin ears devoured the seven rank and full ears. And Pharaoh awoke, and, behold, it was a dream.

8 And it came to pass in the morning that his spirit was troubled; and he sent and called for all the magicians of Egypt, and all the wise men thereof: and Pharaoh told them his dream; but there was none that could interpret it unto Pharaoh.

9 Then spoke the chief butler unto Pharaoh, saying, I do remember my faults this day:

10 Pharaoh was wroth with his servants, and put me in ward in the captain of the guard's house, both me and the chief baker:

11 And we dreamed a dream in one night, I and he; we dreamed each man according to the interpretation of his dream.

12 And there was there with us a young man, a Hebrew, servant to the captain of the guard; and we told him, and he interpreted to us our dreams; to each man according to his dream he did interpret.

13 And it came to pass, as he interpreted to us, so it was; I was restored unto mine office, and he was hanged.

14 Then Pharaoh sent and called Joseph, and they brought him hastily out of the dungeon: and he shaved himself, and changed his raiment, and came in unto Pharaoh.

15 And Pharaoh said unto Joseph, I have dreamed a dream, and there is none that can interpret it: and I have heard say of thee, that thou canst understand a dream to interpret it.

16 And Joseph answered Pharaoh, saying, It is not of me: God will render the peace of Pharaoh.

17 And Pharaoh said unto Joseph, In my dream, behold, I stood upon the bank of the river:

18 And, behold, there came up out of the river seven kine, fatfleshed and well favoured; and they fed in a meadow:

19 And, behold, seven other kine came up after them, poor and very ill favoured and leanfleshed, such as I never saw in all the land of Egypt for badness:

20 And the lean and ill favoured kine ate up the first seven fat kine:

21 And when they had eaten them up, it could not be known that they had eaten them; but they were still ill favoured, as at the beginning. Then I awoke.

22 And I saw in my dream, and, behold, seven ears came up in one stalk, full and good:

23 And, behold, seven ears, withered, thin, and blasted with the east wind, sprung up after them:

24 And the thin ears devoured the seven good ears: and I told this unto the magicians; but there was none that could declare it to me.

25 And Joseph said unto Pharaoh, The dream of Pharaoh is one: God hath shewed Pharaoh what he is about to do.

26 The seven good kine are seven years; and the seven good ears are seven years: the dream is one.

27 And the seven thin and ill favoured kine that came up after them are seven years; and the seven empty ears blasted with the east wind shall be seven years of famine.

28 This is the thing which I have spoken unto Pharaoh: What God is about to do he shewed unto Pharaoh.

29 Behold, there come seven years of great plenty throught all the land of Egypt:

30 And there shall arise after them seven years of famine; and all the plenty shall be forgotten in the land of Egypt; and the famine shall consume the land ;

31 And the plenty shall not be known in the land by reason of that famine following ; for it shall be very grievous.

32 And as to the dream being re-

peated unto Pharaoh twice; it is because the thing is established by God, and God will shortly bring it to pass.

33 Now therefore let Pharaoh look out a man discret and wise, and set him over the land of Egypt.

34 Let Pharaoh do this, and let him appoint officers over the land, and take up the fifth part of the land of Egypt in the seven plenteous years.

35 And let them gather all the food of those good years that come, and lay up corn under the hand of Pharaoh, and let them keep food in the cities.

36 And that food shall be for store to the land against the seven years of famine, which shall be in the land of Egypt; that the land perish not through the famine.

37 And the thing was good in the eyes of Pharaoh, and in the eyes of all his servants.

CHAPTER XLI.

A ND Pharaoh said unto his servants, Can we find such a one as this is, a man in whom the spirit of God is?

2 And Pharaoh said unto Joseph, Forasmuch as God hath shewed thee all this, there is none so discreet and wise as thou art:

3 Thou shalt be over my house, and according unto thy word shall all my people be ruled: only in the throne will I be greater than thou.

4 And Pharaoh said unto Joseph, See, I have set thee over all the land of Egypt.

5 And Pharroh took off his ring from his hand, and put it upon Joseph's hand, and arrayed him in vestures of fine linen, and put a gold chain about his neck;

6 And he made him to ride in the second chariot which he had; and they cried before him, Bow the knee: and he made him ruler over all the land of Egypt.

7 And Pharaoh said unto Joseph, I am Pharaoh, but without thee shall no man lift up his hand or foot in all the land of Egypt.

8 And Pharaoh called Joseph's name Zaphnath-Paaneah; and he gave him to wife Asenath the daughter of Potipherah priest of On. And Joseph went out over all the land of Egypt.

9 And Joseph was thirty years old when he stood before Pharaoh king of Egypt. And Joseph went out from the presence of Pharaoh, and went throughout all the land of Egypt.

10 And in the seven plenteous years the earth brought forth abundantly.

11 And he gathered up all the food of the seven years, which were in the land of Egypt, and laid up the food in the cities: the food of the field, which was round about every city, laid he up in the same.

12 And Joseph gathered corn as the sand of the sea, very much, until he left numbering; for it was without number.

13 And unto Joseph were born two sons, before the years of famine came: which Asenath the daughter of Potipherah priest of On bare unto him,

14 And Joseph called the name of the firstborn Manasseh: For God, said he, hath made me forget all my toil, and all my father's house.

15 And the name of the second called he Ephraim: For God hath caused me to be fruitful in the land of my affliction.

16 And the seven years of plenteousness, that was in the land of Egypt, were ended.

17 And the seven years of dearth began to come, according ·as Joseph had said: and the dearth was in all lands; but in all the land of Egypt there was bread.

18 And when all the land of Egypt was famished, the people cried to Pharaoh for bread: and Pharaoh said unto all the Egyptians, Go unto Joseph; what he sayth to you, do.·

19 And the famine was over all the face of the earth: and Joseph opened all the storehouses, and sold unto the Egyptians; and the famine waxed sore in the land of Egypt.

20 And all countries came into Egypt to Joseph to buy corn; because that the famine was so sore in all lands.

CHAPTER XLII.

NOW when Jacob saw that there was corn in Egypt, Jacob said unto his sons, Why do ye look one upon another?

2 And he said, Behold, I have heard that there is corn in Egypt: get you down thither, and buy for us from thence; that we may live, and not die.

3 And Joseph's ten brethren went down to buy corn in Egypt.

4 But Benjamin, Josep's brother, Jacob sent not with his brethren; for he said, Lest peradventure mischief befall him,

5 And the sons of Israel came to buy corn among those that came: for the famine was in the land of Canaan.

6 And Joseph was the governor over the land, and he it was that sold to all the people of the land: and Joseph's brethren came, and bowed down themselves before him with their faces to the earth.

7 And Joseph saw his brethren, and he knew them, but made himself strange unto them, and spoke roughly unto them; and he said unto them, Whence come ye? And they said, From the land of Canaan to buy food.

8 And Joseph knew his brethren, but they knew not him.

9 And Joseph remembered the dreams which he dreamed of them, and said unto them, Ye are spies; to see the weak places of the land ye are come.

10 And they said unto him, Nay, my lord, but to buy food are thy servants come.

11 We are all one man's sons; we are true men; thy servants are no spies.

12 And he said unto them, Nay, but to see the weak places of the land ye are come.

13 And they said, Thy servants are twelve brethren, the sons of one man in the land of Canaan;' and, behold, the youngest is this day with our father, and one is no more.

14 Joseph said unto them, That is it that I spoke unto you, saying, Ye are spies:

15 Hereby ye shall be proved: By the life of Pharaoh, ye shall not go forth hence, except your youngest brother come hither.

16 Send one of you, and let him fetch your brother, and ye shall be kept in prison, that your words may be proved, whether there be any truth in you: or else, by the life of Pharaoh, surely ye are spies.

17 And he put them all together into ward three days.

18 And Joseph said unto them the third day, This do, and live; for I fear God:

19 If ye be true men, let one of your brethren be bound in the house of your prison: go ye, carry corn for the famine of your houses:

20 But bring your youngest brother unto me ; so shall your words be verified, and ye shall not die. And they did so.

21 And they said one to another, We are verily guilty concerning our brother, in that we saw the anguish of his soul, when he besought us, and we would not hear ; therefore is this distress come upon us.

22 But Reuben answered them, saying, Did I not speak unto you, saying, Do not sin against the child ; and ye would not hear ? therefore, behold, his blood is now required of us.

23 And they knew not that Joseph understood them ; for he spoke unto them by an interpreter.

24 And he turned himself about from them, and wept; and returned to them again, and communed with them, and took from them Simeon, and bound him before their eyes.

25 Then Joseph commanded to fill their sacks with corn, and to restore every man's money into his sack, and to give them provision for the way: and thus it was done unto them.

26 And they loaded their animals with the corn, and departed thence.

27 And as one of them opened his sack to give his animal provender in the inn, he espied his money; for, behold, it was in his sack's mouth.

18 And he said unto his brethren, My money is restored ; and, lo, it is even in my sack : and their heart failed them, and they were afraid, saying one to another, What is this that God hath done unto us ?

29 And they came unto Jacob their father unto the land of Canaan, and told him all that befell unto them, saying,

30 The man, who is the lord of the land, spoke roughly to us, and took us for spies of the country.

31 And we said unto him, We are true men ; we are no spies:

32 We be twelve brethren, sons of one father ; one is no more, and the youngest is this day with our father in the land of Canaan.

33 And the man, the lord of the country, said unto us, Hereby shall I know that ye are true men ; leave one of your brethren here with me, and take food for the famine of your households, and be gone:

34 And bring your youngest brother unto me : then shall I know that ye are no spies, but that ye are true men : so will I deliver you your brother, and ye shall trade in the land.

35 And it came to pass as they emptied their sacks, that, behold, every man's bundle of money was in his sack: and when both they and their father saw the bundles of money, they were afraid.

36 And Jacob their father said unto them, Me have ye bereave of my children : Joseph is not, and Simeon is not, and ye will take Benjamin away; upon me come all these things.

37 And Reuben spoke unto his father, saying, Slay my two sons, if I bring him not to thee: deliver him into my hand and I will bring him to thee again.

38 And he said, My son shall not go down with you: for his brother is dead, and he is left alone: if mischief befall him by the way in the which ye go, then shall ye bring down my gray hairs with sorrow to the grave.

CHAPTER XLIII.

AND the famine was sore in the land. 2 And it came to pass, when they had eaten up the corn which they had brought out of Egypt, their father said unto them, Go again, buy us a little food.

3 And Judah spoke unto him, saying, The man did solemnly protest unto us, saying, Ye shall not see my face, except your brother be with you.

4 If thou wilt send our brother with us, we will go down and buy thee food:

5 But if thou wilt not send him, we will not go down: for the man said unto us, Ye shall not see my face, except your brother be with you.

6 And Israel said, Wherefore dealt ye so ill with me, as to tell the man whether ye had yet a brother?

6 And they said, The man asked us closely of our state, and of our kindred, saying, Is your father yet alive? have ye another brother? and we told him according to the tenor of these words: Could we certainly know that he would say, Bring your brother down?

8 And Judah said unto Israel his father, Send the lad with me, and we will arise and go; that we may live, and not die, both we, and thou, and also our little ones.

9 I will be surety for him; of my hand shalt thou require him: if I bring him not unto thee, and set him before thee, then let me bear the blame for ever:

10 For except we had lingered, surely now we had returned this second time.

11 And their father Israel said unto them, If it must be so now, do this; take of the best fruits in the land in your vessels, and carry down to the man a present, a little balm, and a little honey, spices and myrrh, nuts and almonds:

12 And take double money in your hand; and the money that was brought again in the mouth of your sacks, carry it again in your hand; peradventure it was an oversight.

13 Take also your brother, and arise, go again unto the man:

14 And God Almighty give you mercy before the man, that he may send away your other brother, and Benjamin. And I—if I be bereaved of my children, I am bereaved.

15 And the men took that present, and they took double money in their hand, and Benjamin; and rose up, and went down to Egypt, and stood before Joseph.

16 And when Joseph saw Benjamin with them, he said to the ruler of his house, Bring these men home, and slay, and make ready; for these men shall dine with me at noon.

17 And the man did as Joseph bade; and the man brought the men into Joseph's house.

18 Now the men were afraid, because they were brought into Joseph's house; and they said, Because of the money that was returned in our sacks at the first time are we brought in; that he may seek occasion against us, and fall upon us, and take us for bondmen, and our asses.

19 And they came near to the steward of Joseph's house, and they communed with him at the door of the house,

20 And said, O sir, we came indeed down at the first time to buy food:

21 And it came to pass, when we came to the inn, that we opened our sacks, and, behold, every man's money was in the mouth of his sack, our money in full weight: and we have brought it again in our hand.

22 And other money have we brought down in our hands to buy food: we cannot tell who put our money in our sacks.

23 And he said, Peace be to you, fear not: your God, and the God of your father, hath given you a treasure in your sacks: I had your money. And he brought Simeon out unto them.

24 And the man brought the men into Joseph's house, and gave them water, and they washed their feet; and he gave their animals provender.

25 And they made ready the present before Joseph came at noon: for they heard that they should eat bread there.

26 And when Joseph came home, they brought him the present which was in their hand into the house, and bowed themselves to him to the earth.

27 And he asked them of their welfare, and said, Is your father well, the old man of whom ye spoke? Is he yet alive?

28 And they answered, Thy servant our father is in good health, he is yet alive. And they bowed down their heads, and made obeisance.

29 And he lifted up his eyes, and saw his brother Benjamin, his mother's son, and said, Is this your younger brother, of whom ye spoke unto me? And he said, God be gracious unto thee, my son.

30 And Joseph made haste; for his heart did yearn upon his brother; and he sought where to weep; and he entered into his chamber, and wept there.

31 And he washed his face, and went out, and restrained himself, and said, Set on bread.

32 And they set on for him by himself, and for them by themselves, and for the Egyptians, which did eat with him, by themselves: because the Egyptians might not eat bread with the Hebrews; for that is an abomination unto the Egyptians.

33 And they sat before him, the first-born according to his birthright, and the youngest according to his youth: and the men marvelled one at another.

34 And he took and sent messes unto them from before him: but Benjamin's mess was five times so much as any of theirs. And they drank, and were merry with him.

CHAPTER XLIV.

AND he commanded the steward of his house, saying, Fill the men's sacks with food, as much as they can carry, and put every man's money in his sack's mouth.

2 And put my cup, the silver cup, in the sack of the youngest, and his corn money. And he did according to the word that Joseph had spoken.

3 As soon as the morning was light, the men were sent away, they and their loads.

4 Hardly were they gone out of the city, they were not yet far off, when Joseph said unto his steward, Up, follow after the men; and when thou dost overtake them, say unto them, Wherefore have ye rewarded evil for good?

5 Is not this the cup out of which my lord drinketh, and whereby indeed he divineth? ye have done evil in so doing.

6 And he overtook them, and he spoke unto them these same words.

7 And they said unto him, Wherefore saith my lord these words? God forbid that thy servants should do according to this thing:

8 Behold, the money, which we found in our sacks' mouths, we brought again unto thee out of the land of Canaan: how then should we steal out of thy lord's house silver or gold?

9 With whomsoever of thy servants

it be found, both let him die, and we also will be my lord's bondmen.

10 And he said, Now also let it be according unto your words: he with whom it is found shall be my servant; but ye shall be blameless.

11 Then they speedily took down every man his sack to the ground, and opened every man his sack.

12 And he searched, and began at the eldest, and left at the youngest: and the cup was found in Benjamin's sack.

13 Then they rent their clothes, and laded every man his ass, and returned to the city.

14 And Judah and his brethren came to Joseph's house; for he was yet there; and they fell before him on the ground.

15 And Joseph said unto them, What deed is this that ye have done? know ye not that such a man as I can certainly divine?

16 And Judah said, What shall we say unto my lord? what shall we speak? or how shall we clear ourselves? God hath found out the iniquity of thy servants: behold, we are my lord's servants, both we, and he also with whom the cup is found.

17 And he said, God forbid that I should do so: but the man in whose hand the cup is found, he shall be my servant; and as for you, get you up in peace unto your father.

18 Then Judah came near unto him, and said, O my lord, let thy servant, I pray thee, speak a word in my lord's ears; and let not thine anger burn against thy servant: for thou art even as Pharaoh.

19 My lord asked his servants, saying, Have ye a father, or a brother?

20 And we said unto my lord, We have a father, an old man, and a child of his old age, a little one; and his brother is dead, and he alone is left of his mother, and his father loveth him.

21 And thou saidst unto thy servants, Bring him down unto me, that I may set mine eyes upon him.

22 And we said unto my lord, The lad cannot leave his father: for if he should leave his father, his father would die.

23 And thou saidst unto thy servants, Except your youngest brother come down with you, ye shall see my face no more.

24 And it came to pass when we came up unto thy servant my father, we told him the words of my lord.

25 And our father said, Go again, and buy us a little food.

26 And we said, We cannot go down: if our youngest brother be with us, then will we go down: for we may not see the man's face, except our youngest brother be with us.

27 And thy servant my father said unto us, Ye know that my wife bare me two sons:

28 And the one went out from me, and I said, Surely he is torn in pieces; and I saw him not since:

29 And if ye take this also from me, and mischief befall him, ye shall bring down my gray hairs with sorrow to the grave.

30 Now therefore when I come to thy servant my father, and the lad be not with us; seeing that his life is bound up in the lad's life;

31 It shall come to pass, when he seeth that the lad is not with us, that he will die: and thy servants shall bring down the gray hairs of thy servant our father with sorrow to the grave.

32 For thy servant became surety for

the lad unto my father, saying, If I bring him not unto thee, then I shall bear the blame to my father for ever.

33 Now therefore, I pray thee, let thy servant abide instead of the lad a bondman to my lord ; and let the lad go up with his brethren.

34 For how shall I go up to my father, and the lad be not with me ? lest peradventure I see the evil that shall come on my father.

CHAPTER XLV.

THEN Joseph could not refrain himself before all that stood by him ; and he cried, Cause every man to go out from me. And there stood no man with him, while Joseph made himself known unto his brethren.

2 And he wept aloud : and the Egyptians and the house of Pharaoh heard of it.

3 And Joseph said unto his brethren, I am Joseph ; doth my father yet live ? And his brethren could not answer him ; for they were troubled at his presence.

4 And Joseph said unto his brethren, Come near to me, I pray you. And they came near. And he said, I am Joseph your brother, whom ye sold into Egypt.

5 Now therefore be not grieved, nor angry with yourselves, that ye sold me hither : for God did send me before you to preserve life.

6 For these two years hath the famine been in the land : and yet there are five years, in the which there shall neither be earing nor harvest.

7 And God sent me before you to preserve you a posterity in the earth, and to save your lives by a great deliverance.

8 So now it was not you that sent me hither, but God : and he hath made me a father to Pharaoh, and lord of all his house, and a ruler throughout all the land of Egypt.

9 Haste ye, and go up to my father, and say unto him, Thus saith thy son Joseph, God hath made me lord of all Egypt : come down unto me, tarry not :

10 And thou shalt dwell in the land of Goshen, and thou shalt be near unto me, thou, and thy children, and thy children's children, and thy flocks, and thy herds, and all that thou hast :

11 And there will I nourish thee ; for yet there are five years of famine ; lest thou, and thy household, and all that thou hast, come to poverty.

12 And, behold, your eyes see, and the eyes of my brother Benjamin, that it is my mouth that speaketh unto you.

13 And ye shall tell my father of all my glory in Egypt, and of all that ye have seen ; and ye shall haste and bring down my father hither.

14 And he fell upon his brother Benjamin's neck, and wept : and Benjamin wept upon his neck.

15 Moreover he kissed all his brethren, and wept upon them : and after that his brethren talked with him.

16 And the report thereof was heard in Pharaoh's house, saying, Joseph's brethren are come : and it pleased Pharaoh well, and his servants.

17 And Pharaoh said unto Joseph, Say unto thy brethren, This shall ye do ; lade your beasts, and go, get you unto the land of Canaan ;

18 And take your father and your households, and come unto me : and I will give you the good of the land of Egypt, and ye shall eat the fat of the land.

19 Now thou commanded them, This do ye ; take you wagons out of the land of Egypt for your little ones, and

for your wives, and bring your father, and come.

20 Also regard not your stuff; for the good of the land of Egypt is yours.

21 And the children of Israel did so: and Joseph gave them wagons, according to the commandment of Pharaoh, and gave them provision for the way.

22 To all of them he gave each man changes of raiment; but to Benjamin he gave three hundred pieces of silver, and five changes of raiment.

23 And to his father he sent after this manner: ten asses laden with the good things of Egypt, and ten asses laden with corn and bread and meat for his father by the way.

24 So he sent his brethren away, and they departed: and he said unto them, See that ye quarrel not by the way.

25 And they went up out of Egypt, and came into the land of Canaan unto Jacob their father,

26 And told him that Joseph is yet alive, and that he is governor over all the land of Egypt. And Jacob's heart fainted, for he believed them not.

27 And they told him all the words of Joseph, which he had said unto them: and when he saw the wagons which Joseph had sent to carry him, the spirit of Jacob their father revived.

28 And Israel said, It is enough; Joseph my son is yet alive! I will go and see him before I die.

CHAPTER XLVI.

AND Israel took his journey with all that he had, and came to Beersheba, and offered sacrifices unto the God of his father Isaac.

2 And God spake unto Israel in the visions of the night, and said, Jacob, Jacob. And he said, Here am I.

3 And he said, I am God, the God of thy father: fear not to go down into Egypt; for I will there make of thee a great nation.

4 I will go down with thee into Egypt; and I will also surely bring thee up again: and Joseph shall put his hand upon thine eyes.

5 And Jacob rose up from Beersheba: and the sons of Israel carried Jacob their father, and their little ones, and their wives, in the wagons which Pharaoh had sent to carry him.

6 And they took their cattle, and their goods, which they had gotten in the land of Canaan, and came into Egypt, Jacob, and all his children with him:

7 His sons, and his son's sons with him, his daughters, and his sons' daughters, and all his offspring brought he with him into Egypt.

8 All the souls that came with Jacob into Egypt, besides Jacob's sons' wives, all the souls were threescore and six;

9 And the sons of Joseph, which were born him in Egypt, were two souls: all the souls of the house of Jacob, which came into Egypt, were threescore and ten.

10 And he sent Judah before him unto Joseph, to direct his face unto Goshen; and they came into the land of Goshen.

11 And Joseph made ready his chariot, and went up to meet Israel his father, to Goshen, and presented himself unto him; and he fell on his neck, and wept on his neck a good while.

12 And Israel said unto Joseph, Now let me die, since I have seen thy face, because thou art yet alive.

13 And Joseph said unto his brethren, and unto his father's house, I will go up, and tell Pharaoh, and say unto him, My brethren, and my father's

house, which were in the land of Canaan, are come unto me;

14 And the men are shepherds, for their trade hath been to feed cattle; and they have brought their flocks, and their herds, and all that they have.

15 And it shall come to pass, when Pharaoh shall call you, and shall say, What is your occupation?

16 That ye shall say, Thy servants' trade hath been about cattle from our youth. even until now, both we, and also our fathers: that ye may dwell in the land of Goshen; for every shepherd is an abomination unto the Egyptians.

CHAPTER XLVII.

THEN Joseph came and told Pharaoh, and said, My father and my brethren, and their flocks, and their herds, and all that they have, are come out of the land of Canaan; and, behold, they are in the land of Goshen.

2 And he took some of his brethren, even five men, and presented them unto Pharaoh.

3 And Pharaoh said unto his brethren, What is your occupation? And they said unto Pharaoh, Thy servants are shepherds, both we, and also our fathers.

4 They said moreover unto Pharaoh, To sojourn in the land are· we come; for thy servants have no pasture for their flocks; for the famine is sore in the land of Canaan: now therefore, we pray thee, let thy servants dwell in the land of Goshen.

5 And Pharaoh spake unto Joseph, saying, Thy father and thy brethren are come unto thee:

6 The land of Egypt is before thee; in the best of the land make thy father and brethren to dwell; in the land of Goshen let them dwell: and if thou

knowest any men of activity among them, then make them rulers over my cattle.

7 And Joseph brought in Jacob his father, and presented him before Pharaoh and Jacob blessed Pharaoh.

8 And Pharaoh said unto Jacob, How old art thou?

9 And Jacob said unto Pharaoh, The days of the years of my pilgrimage are a hundred and thirty years: few and evil have the days of the years of my life b· en, and have not attained unto the days of the years of the life of my fathers in the days of their pilgrimage.

10 And Jacob blessed Pharaoh, and went out from before Pharaoh.

11 And Joseph placed his father and his brethren, and gave them a possession in the land of Egypt, in the best of the land, in the land of Rameses, as Pharaoh had commanded.

12 And Joseph nourished his father, and his brethren, and all his father's household, with bread, according to their families.

13 And there was no bread in all the land; for the famine was very sore, so that the land of Egypt and all the land of Canaan fainted by reason of the famine.

14 And Joseph gathered up all the money that was found in the land of Egypt, and in the land of Canaan, for the corn which they bought: and Joseph brought the money into Pharaoh's house.

15 And when money failed in the land of Egypt, and in the land of Canaan, all the Egyptians came unto Joseph, and said, Give us bread: for why should we die in thy presence? for the money faileth.

16 And Joseph said, Give your cattle;

and I will give you for your cattle, if money fail.

17 And they brought their cattle unto Joseph: and Joseph gave them bread in exchange for horses, and for the flocks, and for the cattle of the herds, and he fed them with bread for all their cattle for that year.

18 When that year was ended, they came unto him the second year, and said unto him, We will not hide it from my lord, how that our money is spent; my lord also hath our herds of cattle; there is not aught left in the sight of my lord, but our bodies, and our lands:

19 Wherefore shall we die before thine eyes, both we and our land? buy us and our land for bread, and we and our land will be servants unto Pharaoh; and give us seed, that we may live, and not die, that the land be not desolate.

20 And Joseph bought all the land of Egypt for Pharaoh; for the Egyptians sold every man his field, because the famine prevailed over them: so the land became Pharaoh's.

21 And as for the people, he removed them to cities from one end of the borders of Egypt even to the other end thereof.

22 Only the land of the priests bought he not; for the priests had a portion assigned them of Pharaoh, and did eat their portion which Pharaoh gave them: wherefore they sold not their lands.

23 Then Joseph said unto the people, Behold, I have bought you this day and your land for Pharaoh: lo, here is seed for you, and ye shall sow the land.

24 And it shall come to pass in the increase, that ye shall give the fifth part unto Pharaoh, and four parts shall be your own, for seed of the field, and for your food, and for them of your households, and for food for your little ones.

25 And they said, Thou hast saved our lives: let us find grace in the sight of my lord, and we will be Pharaoh's servants.

26 And Joseph made it a law over the land of Egypt unto this day, that Pharaoh should have the fifth part; except the land of the priests only, which became not Pharaoh's.

27 And Israel dwelt in the land of Egypt, in the country of Goshen; and they had possessions therein, and grew, and multiplied exceedingly.

28 And Jacob lived in the land of Egypt seventeen years: so the whole age of Jacob was a hundred forty and seven years.

29 And the time drew nigh that Israel must die: and he called his son Joseph, and said unto him, If now I have found grace in thy sight, I pray thee, swear unto me that thou wilt deal kindly and truly with me; bury me not, I pray thee, in Egypt:

30 But I will lie with my fathers, and thou shalt carry me out of Egypt, and bury me in their buryingplace. And he said, I will do as thou hast said.

31 And he said, Swear unto me. And he sware unto him. And Israel bowed himself upon the bed's head.

CHAPTER XLVIII.

AND it came to pass after these things, that Joseph was told, Behold, thy father is sick: and he took with him his two sons, Manasseh and Ephraim.

2 And Jacob was told, Behold, thy son Joseph cometh unto thee: and

Israel strengthened himself, and sat upon the bed.

3 And Jacob said unto Joseph, God Almighty appeared unto me at Luz in the land of Canaan, and blessed me,

4 And said unto me, Behold, I will make thee fruitful, and multiply thee, and I will make of thee a multitude of people; and will give this land to thy children after thee for an everlasting possession.

5 And now thy two sons, Ephraim and Manasseh, which were born unto thee in the land of Egypt, before I came unto thee into Egypt, are mine; as Reuben and Simeon, they shall be mine.

6 And thy issue, which thou hast after them, shall be thine, and shall be called after the name of their brethren in their inheritance.

7 And as for me, when I came from Padan, Rachel died by me in the land of Canaan in the way, when yet there was but a little way to come unto Ephrath: and I buried her there in the way of Ephrath; the same is Bethlehem.

8 And Israel beheld Joseph's sons, and said, Who are these ?

9 And Joseph said unto his father, They are my sons, whom God hath given me in this place. And he said, Bring them, I pray thee, unto me, and I will bless them.

10 Now the eyes of Israel were dim for age, so that he could not see. And he brought them near unto him; and he kissed them, and embraced them.

11 And Israel said unto Joseph, I had not thought to see thy face: and, lo, God hath shewed me also thy children.

12 And Joseph brought them out from between his knees, and he bowed himself with his face to the earth.

13 And Joseph took them both, Ephraim in his right hand toward Israel's left hand, and Manasseh in his left hand toward Israel's right hand, and brought them near unto him.

14 And Israel stretched out his right hand, and laid it upon Ephraim's head, who was the younger, and his left hand upon Manasseh's head, guiding his hands wittingly; for Manasseh was the firstborn.

15 And he blessed Joseph, and said, God, before whom my fathers Abraham and Isaac did walk, the God which fed me all my life long unto this day,

16 The angel which redeemed me from all evil, bless the lads ; and let my name be named on them, and the name of my fathers Abraham and Isaac ; and let them grow into a multitude in the midst of the earth.

17 And when Joseph saw that his father laid his right hand upon the head of Ephraim, it displeased him: and he held up his father's hand, to remove it from Ephraim's head unto Manasseh's head.

18 And Joseph said unto his father, Not so, my father: for this is the firstborn; put thy right hand upon his head.

19 And his father refused, and said, I know it, my son, I know it: he also shall become a people, and he also shall be great: but truly his younger brother shall be greater than he, and his issue shall become a multitude of nations.

20 And he blessed them that day, saying, In thee shall Israel bless, saying, God make thee as Ephraim and Manasseh: and he set Ephraim before Manasseh.

21 And Israel said unto Joseph, Be-

hold, I die; but God shall be with you, and bring you again unto the land of your fathers.

22 Moreover I have given to thee one portion above thy brethren, which I took out of the hand of the Amorite with my sword and with my bow.

CHAPTER XLIX.

AND Jacob called unto his sons, and said:
Assemble, that I may tell you that which shall befall you in the last days.
Assemble, and listen, sons of Jacob; listen to Israel, your father.
Reuben, thou art my first-born, my marrow, the firstling of my strength:
there was pre-eminence of dignity, pre-eminence of power—
Boiling over as water, thou shalt not excel;
for thou ascendedst thy father's stead, dishonoring him who rested on my couch.
5 Simeon and Levi are brethren, their swords are weapons of violence.
In their concert may never be my soul, nor my heart join their assembly.
For in their anger they slay a man, in their self-will they hough a bull.
Cursed be their anger—it is fierce; their wrath—it is cruel.
I divide them in Jacob, I scatter them through Israel.
Judah, thee thy brethren extoll; thy hand is on the neck of thy foes, thy father's sons bow down before thee.
Judah is a lion's whelp; from prey thou risest, my son.
He stoops, couches, like a lion, or a lioness—
who shall rouse him up?
10 The sceptre shall not depart from Judah, nor the ruler's staff from between his feet, until he comes to Shiloh,

and there is a gathering of tribes around him.
He binds his foal to the vine, to a choice plant the colt of his ass
he washes his clothes in wine, his garment in the blood of grapes;
His eyes are red from wine, his teeth white with milk.
Zebulun will dwell at the haven of the sea, and his land be a haven for ships; his side touches Zidon.
Issachar is the beast of strangers, couching between the folds.
15 He saw that rest was good, that the land was pleasant:
so he bent his shoulder to bear, and labored, and paid tribute.
Dan shall judge his people, as one of the tribes of Israel.
Dan will be a serpent by the way, an adder in the path,
which bites the heels of the horse, so that the rider falls backward—
For thy salvation I hope, O Eternal.
Gad—squads invade him, but he cuts their heels.
20 Asher's food is fat; he produces kingly dainties.
Naphtali is a slender hind; he utters beautiful words.
Joseph is a fruitful young plant, a fruitful young plant by a well;
the branches run over the wall.
He was bitterly assailed, and shot at, and hated, by archers;
but his bow abode in strength, and his arms were supple—
through the hand of Jacob's defender, through him, the shepherd and rock of Israel;
25 through thy father's God—he helps thee;
through the Almighty—he blesses thee,
with blessings of heaven above, blessings of the deep spread out below,
with blessings of fruitfulness.
Thy father's blessings go beyond the blessings of my progenitors,
to the utmost bound of the everlasting hills;
they shall rest on the head of Joseph,

On the head of the crowned one
among his brethren.
  Benjamin is a wolf that tears.;
he devours prey in the morning,
divides spoils in the evening.

28. All these are the twelve tribes of
Israel: and this it is what their father
spake unto them, and blessed them;
every one according to his blessing he
blessed them.

29 And he charged them, and said
unto them, I am to be gathered unto
my people: bury me with my fathers
in the cave that is in the field of Ephron the Hittite.

30 In the cave that is in the field of
Machpelah, which is before Mamre,
in the land of Canaan, which Abraham bought with the field of Ephron
the Hittite for a possession of a buryingplace.

31 There they buried Abraham and
Sarah his wife; there they buried
Isaac and Rebekah his wife; and there
I buried Leah.

32 The purchase of the field and of
the cave that is therein was from the
children of Heth.

33 And when Jacob had made an
end of commanding his sons, he gathered up his feet into the bed, and
yielded up the ghost, and was gathered
unto his people.

CHAPTER L.

AND Joseph fell upon his father's
face, and wept upon him, and
kissed him.

2 And Joseph commanded his servants the physicians to embalm his
father: and the physicians embalmed
Israel.

3 And forty days were fulfilled for
him; for so are fulfilled the days of
those which are embalmed: and the
Egyptians mourned for him threescore
and ten days.

4 And when the days of his mourning were past, Joseph spoke unto the
house of Pharaoh, saying, If now I
have found grace in your eyes, speak,
I pray you, for me unto Pharaoh,
saying,

5 My father made me swear, saying,
Lo, I die: in my grave which I have
digged for me in the land of Canaan,
there shalt thou bury me. Now therefore let me go up, I pray thee, and
bury my father, and I will come again.

6 And Pharaoh said, Go up, and
bury thy father, according as he made
thee swear.

7 And Joseph went up to bury his
father: and with him went up all the
servants of Pharaoh, the elders of his
house, and all the elders of the land
of Egypt.

8 And all the house of Joseph, and
his brethren, and his father's house:
only their little ones, and their flocks,
and their herds, they left in the land
of Goshen.

9 And there went up with him both
chariots and horsemen: and it was a
very great company.

10 And they came to the threshing-
floor of Atad, which is beyond Jordan;
and there they mourned with a great
and very sore lamentation: and he
made a mourning for his father seven
days.

11 And when the inhabitants of the
land, the Canaanites, saw the mourning by the floor of Atad, they said, This
is a grievous mourning to the Egyptians: wherefore the name of it was
called Abel-mizraim, which is beyond
Jordan.

12 And his sons did unto him according as he commanded them:

13 For his sons carried him into the land of Canaan, and buried him in the cave of the field of Machpelah, which Abraham bought with the field for a possession of a buryingplace of Ephron the Hittite, before Mamre.

14 And Joseph returned into Egypt, he, and his brethren, and all that went up with him to bury his father, after he had buried his father.

15 And when Joseph's brethren saw that their father was dead, they said, Joseph will peradventure hate us, and will certainly requite us all the evil which we did unto him.

16 And they sent a messenger unto Joseph, saying, Thy father did command before he died, saying,

17 So shall ye say unto Joseph, Forgive, I pray thee now, the trespass of thy brethren, and their sin; for they did unto thee evil: and now, we pray thee, forgive the tresprass of the servants of the God of thy father. And Joseph wept when they spoke unto him.

18 And his brethren also went and fell down before his face; and they said, Behold, we be thy servants.

19 And Joseph said unto them, Fear not: for am I in the place of God?

20 But as for you, ye thought evil against me: but God meant it unto good, to bring to pass, as it is this day, to save much people alive.

21 Now therefore fear ye not: I will nourish you, and your little ones. And he comforted them, and spoke kindly unto them.

22 And Joseph dwelt in Egypt, he, and his father's house: and Joseph lived a hundred and ten years.

23 And Joseph saw Ephraim's children of the third generation: the children also of Machir the son of Manasseh were brought up upon Joseph's knees.

24 And Joseph said unto his brethren, I die; and God will surely visit you, and bring you out of this land unto the land which he sware to Abraham, to Isaac, and to Jacob.

25 And Joseph took an oath of the children of Israel, saying, God will surely visit you, and ye shall carry up my bones from hence.

26 So Joseph died, being a hundred and ten years old: and they embalmed him, and he was put in a coffin in Egypt.

EXODUS,

CALLED THE SECOND BOOK OF MOSES.

CHAPTER I.

NOW these are the names of the children of Israel, who came into Egypt; every man and his household came with Jacob.

2 Reuben, Simeon, Levi, and Judah, Issachar, Zebulun, and Benjamin, Dan, and Naphtali, Gad, and Asher.

3 And all the souls that came of Jacob's house were seventy souls:

4 Now Joseph had died, and all his brethren, and all that generation.

5 And the children of Israel increased abundantly, and multiplied, and waxed exceedingly mighty; and the land was filled with them.

6 Now there rose up a new king over Egypt, which knew not Joseph.

7 And he said unto his people, Behold, the people of the children of Israel are more and mightier than we:

8 Come on, let us deal wisely with them: lest they multiply, and it come to pass, that, when there falleth out any war, they join also unto our enemies, and fight against us, and so rise over the land.

9 Therefore they did set over them taskmasters to afflict them with their burdens. And they built for Pharaoh treasure cities, Pithom and Raamses.

10 But the more they afflicted them, the more they multiplied and grew. And they were grieved because of the children of Israel.

11 And the Egyptians made the children of Israel to serve with rigour:

12 And they made their lives bitter with hard bondage, in mortar, and in brick, and in all manner of service in the field: all their service, wherein they made them serve, was with rigour.

13 And Pharaoh charged all his people, saying, Every Hebrew son that is born ye shall cast into the river, and every daughter ye shall save alive.

CHAPTER II.

AND there went a man of the house of Levi, and took to wife a daughter of Levi.

2 And the woman bare a son: and when she saw him that he was a goodly child, she hid him three months.

3 And when she could not longer hide him, she took for him an ark of bulrushes, and daubed it with slime and with pitch, and put the child therein; and she laid it in the flags by the river's brink.

4 And his sister stood afar off, to watch what would be done to him.

5 And the daughter of Pharaoh came down to wash herself at the river; and her maidens walked along by the river's side: and when she saw the ark among the flags, she sent her maid to fetch it.

6 And when she had opened it, she saw the child: and, behold the babe wept. And she had compassion on

him, and said, This is one of the Hebrews' children.

7 Then said his sister to Pharaoh's daughter, Shall I go and call to thee a nurse of the Hebrew women, that she may nurse the child for thee?

8 And Pharaoh's daughter said to her, Go. And the maid went and called the child's mother.

9 And Pharaoh's daughter said unto her, Take the child away, and nurse it for me, and I will give thee thy wages. And the woman took the child, and nursed it.

10 And the child grew, and she brought him unto Pharaoh's daughter, and he became her son. And she called his name Moses: for she said, Because I drew him out of the water.

11 And it came to pass in those days, when Moses was grown, that he went out unto his brethren, and looked on their burdens: and he spied an Egyptian smiting a Hebrew, one of his brethren.

12 And he looked this way and that way, and when he saw that there was no man, he slew the Egyptian, and hid him in the sand.

13 And when he went out the second day, behold, two men of the Hebrews strove together: and he said to him that did the wrong, Wherefore smitest thou thy fellow?

14 And he said, Who made thee a prince and a judge over us? intendest thou to kill me, as thou killedst the Egyptian? And Moses feared, and said, Surely this thing is known.

15 Now when Pharaoh heard this thing, he sought to slay Moses. But Moses fled from the face of Pharaoh, and dwelt in the land of Midian: and he sat down by a well.

16 Now the priest of Midian had

seven daughters: and they came and drew water, and filled the troughs to water their father's flock.

17 And the shepherds came and drove them away: but Moses stood up and helped them, and watered their flock.

18 And when they came to Rĕuel their father, he said, How is it that ye are come so soon to day?

19 And they said, An Egyptian delivered us out of the hand of the shepherds, and also drew water enough for us, and watered the flock.

20 And he said unto his daughters, And where is he? why is it that ye have left the man? call him, that he may eat bread.

21 And Moses was content to dwell with the man: and he gave Moses Zipporah his daughter to wife.

22 And she bare him a son, and he called his name Gershom; for he said, I have been an alien in a strange land.

23 And she again bare a son, and he called his name Eliezer, for, said he, the God of my father was my help, and delivered me from the sword of Pharaoh.

24 And it came to pass in process of time, that the king of Egypt died: and the children of Israel sighed by reason of the bondage, and they cried, and their cry came up unto God from their bondage.

25 And God heard their groaning, and God remembered his covenant with Abraham, with Isaac, and with Jacob.

26 And God looked upon the children of Israel, and God had respect unto them.

CHAPTER III.

NOW Moses kept the flock of Jethro his father in law, the priest of Midian: and he led the flock toward the desert, and came to the mountain of God, even to Horeb.

2 And an angel of the LORD appeared unto him in a flame of fire out of the midst of a bush: and he looked, and, behold, the bush burned with fire, and the bush was not consumed.

3 And Moses said, I will now turn aside and see this great sight, why the bush is not burnt.

4 And when the LORD saw that he turned aside to see, God called unto him out of the midst of the bush, and said, Moses, Moses. And he said, Here am I.

5 And he said, Draw not nigh hither: put off thy shoes from off thy feet; for the place whereon thou standest is holy ground.

6 Moreover he said, I am the God of thy father, the God of Abraham, the God of Isaac, and the God of Jacob. And Moses hid his face; for he was afraid to look upon God.

7 And the LORD said, I have surely seen the affliction of my people which are in Egypt, and have heard their cry by reason of their taskmasters; for I know their sorrows;

8 And I am come down to deliver them out of the hand of the Egyptians, and to bring them up out of that land unto a good land and a large, unto a land flowing with milk and honey; unto the place of the Canaanites, and the Hittites, and the Amorites, and the Perizzites, and the Hivites, and the Jebusites.

9 Now therefore, behold, the cry of the children of Israel is come unto me: and I have also seen the oppression wherewith the Egyptians oppress them.

10 Come now therefore, and I will send thee unto Pharaoh, that thou mayest bring forth my people the children of Israel out of Egypt.

11 And Moses said unto God, Who am I, that I should bring forth the children of Israel out of Egypt?

12 And he said, I will certainly be with thee; and this shall be a token unto thee, that I have sent thee: When thou hast brought forth the people out of Egypt, ye shall serve God upon this mountain.

13 And Moses said unto God, Behold, when I come unto the children of Israel, and shall say unto them, The God of your fathers hath sent me unto you; and they shall say to me, What is his name? what shall I say unto them?

14 And God said unto Moses, I AM THAT I AM: and he said, Thus shalt thou say unto the children of Israel, I AM hath sent me unto you.

15 And God said moreover unto Moses, Thus shalt thou say unto the children of Israel, The LORD God of your fathers, the God of Abraham, the God of Isaac, and the God of Jacob, hath sent me unto you: this is my name for ever, and this is my memorial unto all generations.

16 Go, and gather the elders of Israel together, and say unto them, The LORD God of your fathers, the God of Abraham, of Isaac, and of Jacob, appeared unto me, saying, I have surely visited you, and seen that which is done to you in Egypt:

17 And I have said, I will bring you up out of the affliction of Egypt unto the land of the Canaanites, and the Hittites and the Amorites, and the Perizzites, and the Hivites, and the Jebusites, unto a land flowing with milk and honey.

18 And they shall hearken to thy

voice: and thou shalt come, thou and the elders of Israel, unto the king of Egypt, and ye shall say unto him, The LORD God of the Hebrews hath met with us: and now let us go, we beseech thee, three days' yourney into the wilderness, that we may sacrifice to the LORD our God.

19 And I am sure that the king of Egypt will not let you go, no, not by a mighty hand.

20 And I will stretch out my hand, and smite Egypt with all my wonders which I will do in the midst thereof: and after that he will let you go.

CHAPTER IV.

AND Moses answered and said, But, behold, they will not believe me, nor hearken unto my voice: for they will say, The LORD hath not appeared unto thee.

2 And the LORD said unto him, What is that in thine hand? And he said, A rod.

3 And he said, Cast it on the ground. And he cast it on the ground, and it became a serpent: and Moses fled from before it.

4 And the LORD said unto Moses, Put forth thine hand, and take it by the tail. And he put forth his hand, and caught it, and it became a rod in his hand:

5 That they may believe that the LORD God of their fathers, the God of Abraham, the God of Isaac, and the God of Jacob, hath appeared unto thee.

6 And the LORD said furthermore unto him, Put now thine hand into thy bosom. And he put his hand into his bosom: and when he took it out, behold, his hand was leprous as snow.

7 And he said, Put thine hand into thy bosom again. And he put his hand into his bosom again; and brought it out of his bosom, and, behold, it was turned again as his other flesh.

8 And it shall come to pass, if they will not believe thee, neither hearken to the voice of the first sign, that they will believe the voice of the latter sign.

9 And it shall come to pass, if they will not believe also these two signs, neither hearken unto thy voice, that thou shalt take of the water of the river, and pour it upon the dry land: and the water which thou takest out of the river shall become blood upon the dry land.

10 And Moses said unto the LORD, O my Lord, I am not eloquent, neither heretofore, nor since thou hast spoken unto thy servant; but I am slow of speech, and of a slow tongue.

11 And the LORD said unto him, Who hath made man's mouth? or who maketh the dumb, or deaf, or the seeing, or the blind? Is it not I the LORD?

12 Now therefore go, and I will be with thy mouth, and teach thee what thou shalt say.

13 And he said, O my Lord, send, I pray thee, by the hand of him whom thou wilt send.

14 And the anger of the LORD was kindled against Moses, and he said, Is not Aaron the Levite thy brother? I know that he can speak well. And also, behold, he cometh forth to meet thee: and when he seeth thee, he will be glad in his heart.

15 And thou shalt speak unto him, and put words in his mouth: and I will be with thy mouth, and with his mouth, and will teach you what ye shall do.

16 And he shall be thy spokesman unto the people: and he shall be, to

thee instead of a mouth, and thou shalt be to him instead of God.

17 And thou shalt take this rod in thine hand, wherewith thou shalt do signs.

18 And Moses went and returned to Jethro his father in law, and said unto him, Let me go, I pray thee, and return unto my brethren which are in Egypt, and see whether they be yet alive. And Jethro said to Moses, Go in peace.

19 And the LORD said unto Moses in Midian, Go, return into Egypt: for all the men are dead which sought thy life.

20 And Moses took his wife and his sons, and set them upon an ass, and he returned to the land of Egypt: and Moses took the rod of God in his hand.

21 And the LORD said unto Moses, When thou goest to return into Egypt, see that thou do all those wonders before Pharaoh, which I have put in thine hand.

22 And thou shalt say unto Pharaoh, Thus saith the LORD, Israel is my son, even my firstborn:

23 And I say unto thee, Let my son go, that he may serve me: and if thou refuse to let him go, behold, I will slay thy son, even thy firstborn.

24 And the LORD said to Aaron, Go into the wilderness to meet Moses. And he went, and met him in the mount of God, and kissed him.

25 And Moses told Aaron all the words of the LORD who had sent him, and all the signs which he had commanded him.

26 And Moses and Aaron went and gathered together all the elders of the children of Israel:

27 And Aaron spoke all the words which the LORD had spoken unto Moses, and did the signs in the sight of the people.

28 And the people believed: and when they heard that the LORD had visited the children of Israel, and that he had looked upon their affliction, then they bowed their heads and worshipped.

CHAPTER V.

AND afterward Moses and Aaron went in, and told Pharaoh, Thus saith the LORD God of Israel, Let my people go, that they may hold a feast unto me in the wilderness.

2 And Pharaoh said, Who is the LORD, that I should obey his voice to let Israel go? I know not the LORD, neither will I let Israel go.

3 And they said, The God of the Hebrews hath met with us: let us go, we pray thee, three days' journey into the desert, and sacrifice unto the LORD our God; lest he fall upon us with pestilence, or with the sword.

4 And the king of Egypt said unto them, Wherefore do ye, Moses and Aaron, detain the people from their works? get you unto your burdens,

5 And Pharaoh said, Behold, the people of the land now are many, and ye make them rest from their burdens.

6 And Pharaoh commanded the same day the taskmasters of the people, and their officers, saying,

7 Ye shall no more give the people straw to make brick, as heretofore: let them go and gather straw for themselves.

8 And the tale of the bricks, which they did make heretofore, ye shall lay upon them; ye shall not diminish aught thereof: for they are idle; therefore they cry, saying, Let us go and sacrifice to our God.

9 Let there more work be laid upon the men, that they may labour therein; and let them not regard vain words.

10 And the taskmasters of the people went out, and their officers, and they spoke to the people, saying, Thus saith Pharaoh, I will not give you straw.

11 Go ye, get you straw where ye can find it: yet not aught of your work shall be diminished.

12 So the people were scattered abroad throughout all the land of Egypt to gather stubble instead of straw.

13 And the taskmasters hasted them, saying, Fulfill your works, your daily tasks, as when there was straw.

14 And the officers of the children of Israel, which Pharaoh's taskmasters had set over them, were beaten, and demanded, Wherefore have ye not fulfilled your task in making brick both yesterday and to day, as heretofore?

15 Then the officers of the children of Israel came and cried unto Pharaoh, saying, Wherefore dealest thou thus with thy servants?

16 There is no straw given unto thy servants, and they say to us, Make brick: and, behold, thy servants are beaten, and sin is laid on thy people.

17 But he said, Ye are idle, ye are idle: therefore ye say, Let us go and do sacrifice to the LORD.

18 Go therefore now, and work; for there shall no straw be given you, yet shall ye deliver the tale of bricks.

19 And the officers of the children of Israel did see that they were in evil case, after it was said, Ye shall not diminish aught from your bricks of your daily task.

20 And they met Moses and Aaron, who stood in the way, as they came forth from Pharaoh:

21 And they said unto them, The LORD look upon you, and judge; because ye have made our savour to be abhorred in the eyes of Pharaoh, and in the eyes of his servants, to put a sword in their hand to slay us.

22 And Moses returned unto the LORD, and said, Lord, wherefore hast thou so evil treated this people? why is it that thou hast sent me?

23 For since I came to Pharaoh to speak in thy name, he hath done evil to this people: neither hast thou delivered thy people at all.

CHAPTER VI.

THEN the LORD said unto Moses, Now shalt thou see what I will do to Pharaoh: for with a strong hand shall he let them go, and with a strong hand shall he drive them out of his land.

2 And God spake unto Moses, and said unto him, I am the LORD:

3 And I appeared unto Abraham, unto Isaac, and unto Jacob, by the name of EL-SHADDAI (God Almighty); but by my name JEHOVAH* (The Eternal) was I not known to them.

4 And I have also established my covenant with them, to give them the land of Canaan, the land of their pilgrimage, wherein they were strangers.

5 And I have also heard the groaning of the children of Israel, whom the Egyptians keep in bondage; and I have remembered my covenant.

6 Wherefore say unto the children of Israel, I am the Eternal, and I will bring you out from under the burdens of the Egyptians, and I will rid you out of their bondage, and I will redeem you with an outstretched arm, and with great judgments:

7 And I will take you to me for a

*JHVH with the vowels of Adonai.

people, and I will be to you a God: and ye shall know that I am the LORD your God, which bringeth you out from under the burdens of the Egyptians.

8 And I will bring you in unto the land, concerning which I did swear to give it to Abraham, to Isaac, and to Jacob; and I will give it you for a heritage: I am the Eternal.

9 And Moses spoke so unto the children of Israel: but they hearkened not unto Moses for anguish of spirit, and for cruel bondage.

10 And when the LORD spake unto Moses, saying, Go in, speak unto Pharaoh king of Egypt, that he let the children of Israel go out of his land;

11 Moses answered the LORD, saying, Behold, the children of Israel have not hearkened unto me; how then shall Pharaoh hear me, and I am slow of speech and of a slow tongue?

CHAPTER VII.

AND the LORD said unto Moses, See, I have made thee a god to Pharaoh; and Aaron thy brother shall be thy prophet.

2 Thou shalt speak all that I command thee: and Aaron thy brother shall speak unto Pharaoh, that he send the children of Israel out of his land.

3 But Pharaoh shall not hearken unto you, that I will lay my hand upon Egypt, and bring forth mine armies, my people the children of Israel, out of the land of Egypt by great judgments.

4 And Pharaoh will harden his heart, and I will multiply my signs and my wonders in the land of Egypt.

5 And the Egyptians shall know that I am the LORD, when I stretch forth mine hand upon Egypt, and bring out the children of Israel from among them.

6 And Moses and Aaron did as the LORD commanded them, so did they.

7 And Moses was fourscore years old, and Aaron fourscore and three years old, when they spoke unto Pharaoh.

8 And the LORD spake unto Moses and unto Aaron, saying,

9 When Pharaoh shall speak unto you, saying, Shew a miracle for you: then thou shalt say unto Aaron, Take thy rod, and cast it before Pharaoh, and it shall become a serpent.

10 And Moses and Aaron went in unto Pharaoh, and they did so as the LORD had commanded: and Aaron cast down his rod before Pharaoh, and before his servants, and it became a serpent.

11 Then Pharaoh also called the wise men and the sorcerers: now the magicians of Egypt, they also did in like manner with their enchantments.

12 For they cast down every man his rod, and they became serpents: but Aaron's rod swallowed up their rods.

13 And Pharaoh's heart was hardened, that he hearkened not unto them; as the LORD had said,

14 And the LORD said unto Moses, Pharaoh's heart is hardened, he refuseth to let the people go.

15 Get thee unto Pharaoh in the morning; lo, he goeth out unto the water; and thou shalt stand by the river's brink as he cometh; and the rod which was turned to a serpent shalt thou take in thine hand.

16 And thou shalt say unto him, The LORD God of the Hebrews hath sent me unto thee, saying, Let my people go, that they may serve me in the wilderness: and, behold, hitherto thou wouldest not hear.

17 Thus saith the LORD, In this thou shalt know that I am the LORD:

behold, I will smite with the rod that is in mine hand upon the waters which are in the river, and they shall be turned to blood.

18 And the fish that is in the river shall die, and the Egyptians shall loathe to drink of the water of the river.

19 And the LORD spake unto Moses, Say unto Aaron, Take thy rod, and stretch out thine hand upon the waters of Egypt, upon their streams, upon their rivers, and upon their ponds, and upon all their pools of water, that they may become blood; and that there may be blood throughout all the land of Egypt, both in vessels of wood, and in vessels of stone.

20 And Moses and Aaron did so, as the LORD commanded; and he lifted up the rod, and smote the waters that were in the river, in the sight of Pharaoh, and in the sight of his servants; and all the waters that were in the river were turned to blood.

21 And the fish that was in the river died; and the river stank, and the Egyptians could not drink of the water of the river; and there was blood throughout all the land of Egypt.

22 And the magicians of Egypt did so with their enchantments: and Pharaoh's heart was hardened, neither did he hearken unto them; as the LORD had said.

23 And Pharaoh turned and went into his house, neither did he set his heart to this also.

24 And all the Egyptians digged round about the river for water to drink; for they could not drink of the water of the river.

25 And seven days were fulfilled, after that the LORD had smitten the river.

CHAPTER VIII.

AND the LORD spake unto Moses, Go unto Pharaoh, and say unto him, Thus saith the LORD, Let my people go, that they may serve me.

2 And if thou refuse to let them go, behold, I will smite all thy borders with frogs:

3 And the river shall bring forth frogs abundantly, which shall go up and come into thine house, and into thy bedchamber, and upon thy bed, and into the house of thy servants, and upon thy people, and into thine ovens, and into thy kneadingtroughs:

4 And the frogs shall come up both on thee, and upon thy people, and upon all thy servants.

5 And the LORD spake unto Moses, Say unto Aaron, Stretch forth thine hand with thy rod over the streams, over the rivers, and over the ponds, and cause frogs to come up upon the land of Egypt.

6 And Aaron stretched out his hand over the waters of Egypt; and the frogs came up, and covered the land of Egypt.

7 And the magicians did so with their enchantments, and brought up frogs upon the land of Egypt.

8 Then Pharaoh called for Moses and Aaron, and said, Entreat the LORD, that he may take away the frogs from me, and from my people; and I will let the people go, that they may do sacrifice unto the LORD.

9 And Moses said unto Pharaoh, Glory over me: when shall I entreat for thee, and for thy servants, and for thy people, to destroy the frogs from thee and thy houses, that they may remain in the river only?

10 And he said, To morrow. And

he said, Be it according to thy word; that thou mayest know that there is none like unto the LORD our God.

11 And the frogs shall depart from thee, and from thy houses, and from thy servants, and from thy people; they shall remain in the river only.

12 And Moses and Aaron went out from Pharaoh: and Moses cried unto the LORD because of the frogs which he had brought against Pharaoh.

13 And the LORD did according to the word of Moses; and the frogs died out of the houses, out of the villages, and out of the fields.

14 And they gathered them together upon heaps; and the land stank.

15 But when Pharaoh saw that there was respite, he hardened his heart, and hearkened not unto them; as the LORD had said.

16 And the LORD said unto Moses, Say unto Aaron, Stretch out thy rod, and smite the dust of the land, that it may become vermin throughout all the land of Egypt.

17 And they did so; for Aaron stretched out his hand with his rod, and smote the dust of the earth, and it became vermin in man, and in beast; all the dust of the land became vermin throughout all the land of Egypt.

18 And the magicians did so with their enchantments to bring forth vermin, but they could not.

19 Then the magicians said unto Pharaoh, This is the finger of God: and Pharaoh's heart was hardened, and he hearkened not unto them; as the LORD had said.

20 And the Lord said unto Moses, Rise up early in the morning, and stand before Pharaoh; lo, he cometh forth to the water; and say unto him, Thus saith the LORD, Let my people go, that they may serve me.

21 Else, if thou wilt not let my people go, behold, I will send swarms of flies upon thee, and upon thy servants, and upon thy people, and into thy houses: and the houses of the Egyptians shall be full of swarms of flies, and also the ground whereon they are.

22 And I will sever in that day the land of Goshen, in which my people dwell, that no swarms of flies shall be there; to the end thou mayest know that I am the LORD in the midst of the earth.

23 And I will put a division between my people and thy people: to morrow shall this sign be.

24 And the LORD did so; and there came a grievous swarm of flies into the house of Pharaoh, and into his servants' houses, and into all the land of Egypt: the land was corrupted by reason of the swarm of flies.

25 And Pharaoh called for Moses and for Aaron, and said, Go ye, sacrifice to your God in the land.

26 And Moses said, It is not meet so to do; for we shall sacrifice the gods of the Egyptians to the LORD our God: lo, shall we sacrifice the gods of the Egyptians before their eyes, and will they not stone us?

27 We will go three days' journey into the wilderness, and sacrifice to the LORD our God, as he shall command us.

28 And Pharaoh said, I will let you go, that ye may sacrifice to the LORD your God in the wilderness; only ye shall not go very far away: entreat for me.

29 And Moses said, Behold, I go out from thee, and I will entreat the LORD that the swarms of flies may

depart from Pharaoh, from his servants, and from his people, to morrow: but let not Pharaoh deal deceitfully any more in not letting the people go to sacrifice to the LORD.

30 And Moses went out from Pharaoh, and entreated the LORD

31 And the LORD did according to the word of Moses; and he removed the swarms of flies from his people; there remained not one.

32 And Pharaoh hardened his heart at this time also, neither would he let the people go.

CHAPTER IX.

THEN the LORD said unto Moses, Go in unto Pharaoh, and tell him, Thus saith the LORD God of the Hebrews, Let my people go, that they may serve me.

2 For if thou refuse to let them go, and wilt hold them still,

3 Behold, the hand of the LORD is upon thy cattle which is in the field, upon the horses, upon the asses, upon the camels, upon the oxen, and upon the sheep: there shall be a very grievous murrain.

4 And the LORD shall sever between the cattle of Israel and the cattle of Egypt; and there shall nothing die of all that is the children's of Israel.

5 And the LORD appointed a set time, saying, To morrow the LORD shall do this thing in the land.

6 And the LORD did that thing on the morrow, and all the cattle of Egypt died: but of the cattle of the children of Israel died not one.

7 And Pharaoh sent, and, behold, there was not one of the cattle of the Israelites dead. And yet the heart of Pharaoh was hardened, and he did not let the people go.

8 And the LORD said unto Moses and unto Aaron, Take to you handfuls of ashes of the furnace, and let Moses sprinkle it toward the heaven in sight of Pharaoh.

9 And it shall become small dust in all the land of Egypt, and shall be a boil breaking forth with blains upon man, and upon beast, throughout all the land of Egypt.

10 And they took ashes of the furnace, and stood before Pharaoh; and Moses sprinkled it up toward heaven; and it became a boil breaking forth with blains upon man, and upon beast.

11 And the magicians could not stand before Moses because of the boils; for the boil was upon the magicians, and upon all the Egyptians.

12 And Pharaoh hardened his heart, and he hearkened not unto them; as the LORD had spoken unto Moses.

13 And the LORD said unto Moses, Rise up early in the morning, and stand before Pharaoh, and say unto him, Thus saith the LORD God of the Hebrews, Let my people go, that they may serve me.

14 For I will at this time send all my plagues upon thine heart, and upon thy servants, and upon thy people; that thou mayest know that there is none like me in all the earth.

15 For now I will stretch out my hand, that I may smite thee and thy people with pestilence; and thou shalt be cut off from the earth.

16 As yet exaltest thou thyself against my people, that thou wilt not let them go?

17 Behold, to morrow about this time I will cause it to rain a very grievous hail, such as hath not been in Egypt since the foundation thereof even until now.

18 Send therefore now, and gather thy cattle, and all that thou hast in the field; for upon every man and beast which shall be found in the field, and shall not be brought home, the hail shall come down upon them, and they shall die.

19 He that feared the word of the LORD among the servants of Pharaoh made his servants and his cattle flee into the houses:

20 And he that regarded not the word of the LORD left his servants and his cattle in the field.

21 And the LORD said unto Moses, Stretch forth thine hand toward heaven, that there may be hail in all the land of Egypt, upon man, and upon beast, and upon every herb of the field, throughout all the land of Egypt.

22 And Moses stretched forth his rod toward heaven: · and the LORD sent thunder and hail, and the fire ran along upon the ground; and the LORD rained hail upon the land of Egypt.

23 So there was hail, and fire mingled with the hail, very grievous, such as there was none like it in all the land of Egypt since it became a nation.

24 And the hail smote throughout all the land of Egypt all that was in the field, both man and beast; and the hail smote every herb of the field, and broke every tree of the field.

25 Only in the land of Goshen, where the children of Israel were, was there no hail.

26 And Pharaoh sent, and called for Moses and Aaron, and said unto them, I have sinned this time: the LORD is righteous, and I and my people are wicked.

27 Entreat the LORD, for it is enough, that there be no more mighty thunderings and hail; and I will let you go, and ye shall stay no longer.

28 And Moses said unto him, As soon as I am gone out of the city, I will spread abroad my hands unto the LORD; and the thunder shall cease, neither shall there be any more hail; that thou mayest know that the earth is the LORD'S.

29 But as for thee and thy servants, I know that ye will not yet fear the LORD God.

30 And the flax and the barley was smitten: for the barley was in the ear, and the flax was bolled.

31 But the wheat and the rye were not smitten; for they were not grown up.

32 And Moses went out of the city from Pharaoh, and spread abroad his hands unto the LORD: and the thunders and hail ceased, and the rain ceased to pour down upon the earth.

33 And when Pharaoh saw that the rain and the hail and the thunders were ceased, he sinned yet more, and hardened his heart, he and his servants.

34 And the heart of Pharaoh was hardened, neither would he let the children of Israel go; as the LORD had spoken by Moses.

CHAPTER X.

AND the LORD said unto Moses, Go in unto Pharaoh: his heart is hardened, and the heart of his servants, that I might show these my signs before him :

2 And that thou mayest tell in the ears of thy son, and of thy son's son, what things I have wrought in Egypt, and my signs which I have done among them; that ye may know that I am the LORD.

3 And Moses and Aaron came in unto Pharaoh, and said unto him,

Thus saith the LORD God of the Hebrews, How long wilt thou refuse to humble thyself before me? let my people go, that they may serve me.

4 Else, if thou refuse to let my people go, behold, to morrow will I bring the locusts into thy coast:

5 And they shall cover the face of the earth, that one cannot be able to see the earth: and they shall eat the residue of that which is escaped, which remaineth unto you from the hail, and shall eat every tree which groweth for you out of the field:

6 And they shall fill thy houses, and the houses of all thy servants, and the houses of all the Egyptians; which neither thy fathers, nor thy fathers' fathers have seen, since the day that they were upon the earth unto this day. And he turned himself, and went out from Pharaoh.

7 And Pharaoh's servants said unto him, How long shall this man be a snare unto us? let the men go, that they may serve the LORD their God: knowest thou not yet that Egypt is destroyed?

8 And Moses and Aaron were brought again unto Pharaoh: and he said unto them, Go, serve the LORD your God: but who are they that shall go?

9 And Moses said, We will go with our young and with our old, with our sons and with our daughters, with our flocks and with our herds will we go; for we must hold a feast unto the LORD.

10 And he said unto them, Let the LORD be so with you, as I will let you go, and your little ones: look to it; for evil is before you.

11 Not so: go now ye, the men, and serve the LORD; for that ye did desire. And they were driven out from Pharaoh's presence.

12 And the LORD said unto Moses, Stretch out thine hand over the land of Egypt for the locusts, that they may come up upon the land of Egypt, and eat every herb of the land, even all that the hail hath left.

13 And Moses stretched forth his rod over the land of Egypt, and the LORD brought an east wind upon the land all that day, and all that night; and when it was morning, the east wind brought the locusts.

14 And the locusts went up over all the land of Egypt, and rested in all the coasts of Egypt: very grievous were they; before them there were no such locusts as they, neither after them shall be such.

15 For they covered the face of the whole land, so that the land was darkened; and they did eat every herb of the land, and all the fruit of the trees which the hail had left: and there remained not any green thing in the trees, or in the herbs of the field, through all the land of Egypt.

16 Then Pharaoh called for Moses and Aaron in haste; and he said, I have sinned against the LORD your God, and against you.

17 Now therefore forgive, I pray thee, my sin only this once, and entreat the LORD your God, that he may but take away from me this death.

18 And he went out from Pharaoh, and entreated the LORD.

19 And the LORD turned a mighty strong west wind, which took away the locusts, and cast them into the Red sea; there remained not one locust in all the coasts of Egypt.

20 But still Pharaoh hardened his heart, so that he would not let the children of Israel go.

CHAPTER XI.

AND the LORD said unto Moses, Stretch out thine hand toward heaven, that there may be darkness over the land of Egypt, even darkness which may be felt.

2 And Moses stretched forth his hand toward heaven ; and there was a thick darkness in all the land of Egypt three days :

3 They saw not one another, neither rose any from his place for three days : but all the children of Israel had light in their dwellings.

4 And Pharaoh called unto Moses, and said, Go ye, serve the LORD ; only let your flocks and your herds be stayed : let your little ones also go with you.

5 And Moses said, Thou must give us also sacrifices and burnt offerings, that we may sacrifice unto the LORD our God.

6 Our cattle also shall go with us ; there shall not a hoof be left behind ; for thereof must we take to serve the LORD our God ; and we know not with what we must serve the LORD, until we come thither.

7 But Pharaoh said unto him, Get thee from me, take heed to thyself, see my face no more ; for in that day thou seest my face thou shalt die.

8 And Moses said, It shall be as thou hast spoken, I will see thy face again no more.

9 And the LORD said unto Moses, Yet one plague more will I bring upon Pharaoh, and upon Egypt ; afterwards he will let you go hence : when he shall let you go, he shall surely thrust you out hence altogether.

10 And Moses said, Thus saith the LORD, About midnight will I go out into the midst of Egypt :

11 And all the firstborn in the land of Egypt shall die, from the firstborn of Pharaoh that sitteth upon his throne, even unto the firstborn of the maid-servant that is behind the mill ; and all the firstborn of beasts.

12 And there shall be a great cry throughout all the land of Egypt, such as there was none like it, nor shall be like it any more.

13 But against any of the children of Israel shall not a dog move his tongue, against man or beast : that ye may know that the LORD doth put a difference between the Egyptians and Israel.

14 And all these thy servants shall come down unto me, and bow down themselves unto me, saying, Get thee out, and all the people that follow thee : and after that I will go out. And he went out from Pharaoh in a great anger.

CHAPTER XII.

AND the LORD spake unto Moses and Aaron in the land of Egypt, saying,

2 This month shall be unto you the beginning of months : it shall be the first month of the year to you.

3 Speak ye unto all the congregation of Israel, saying, In the tenth day of this month they shall take to them every man a lamb, according to the house of their fathers, a lamb for a house :

4 And if the household be too little for the lamb, let him and his neighbour next unto his house take it according to the number of the souls ; every man according to his eating shall make your count for the lamb.

5 And ye shall keep it up until the fourteenth day of the same month: and the whole assembly of the congregation of Israel shall kill it in the evening.

6 And ye shall eat the flesh in that night, roast with fire, and unleavened bread; and with bitter herbs they shall eat it.

7 Eat not of it raw, nor sodden at all with water, but roast with fire; his head with his legs, and with the purtenance thereof.

8 And ye shall let nothing of it remain until the morning; and that which remaineth of it until morning ye shall burn with fire.

9 And thus shall ye eat it; with your loins girded, your shoes on your feet, and your staff in your hand; and ye shall eat it in haste: it is the Passover unto the LORD.

10 For I will pass through the land of Egypt this night, and will smite all the firstborn in the land of Egypt, both man and beast; and against all the gods of Egypt I will execute judgment: I am the LORD.

11 I will pass over you, and the plague shall not be upon you to destroy you, when I smite the land of Egypt.

12 And this day shall be unto you for a memorial; and ye shall keep it a feast to the LORD throughout your generations: ye shall keep it a feast by an ordinance for ever.

13 Seven days shall ye eat unleavened bread; even the first day ye shall put away leaven out of your houses;

14 And in the first day there shall be a holy convocation, and in the seventh day there shall be a holy convocation to you; no manner of work shall be done in them, save that which every man must eat — that only may be done of you.

15 And ye shall observe the feast of unleavened bread; for in this selfsame day have I brought your armies out of the land of Egypt: therefore shall ye observe this day in your generations by an ordinance for ever.

16 In the first month, on the fourteenth day of the month at even, ye shall eat unleavened bread, until the one and twentieth day of the month at even.

17 Then Moses called for all the elders of Israel, and said unto them, Draw out and take you a lamb according to your families, and kill the passover.

18 For the LORD will pass through to smite the Egyptians; and the LORD will pass over your doors, and will not suffer the destroyer to come in unto your houses to smite you.

19 And ye shall observe this thing for an ordinance to thee and to thy sons for ever.

20 And it shall come to pass, when ye be come to the land which the LORD will give you, according as he hath promised, that ye shall keep this service.

21 And it shall come to pass, when your children shall say unto you, What mean ye by this service?

22 That ye shall say, It is the sacrifice of the LORD'S passover, who passed over the houses of the children of Israel in Egypt, when he smote the Egyptians, and delivered our houses. And the people bowed the head and worshipped.

23 And the children of Israel went away, and did as the LORD had commanded Moses and Aaron, so did they.

24 And it came to pass, that at midnight the LORD smote all the firstborn in the land of Egypt, from the firstborn of Pharaoh that sat on his throne unto the firstborn of the captive that was in the dungeon ; and all the firstborn of cattle.

25 And Pharaoh rose up in the night, he, and all his servants, and all the Egyptians; and there was a great cry in Egypt: for there was not a house where there was not one dead.

26 And he called for Moses and Aaron by night, and said, Rise up, and get you forth from among my people, both ye and the children of Israel; and go, serve the LORD as ye have said.

27 Also take your flocks and your herds, as ye have said, and be gone; and bless me also.

28 And the Egyptians were urgent upon the people, that they might send them out of the land in haste; for they said, We be all dead men.

29 And the people took their dough before it was leavened, out of their kneadingtroughs, and bound it up in their clothes upon their shoulders.

30 And the children of Israel journeyed from Rameses to Succoth, about six hundred thousand men on foot, beside children.

31 And a mixed multitude went up also with them; and flocks, and herds, even very much cattle.

32 And they baked unleavened cakes of the dough which they brought forth out of Egypt, for it was not leavened; because they were thrust out of Egypt, and could not tarry, neither had they prepared for themselves any victuals.

33 Now the sojourning of the children of Israel, who dwelt in Egypt, was four hundred and thirty years.

34 And it came to pass at the end of the four hundred and thirty years, even the selfsame day it came to pass, that all the hosts of the LORD went out from the land of Egypt.

35 It is a night to be much observed unto the LORD for bringing them out from the land of Egypt: this is that night of the LORD to be observed of all the children of Israel in their generations.

36 And it came to pass the selfsame day, that the LORD did bring the children of Israel out of the land of Egypt by their armies.

CHAPTER XIII.

AND Moses said unto the people, Remember this day, in which ye came out from Egypt, out of the house of bondage ; for by great might the LORD brought you out from this place: there shall no leavened bread be eaten.

2 This day came ye out in the month Abib.

3 And it shall be when the LORD shall bring thee into the land of the Canaanites, and the Hittites, and the Amorites, and the Hivites, and the Jebusites, which he sware unto thy fathers to give thee, a land flowing with milk and honey, that thou shalt keep this service in this month.

4 Seven days thou shalt eat unleavened bread, and in the seventh day shall be a feast to the LORD.

5 Unleavened bread shall be eaten seven days ; and there shall no leavened bread be seen with thee, neither shall there be leaven seen with thee in all thy quarters.

6 And thou shalt tell thy son in that day, saying, This is done because

of that which the LORD did unto me when I came forth out of Egypt.

7 And it shall be for a sign unto thee upon thine hand, and for a memorial between thine eyes, that the LORD's law may be in thy mouth: for with great might hath the LORD brought thee out of Egypt.

8 Thou shalt therefore keep this ordinance in his season from year to year.

9 And it came to pass, when Pharaoh had let the people go, that God led them not through the way of the land of the Philistines, although that was near; for God said, Lest peradventure the people repent when they see war, and they return to Egypt:

10 But God led the people about, through the way of the wilderness of the Red sea: and the children of Israel went up armed out of the land of Egypt.

11 And Moses took the bones of Joseph with him: for he had solemnly sworn the children of Israel, saying, God will surely visit you; and ye shall carry up my bones hence with you.

12 And they took their journey from Succoth, and encamped in Etham, in the edge of the wilderness.

13 And the LORD went before them by day in a pillar of a cloud, to lead them the way; and by night in a pillar of fire, to give them light; to go by day and night.

14 The pillar of the cloud did not depart by day, nor the pillar of fire by night, from before the people.

CHAPTER XIV.

AND the LORD spake unto Moses, saying,

2 Speak unto the children of Israel, that they turn and encamp before Pi-hahiroth, between Migdol and the sea, over against Baal-zephon: before it shall ye encamp by the sea.

3 For Pharaoh will say of the children of Israel, They are entangled in the land, the wilderness hath shut them in.

4 And Pharaoh shall follow after them; and I will be honoured upon Pharaoh, and upon all his host; that the Egyptians may know that I am the LORD. And they did so.

5 And it was told the king of Egypt that the people fled: and the heart of Pharaoh and of his servants was turned against the people, and they said, Why have we done this, that we have let Israel go from serving us?

6 And he made ready his chariot, and took his people with him;

7 And he took six hundred chosen chariots, and all the chariots of Egypt, and captains over every one of them.

8 And he pursued after the children of Israel: and the children of Israel went out with a high hand.

9 But the Egyptians pursued after them, all the horses and chariots of Pharaoh, and his horsemen, and his army, and overtook them encamping by the sea, beside Pi-hahiroth, before Baal-zephon.

10 And Pharaoh drew nigh; and the children of Israel lifted up their eyes, and, behold, the Egyptians marched after them; and they were sore afraid: and the children of Israel cried out unto the LORD.

11 And they said unto Moses, Is it because there were no graves in Egypt, that thou hast taken us away to die in the wilderness? wherefore hast thou dealt thus with us, to carry us forth out of Egypt?

12 Is not this the word that we did tell thee in Egypt, saying, Let us alone, that we may serve the Egyptians? For it had been better for us to serve the Egyptians, than that we should die in the wilderness.

13 And Moses said unto the people, Fear ye not, stand still, and see the salvation of the LORD, which he will shew to you, to day: for the Egyptians whom ye have seen to day, ye shall see them again no more for ever.

14 The LORD shall fight for you, and ye shall hold your peace.

15 And the LORD said unto Moses, Wherefore criest thou unto me? speak unto the children of Israel, that they go forward:

16 But lift thou up thy rod, and stretch out thine hand over the sea, and divide it: and the children of Israel shall go on dry ground through the midst of the sea.

17 And, behold, I will harden the hearts of the Egyptians will be hardened, and they shall follow them: and I will be honoured upon Pharaoh, and upon all his host, upon his chariots, and upon his horsemen.

18 And the Egyptians shall know that I am the LORD, when I have been honoured upon Pharaoh, upon his chariots, and upon his horsemen.

19 And the angel of God, which went before the camp of Israel, removed and went behind them; and the pillar of the cloud went from before their face, and stood behind them:

20 And it came between the camp of the Egyptians and the camp of Israel; and it was a cloud and darkness to them, but it gave light by night to these: so that the one came not near the other all the night,

21 And Moses stretched out his hand over the sea; and the LORD caused the sea to go back by a strong east wind all that night, and made the sea dry land, and the waters were divided.

22 And the children of Israel went into the midst of the sea upon the dry ground: and the waters were a wall unto them on their right hand, and on their left.

23 And the Egyptians pursued, and went in after them to the midst of the sea, even all Pharaoh's horses, his chariots, and his horsemen.

24 And it came to pass, that in the morning watch the LORD looked unto the host of the Egyptians through the pillar of fire and of the cloud, and troubled the host of the Egyptians,

25 And took off their chariot wheels, that they drove them heavily: so that the Egyptians said, Let us flee from the face of Israel; for the LORD fighteth for them against the Egyptians.

26 And the LORD said unto Moses, Stretch out thine hand over the sea, that the waters may come again upon the Egyptians, upon their chariots, and upon their horsemen.

27 And Moses stretched forth his hand over the sea, and the sea returned to his strength when the morning appeared; and the Egyptians fled against it; and the LORD overthrew the Egyptians in the midst of the sea,

28 And the waters returned, and covered the chariots, and the horsemen, and all the host of Pharaoh that came into the sea after them; there remained not so much as one of them.

29 But the children of Israel walked upon dry land in the midst of the sea; and the waters were a wall unto them on their right hand, and on their left.

30 Thus the LORD saved Israel that

day. out of the hand of the Egyptians;
and Israel saw the Egyptians dead
upon the sea shore.

31 And Israel saw that great work
which the LORD did upon the Egyptians: and they feared the LORD,
and believed in the LORD, and his
servant Moses.

CHAPTER XV.

THEN sang Moses and the children
of Israel this song unto the LORD,
and spoke, saying,

I sing to the Eternal,
for he is grandly triumphant:
horse and rider
he has dashed into the sea.
God is my triumph, my song;
he has become my deliverance.
Here is my God—him I glorify;
my father's God—I extol him.
The Eternal is a warrior,
The Eternal is his name.
Pharaoh's chariots and host
he has hurled into the sea;
his choicest knights
have sunk into the Sea of Weeds;
5 floods cover them,
they sank into the deeps as a stone.
Thy right hand, O Eternal,
shines forth with strength;
thy right hand, O Eternal,
crushes the foe.
In the height of thy greatness
thou destroyest thy enemies;
thou sendest thy wrath,
it consumes them as stubble.
At a breath from thy presence
the waters rose in piles,
waves stood like dikes,
the depths congealed
in the heart of the sea.
The foe said,
'I will pursue, overtake,
divide the booty—
they shall satiate my desire;
I draw my sword,
my hand destroys them.'
10 Thou madest thy wind blow,
and the sea covered them;
they sank as lead
into the mighty floods.

Who is like thee among the mighty,
O Eternal?
who is like thee resplendent in
holiness,
glorified in hymns,
a worker of wonders?
At the move of thy right hand,
the earth swallowed them.
Thou ledst in thy mercy
the people redeemed by thee;
thou guidedst it triumphantly
to thy holy abode.
The nations heard, and trembled;
a quiver seized on the dwellers in
Philistia,
15 Edom's princes were amazed,
of Moab's mighty men a tremor took
hold,
all the inhabitants of Canaan were
undone.
Fear and dread befell them,
at the grand appearance of thy arm
they were still as a stone—
while thy people marched on, O
Eternal,
the people thou hadst made thy own.
Thou carriedst them, and plantedst
them
on the hill of thy possession;
on the spot formed, O Eternal, into
a seat for thee,
the sanctuary, O Lord, established
by thy hands.—
God will reign for ever and ever.

19 For the horse of Pharaoh went
in with his chariots and with his horsemen into the sea, and the LORD brought
again the waters of the sea upon them;
but the children of Israel went on dry
land in the midst of the sea.

20 And Miriam the prophetess, the
sister of Aaron, took a timbrel in her
hand; and all the women went out
after her with timbrels and with
dances.

21 And Miriam answered them:

Sing to the Eternal,
for he is grandly triumphant:
horse and rider
he has dashed into the sea.

22 Then Moses made Israel move

from the Red sea, and they went out into the wilderness of Shur; and they went three days in the wilderness, and found no water.

23 And when they came to Marah, they could not drink of the waters of Marah, for they were bitter: therefore the name of it was called Marah.

24 And the people murmured against Moses, saying, What shall we drink?

25 And he cried unto the LORD; and the LORD shewed him a tree, which, when he had cast into the waters, the waters were made sweet: there he made for them a statute and an ordinance, and there he proved them,

26 And said, If thou wilt diligently hearken to the voice of the LORD thy God, and wilt do that which is right in his sight, and wilt give ear to his commandments, and keep all his statutes, I will put none of these diseases upon thee, which I have brought upon the Egyptians: for I am the LORD that healeth thee.

27 And they came to Elim, where were twelve wells of water, and threescore and ten palm trees: and they encamped there by the waters.

CHAPTER XVI.

AND they took their journey from Elim, and all the congregation of the children of Israel came unto the wilderness of Sin, which is between Elim and Sinai, on the fifteenth day of the second month after their departing out of the land of Egypt.

2 And the whole congregation of the children of Israel murmured against Moses and Aaron in the wilderness:

3 And the children of Israel said unto them, Would to God we had died by the hand of the LORD in the land of Egypt, when we sat by the flesh pots, and when we did eat bread to the full; for ye have brought us forth into this wilderness, to kill this whole assembly with hunger.

4 Then said the LORD unto Moses, Behold, I will rain bread from heaven for you; and the people shall go out and gather a certain rate every day, that I may prove them, whether they will walk in my law, or not.

5 And it shall come to pass, that on the sixth day they shall prepare that which they shall bring in; and it shall be twice as much as they gather daily.

6 And Moses and Aaron said unto all the children of Israel, At even, then ye shall know that the LORD hath brought you out from the land of Egypt:

7 And in the morning, then ye shall see the glory of the LORD; for he hath heard your murmurings against the LORD: and what are we, that ye murmur against us?

8 And Moses said, This shall be, when the LORD shall give you in the evening flesh to eat, and in the morning bread to the full; for the LORD hath heard your murmurings which ye murmur against him: and what are we? your murmurings are not against us, but against the LORD.

9 And Moses spake unto Aaron, Say unto all the congregation of the children of Israel, Come near before the LORD: for he hath heard your murmurings.

10 And it came to pass, as Aaron spake unto the whole congregation of the children of Israel, that they looked toward the wilderness, and, behold, the glory of the LORD appeared in the cloud.

11 And the LORD spake unto Moses, saying,

12 I have heard the murmurings of the children of Israel: speak unto them, saying, At even ye shall eat flesh, and in the morning ye shall be filled with bread; and ye shall know that I am the LORD your God.

13 And it came to pass, that at even the quails came up, and covered the camp: and in the morning the dew lay round about the camp.

14 And when the dew that lay was gone up, behold, upon the face of the wilderness their lay a small round thing, as small as the hoar frost on the ground.

15 And when the children of Israel saw it, they said one to another, It is food: for they knew not what it was. And Moses said unto them, This is the bread which the LORD hath given you to eat.

16 This is the thing which the LORD hath commanded, Gather of it every man according to his eating, an omer for every man, according to the number of your persons; take ye every man for them which are in his tents.

17 And the children of Israel did so, and gathered, some more, some less.

18 And when they did mete it with an omer, he that gathered much had nothing over, and he that gathered little had no lack; they gathered every man according to his eating.

19 And Moses said, Let no man leave of it till the morning.

20 Notwithstanding they hearkened not unto Moses; but some of them left of it until the morning, and it bred worms and stank: and Moses was wroth with them.

21 And they gathered it every morning every man according to his eating: and when the sun waxed hot, it melted.

22 And it came to pass, that on the sixth day they gathered twice as much bread, two omers for one man: and all the rulers of the congregation came and told Moses.

23 And he said unto them, This is that which the LORD hath said, To morrow is the rest of the holy sabbath unto the LORD: bake that which ye will bake to day, and seethe that ye will seethe; and that which remaineth over lay up for you to be kept until the morning.

24 And they laid it up till the morning, as Moses bade: and it did not rot, neither was there any worm therein.

25 And Moses said, Eat that to day; for to day is a sabbath unto the LORD: to day ye shall not find it in the field.

26 Six days ye shall gather it; but on the seventh day, which is the sabbath, in it there shall be none.

27 And it came to pass, that there went out some of the people on the seventh day to gather, and they found none.

28 And the LORD said unto Moses, How long refuse ye to keep my commandments and my laws?

29 See, for that the LORD hath given you the sabbath, therefore he giveth you on the sixth day the bread of two days: abide ye every man in his place, let no man go out of his place on the seventh day.

30 So the people rested on the seventh day.

31 And the house of Israel called the name thereof Manna: and it was like coriander seed, white; and the taste of it was like wafers made with honey.

32 And Moses said, This is the thing which the LORD commandeth, Fill an omer of it to be kept for your genera-

tions; that they may see the bread wherewith I have fed you in the wilderness, when I brought you forth from the land of Egypt.

33 And Moses said unto Aaron, Take a pot, and put an omer full of manna therein, and lay it up before the LORD, to be kept for your generations.

34 As the LORD commanded Moses, so Aaron laid it up before the Testimony, to be kept.

35 And the children of Israel did eat manna forty years, until they came to a land inhabited: they did eat manna, until they came unto the borders of the land of Canaan.

36 Now an omer is the tenth part of an ephah.

CHAPTER XVII.

AND all the congregation of the children of Israel journeyed from the wilderness of Sin, after their journeys, according to the commandment of the LORD, and pitched in Rephidim: and there was no water for the people to drink.

2 Wherefore the people did chide with Moses, and said, Give us water that we may drink. And Moses said unto them, Why chide ye with me? wherefore do ye tempt the LORD?

3 And the people thirsted there for water; and the people murmured against Moses, and said, Wherefore hast thou brought us up out of Egypt, to kill us and our children and our cattle with thirst?

4 And Moses cried unto the LORD, saying, What shall I do unto this people? they be almost ready to stone me.

5 And the LORD said unto Moses, Go on before the people, and take with thee of the elders of Israel; and thy rod, wherewith thou smotest the river, take in thine hand, and go.

6 Behold, I will stand before thee there upon the rock in Horeb; and thou shalt smite the rock, and there shall come water out of it, that the people may drink. And Moses did so in the sight of the elders of Israel.

7 And he called the name of the place Massah and Meribah, because of the chiding of the children of Israel, and because they tempted the LORD, saying, Is the LORD among us, or not?

8 Then came Amalek, and fought with Israel in Rephidim.

9 And Moses said unto Joshua, Choose us out men, and go out, fight with Amalek: to morrow I will stand on the top of the hill with the rod of God in mine hand.

10 So Joshua did as Moses had said to him, and fought with Amalek: and Moses, Aaron, and Hur went up to the top of the hill.

11 And it came to pass, when Moses held up his hand, that Israel prevailed: and when he let down his hand, Amalek prevailed.

12 But Moses' hands were heavy; and they took a stone, and put it under him, and he sat thereon; and Aaron and Hur stayed up his hands, the one on the one side, and the other on the other side; and his hands were steady until the going down of the sun.

13 And Joshua discomfited Amalek and his people with the edge of the sword.

14 And the LORD said unto Moses, Write this for a memorial in a book, and repeat it in the ears of Joshua: for I will utterly put out the remembrance of Amalek from under heaven.

15 And Moses built an altar, and called the name of it JEHOVAH-nissi:

16 For he said, Because the LORD hath sworn that the LORD will have war with Amalek from generation to generation.

CHAPTER XVIII.

WHEN Jethro, the priest of Midian, Moses' father in law, heard of all that God had done for Moses, and for Israel his people, and that the LORD had brought Israel out of Egypt:

2 Then Jethro, Moses' father in law, took Zipporah, Moses' wife, after he had sent her back,

3 And her two sons: of which the name of the one was Gershom; for he said, I have been an alien in a strange land;

4 And the name of the other was Eliezer; for the God of my father, said he, was mine help, and delivered me from the sword of Pharaoh:

5 And Jethro, Moses' father in law, came with his sons and his wife unto Moses into the wilderness, where he encamped at the mount of God:

6 And he sent word unto Moses, saying, I thy father in law Jethro am come unto thee, and thy wife, and her two sons with her.

7 And Moses went out to meet his father in law, and did obeisance, and kissed him; and they asked each other of their welfare; and they came into the tent.

8 And Moses told his father in law all that the LORD had done unto Pharaoh and to the Egyptians for Israel's sake, and all the travail that had come upon them by the way, and how the LORD delivered them.

9 And Jethro rejoiced for all the goodness which the LORD had done to Israel, whom he had delivered out of the hand of the Egyptians.

10 And Jethro said, Blessed be the LORD, who hath delivered you out of the hand of the Egyptians, and out of the hand of Pharaoh, who hath delivered the people from under the hand of the Egyptians.

11 Now I know that the LORD is greater than all gods: for the thing wherein they dealt proudly came over them.

12 And Jethro, Moses' father in law, took a burnt offering and sacrifices for God: and Aaron came, and all the elders of Israel, to eat bread with Moses' father in law before God.

13 And it came to pass on the morrow, that Moses sat to judge the people: and the people stood by Moses from the morning unto the evening.

14 And when Moses' father in law saw all that he did to the people, he said, What is this thing that thou doest to the people? Why sittest thou thyself alone, and all the people stand by thee from morning unto even?

15 And Moses said unto his father in law, Because the people come unto me to inquire of God:

16 When they have a matter, they come unto me; and I judge between one and another, and I do make them know the statutes of God, and his laws.

17 And Moses' father in law said unto him, The thing that thou doest is not good.

18 Thou wilt surely wear away, both thou, and this people that is with thee: for this thing is too heavy for thee; thou art not able to perform it thyself alone.

19 Hearken now unto my voice, I will give thee counsel, and God shall be with thee: Be thou for the people to God-ward, that thou mayest bring the causes unto God:

20 And thou shalt teach them ordinances and laws, and shalt shew them the way wherein they must walk, and the work that they must do.

21 Moreover thou shalt provide out of all the people able men, such as fear God, men of truth, hating covetousness; and place such over them, to be rulers of thousands, and rulers of hundreds, rulers of fifties, and rulers of tens:

22 And let them judge the people at all seasons: and it shall be, that every great matter they shall bring unto thee, but every small matter they shall judge: so shall it be easier for thyself, and they shall bear the burden with thee.

23 If thou shalt do this thing, and God command thee so, then thou shalt be able to endure, and all this people shall also go to their place in peace.

24 So Moses hearkened to the voice of his father in law, and did all that he had said.

25 And Moses chose able men out of all Israel, and made them heads over the people, rulers of thousands, rulers of hundreds, rulers of fifties, and rulers of tens.

26 And they judged the people at all seasons: the hard causes they brought unto Moses, but every small matter they judged themselves.

27 And Moses let his father in law depart; and he went his way into his own land.

CHAPTER XIX.

IN the third month, when the children of Israel were gone forth out of the land of Egypt, the same day came they into the wilderness of Sinai.

2 For they were departed from Rephidim, and were come to the desert of Sinai, and had pitched in the wilderness; and there Israel camped before the mount.

3 And Moses went up unto God, and the LORD called unto him out of the mountain, saying, Thus shalt thou say to the house of Jacob, and tell the children of Israel;

4 Ye have seen what I did unto the Egyptians, and how I bare you on eagles' wings, and brought you unto myself.

5 Now therefore, if ye will obey my voice indeed, and keep my covenant, then ye shall be a peculiar treasure unto me above all people: for all the earth is mine:

6 And ye shall be unto me a kingdom of priests, and a holy nation. These are the words which thou shalt speak unto the children of Israel.

7 And Moses came and called for the elders of the people, and laid before them all these words which the LORD commanded him.

8 And all the people answered together, and said, All that the LORD hath spoken we will do. And Moses returned the words of the people unto the LORD.

9 And the LORD said unto Moses, Go unto the people, and sanctify them to day and to morrow, and let them wash their garments.

10 And be ready for the third day: for on the third day the LORD will appear in the sight of all the people upon mount Sinai.

11 And Moses went down from the mount unto the people; and sanctified the people; and they washed their raiments.

12 And he said unto the people, Be ready against the third day.

13 And it came to pass on the third day in the morning, that there were

thunders and lightnings, and a thick cloud upon the mount, and the voice of the trumpet exceeding loud; so that all the people that were in the camp trembled.

14 And Moses brought forth the people out of the camp to meet with God; and they stood at the nether part of the mount.

.15 And mount Sinai was altogether on a smoke, because the LORD appeared upon it in fire: and the smoke thereof ascended as the smoke of a furnace, and the whole mount quaked greatly.

16 And the voice of the trumpet sounded long, and waxed louder and louder, and Moses spake, and God answered him by a voice.

17 And the LORD appeared upon mount Sinai, and the LORD called Moses up to the top of the mount; and Moses went up.

CHAPTER XX.

AND God spake all these words, saying,

2 I am the Eternal thy God, who brought thee out of the land of Egypt, out of the house of bondage.

3 Thou shalt have no other gods before me.

4 Thou shalt not make unto thee any graven image, or any likeness of any thing that is in heaven above, or that is in the earth beneath, or that is in the water under the earth:

5 Thou shalt not bow down thyself to them, nor serve them: for I. the LORD thy God am a jealous God, visiting the iniquity of the fathers upon the children unto the third and fourth generation of them that hate me;

6 And shewing mercy unto thousands of them that love me, and keep my commandments.

7 Thou shalt not take the name of the LORD thy God in vain: for the LORD will not let him go unpunished that taketh his name in vain.

8 Remember the Sabbath day, to keep it holy.

9 Six days shalt thou labour, and do all thy work:

10 But the seventh day is the Sabbath of the LORD thy God: in it thou shalt not do any work, thou, nor thy son, nor thy daughter, thy manservant, nor thy maidservant, nor thy cattle, nor thy stranger that is within thy gates:

11 For in six days the LORD made heaven and earth, the sea, and all that is therein, and rested the seventh day: wherefore the LORD blessed the Sabbath day, and hallowed it,

12 Honour thy father and thy mother: that thy days may be prolonged upon the land which the LORD thy God giveth thee.

13 Thou shalt not kill.

14 Thou shalt not commit adultery.

15 Thou shalt not steal.

16 Thou shalt not bear false witness against thy neighbour.

17 Thou shalt not covet thy neighbour's house, thou shalt not covet thy neighbour's wife, nor his manservant, nor his maidservant, nor his ox, nor his ass, nor any thing that is thy neighbour's.

18 And all the people saw the thunderings, and the lightnings, and the noise of the trumpet, and the mountain smoking: and when the people saw it, they removed, and stood afar off.

19 And they said unto Moses, Speak thou with us, and we will hear: but let not God speak with us, lest we die.

·20 And Moses said unto the people, Fear not: for God is come to prove you, and that his fear may be before your faces, that ye sin not.

21 And the people stood afar off, and Moses drew near unto the thick darkness where God was.

22 And the LORD said unto Moses, Thus thou shalt say unto the children of Israel, Ye have seen that I have spoken with you from heaven.

23 Ye shall not make with me gods of silver, neither shall ye make unto you gods of gold.

24 An altar of earth thou shalt make unto me, and shalt sacrifice thereon thy burnt offerings, and thy peace offerings, thy sheep, and thine oxen: in all places where I have my name called I will come unto thee, and I will bless thee.

25 And if thou wilt make me an altar of stone, thou shalt not build it of hewn stone: for if thou lift up thy iron upon it, thou hast polluted it.

CHAPTER XXI.

NOW these are the judgments which thou shalt set before them.

2 If thou buy a Hebrew servant, six years he shall serve: and in the seventh he shall go out free for nothing.

3 If he came in by himself, he shall go out by himself: if he were married, then his wife shall go out with him.

4 If his master have given him a wife, and she have born him sons or daughters; the wife and her children shall be her master's, and he shall go out by himself.

5 And if the servant shall plainly say, I love my master, my wife, and my children; I will not go out free:

6 Then his master shall bring him unto the judges; he shall also bring him to the door, or unto the door post; and his master shall bore his ear through with an awl; and he shall serve him for ever.

7 And if a man sell his daughter to be a maidservant, she shall not go out as the menservants do.

8 If she please not her master, who hath betrothed her to himself, then shall he let her be redeemed: to sell her unto a strange nation he shall have no power, seeing he hath dealt deceitfully with her.

9 And if he have betrothed her unto his son, he shall deal with her after the manner of daughters.

10 If he take him another wife, her food, her raiment, and her honour, shall he not diminish.

11 And if he do not these three unto her, then shall she go out free without money.

12 He that smiteth a man, so that he die, shall be surely put to death.

13 And if a man lie not in wait, then I will appoint thee a place whither he shall flee.

14 But if a man come presumptuously upon his neighbour, to slay him with guile; thou shalt take him from mine altar, that he be put to death.

15 And he that smiteth his father, or his mother, shall be surely put to death.

16 And he that stealeth a man, and selleth him, or if he be found in his hand, he shall surely be put to death.

17 And he that curseth his father, or his mother, shall surely be put to death.

18 And if men strive together, and one smite another with a stone, or with his fist, and he die not, but keepeth his bed:

19 If he rise again, and walk abroad

upon his staff, then shall he that smote him be quit: only he shall pay for the loss of his time, and shall cause him to be thoroughly healed.

20 And if a man smite his servant, or his maid, with a rod, and he die under his hand; he shall be surely punished.

21 And if a man smite the eye of his servant, or the eye of his maid, that it perish; he shall let him go free for his eye's sake.

22 And if he smite out his manservant's tooth; he shall let him go free for his tooth's sake.

23 If an ox gore a man or a woman, that they die: then the ox shall be surely stoned, and his flesh shall not be eaten; but the owner of the ox shall be quit.

24 But if the ox were wont to push with his horn in time past, and it hath been testified to his owner, and he hath not kept him in, and the ox hath killed a man or a woman; the ox shall be stoned, and his owner also shall be put to death.

25 If there be laid on him a sum of money, then he shall give for the ransom of his life whatsoever is laid upon him.

26 Whether he have gored a son, or have gored a daughter, according to this judgment shall it be done unto him.

27 If the ox shall push a manservant or a maidservant; the owner shall give unto their master thirty shekels of silver, and the ox shall be stoned.

28 And if a man shall open a pit, or if a man shall dig a pit, and not cover it, and an ox or an ass fall therein;

29 The owner of the pit shall make it good, and give money unto the owner of them; and the dead beast shall be his.

30 And if one man's ox hurt another's, that he die: then they shall sell the live ox, and divide the money of it; and the dead ox also they shall divide.

31 Or if it be known that the ox hath used to push in time past, and his owner hath not kept him in; he shall surely pay ox for ox; and the dead shall be his own.

CHAPTER XXII.

IF a man shall steal an ox, or a sheep, and kill it, or sell it; he shall restore five oxen for an ox, and four sheep for a sheep.

2 If a thief be found breaking in, and be smitten that he die, there shall no blood be shed for him.

3 If the sun be risen upon him, it is murder; for what he has stolen he should make full restitution: if he have nothing, then he shall be sold for his theft.

4 If the theft be certainly found in his hand alive, whether it be ox, or ass, or sheep; he shall restore double.

5 If a man shall cause a field or vineyard to be eaten, and shall put in his beast, and shall feed in another man's field; of the best of his own field, and of the best of his own vineyard, shall he make restitution.

6 If fire break out, and catch in thorns, so that the stacks of corn, or the standing corn, or the field, be consumed therewith; he that kindled the fire shall surely make restitution.

7 If a man shall deliver unto his neighbour money or stuff to keep, and it be stolen out of the man's house; if the thief be found, let him pay double.

8 If the thief be not found, then the

master of the house shall be brought unto the judges, to see whether he have put his hand unto his neighbour's goods.

9 For all manner of trespass, whether it be for ox, for ass, for sheep, for raiment, or for any manner of lost thing, which another challengeth to be his, the cause of both parties shall come before the judges; and whom the judges shall condemn, he shall pay double unto his neighbour.

10 If a man deliver unto his neighbour an ass, or an ox, or a sheep, or any beast, to keep ; and it die, or be hurt, or driven away, no man seeing it:

11 Then shall an oath of the LORD be between them both, that he hath not put his hand unto his neighbour's goods; and the owner of it shall accept thereof, and he shall not make it good.

12 And if it be stolen from him, he shall make restitution unto the owner thereof.

13 If it be torn in pieces, then let him bring it for witness, and he shall not make good that which was torn.

14 And if a man borrow aught of his neighbour, and it be hurt, or die, the owner thereof not being with it, he shall surely make it good.

15 But if the owner thereof be with it, he shall not make it good: if he be hired to keep the thing, he looses his hire.

16 Thou shalt not vex a stranger, nor oppress him: for ye were strangers in the land of Egypt.

17 Ye shall not afflict any widow, or fatherless child.

18 If thou afflict them in any wise, and they cry unto me, I will surely hear their cry;

19 And my wrath shall wax hot, and I will kill you with the sword;

and your wives shall be widows, and your children fatherless.

20 If thou lend money to any of my people that is poor by thee, thou shalt not be to him as a usurer, neither shalt thou lay upon him usury.

21 If thou at all take thy neighbour's raiment to pledge, thou shalt deliver it unto him when the sun goeth down :

22 For that is his covering only, it is his raiment for his skin: wherein shall he sleep ? and it shall come to pass, when he crieth unto me, that I will hear; for I am gracious.

23 Thou shalt not revile the judges, nor curse the ruler of thy people.

24 Thou shalt not delay to offer the first of thy ripe fruits, and of thy wine : the firstborn of thy sons shalt thou sanctify unto me.

25 Likewise shalt thou do with thine oxen, and with thy sheep: seven days it shall be with his mother; on the eighth day thou shalt give it me.

26 And ye shall be holy men unto me : neither shall ye eat any flesh that is torn of beasts in the field; ye shall cast it to the dogs.

CHAPTER XXIII.

THOU shalt not raise a false report : put not thine hand with the wicked to be an unrighteous witness.

2 Thou shalt not follow a multitude to do evil: neither shalt thou speak in a cause to incline after many to wrest judgment.

3 Neither shalt thou countenance a poor man in his cause on account of his poverty.

4 If thou meet thine enemy's ox or his ass going astray, thou shalt surely bring it back to him again.

5 If thou see the beast of him that hateth thee lying under his burden,

and wouldest forbear to help him, thou shalt surely help with him.

6 Thou shalt not wrest the judgment of thy poor in his cause.

7 Keep thee far from a false matter; and the innocent and righteous slay thou not: for I will not justify the wicked.

8 And thou shalt take no gift: for the gift blindeth the wise, and perverteth the words of the righteous.

9 Also thou shalt not oppress a stranger: for ye know the heart of a stranger, seeing ye were strangers in the land of Egypt.

10 And six years thou shalt sow thy land, and shalt gather in the fruits thereof:

11 But the seventh year thou shalt let it rest and lie still; that the poor of thy people may eat: and what they leave the beasts of the field shall eat. In like manner thou shalt deal with thy vineyard, and with thy oliveyard.

12 Six days thou shalt do thy work, and on the seventh day thou shalt rest: that thine ox and thine ass may rest, and the son of thy handmaid, and the stranger, may be refreshed.

13 And in all things that I have said unto you be circumspect: and make no mention of the name of other gods, neither let it be heard out of thy mouth.

14 Three times thou shalt keep a feast unto me in the year.

15 Thou shalt keep the feast of unleavened bread: thou shalt eat unleavened bread seven days, as I commanded thee, in the time appointed of the month Abib; for in it thou camest out from Egypt: and none shall appear before me empty:

16 And the feast of harvest, the firstfruits of thy labours, which thou hast sown in the field: and the feast of ingathering, which is at the end of the year, when thou hast gathered in thy labours out of the field.

17 Three times in the year all thy males shall appear before the Lord GOD.

18 Thou shalt not offer the blood of my sacrifice with leavened bread; neither shall the fat of my sacrifice remain until the morning.

19 The first of the firstfruits of thy land thou shalt bring into the house of the LORD thy God. Thou shalt not seethe a kid in his mother's milk.

CHAPTER XXIV.

AND God said unto Moses, Come up, thou, and Aaron, Nadab, and Abihu, and seventy of the elders of Israel; and worship ye afar off.

2 And Moses alone shall come near the LORD: but they shall not come nigh; neither shall the people go up with him.

3 And Moses came and told the people all the words of the LORD, and all the judgments: and all the people answered with one voice, and said, All the words which the LORD hath said, will we do.

4 And Moses wrote all the words of the LORD, and rose up early in the morning, and built an altar under the hill, and twelve pillars, according to the twelve tribes of Israel.

5 And he sent young men of the children of Israel, which offered burnt offerings, and sacrificed peace offerings of oxen unto the LORD.

6 And he took the book of the covenant, and read in the audience of the people: and they said, All that the LORD hath said will we do, and be obedient.

7 And the LORD said unto Moses,

Come up to me into the mount, and be there: and I will give thee tables of stone, and a law, and commandments which I have written ; that thou mayest teach them.

8 And Moses rose up, and his disciple Joshua ; and Moses went up into the mount of God.

9 And he said unto the elders, Tarry ye here for us, until we come again unto you: and, behold, Aaron and Hur are with you: if any man have any matters to do, let him come unto them.

10 And Moses went up into the mount, and a cloud covered the mount.

11 And the glory of the LORD abode upon mount Sinai, and the cloud covered it six days : and the seventh day he called unto Moses out of the midst of the cloud.

12 And the sight of the glory of the LORD was like devouring fire on the top of the mount in the eyes of the children of Israel.

13 And Moses went into the midst of the cloud, and went up into the mount : and Moses was in the mount forty days and forty nights.

CHAPTER XXV.

AND the LORD spake unto Moses, saying,

2 Speak unto the children of Israel, that they bring me an offering: of every man that giveth it willingly with his heart ye shall take my offering.

3 And this is the offering which ye shall take of them; gold, and silver, and brass,

4 And blue, and purple, and scarlet, and fine linen, and goats' hair,

5 And rams' skins dyed red, and badgers' skins, and cedar wood,

6 Oil for the light, spices for anointing oil, and for sweet incense,

7 Onix stones, and stones to be set in he ephod, and in the breastplate.

8 And let them make me a sanctuary; that I may dwell among them.

9 According to all that I shew thee, after the pattern of the tabernacle, and the pattern of all the instruments thereof, even so shall ye make it

10 See, I have called by name Bezaleel the son of Uri, the son of Hur, of the tribe of Judah :

11 And I have filled him with the spirit of God, in wisdom, and in understanding, and in knowledge, and in all manner of workmanship,

12 To devise cunning works, to work in gold, and in silver, and in brass,

13 And in cutting of stones, to set them, and in carving of timber, to work in all manner of workmanship.

14 And I, behold, I have given with him Aholiab, the son of Ahisamach, of the tribe of Dan: and in the hearts of all that are wise hearted I have put wisdom, that they may make all that I have commanded thee ;

15 The tabernacle of the congregation, and the ark of the testimony, and the mercy seat that is thereupon, and all the furniture of the tabernacle,

16 And the table and his furniture, and the pure candlestick with all his furniture, and the altar of incense,

17 And the altar of burnt offering with all his furniture, and the laver and his foot,

18 And the clothes of service, and the holy garments for Aaron the priest, and the garments of his sons, to minister in the priest's office,

19 And the anointing oil, and sweet incense for the holy place: according to all that I have commanded thee shall they do.

20 And I will sanctify the taber-

nacle of the congregation, and the altar: I will sanctify also both Aaron and his sons, to minister to me in the priest's office.

21 And I will dwell among the children of Israel, and will be their God.

22 And they shall know that I am the LORD their God, that brought them forth out of the land of Egypt, that I may dwell among them: I am the LORD their God.

23 When thou takest the sum of the children of Israel after their number, then shall they give every man a ransom for his soul unto the LORD, when thou numberest them; that there be no plague among them, when thou numberest them.

24 This they shall give, every one that passeth among them that are numbered, half a shekel after the shekel of the sanctuary: (a shekel is twenty gerahs:) a half shekel shall be the offering of the LORD.

25 Every one that passeth among them that are numbered, from twenty years old and above, shall give an offering unto the LORD.

26 The rich shall not give more, and the poor shall not give less, than half a shekel, when they give an offering unto the LORD, to make an atonement for your souls.

27 And thou shalt take the atonement money of the children of Israel, and shalt appoint it for the service of the tabernacle of the congregation; that it may be a memorial unto the children of Israel before the LORD, to make an atonement for your souls.

28 And the LORD spake unto Moses, saying,

29 Speak thou also unto the children of Israel, saying, Verily my sabbaths ye shall keep: for it is a sign between me and you throughout your generations; that ye may know that I am the LORD that doth sanctify you.

30 Ye shall keep the sabbath therefore; for it is holy unto you. Every one that defileth it shall surely be put to death: for whosoever doeth any work therein, that soul shall be cut off from among his people.

31 Six days may work be done; but in the seventh is the sabbath of rest, holy to the LORD: whosoever doeth any work in the sabbath day, he shall surely be put to death.

32 Wherefore the children of Israel shall keep the sabbath, to observe the sabbath throughout their generations, for a perpetual covenant.

33 It is a sign between me and the children of Israel for ever: for in six days the LORD made heaven and earth, and on the seventh day he rested, and was satisfied.

34 And he gave unto Moses, when he had made an end of communing with him upon mount Sinai, two tables of testimony, tables of stone, written with the finger of God.

CHAPTER XXVI.

AND when the people saw that Moses delayed to come down out of the mount, the people gathered themselves together unto Aaron, and said unto him, Up, make us gods, which shall go before us; for as for this Moses, the man that brought us up out of the land of Egypt, we know not what is become of him.

2 And Aaron said unto them, Take off the golden earrings, which are in the ears of your wives, of your sons, and of your daughters, and bring them unto me.

3 And all the people took off the golden earrings which were in their ears, and brought them unto Aaron.

4 And he received them at their hand, and fashioned it with a graving tool, after he had made it a molten calf: and they said, These be thy gods, O Israel, which brought thee up out of the land of Egypt.

5 And when Aaron saw it, he built an altar before it; and Aaron made proclamation, and said, To-morrow is a feast to the-LORD.

6 And they rose up early on the morrow, and offered burnt offerings, and brought peace offerings; and the people sat down to eat and to drink, and rose up to play.

7 And the LORD said unto Moses, Go, get thee down; for thy people, which thou broughtest out of the land of Egypt, have corrupted themselves:

8 They have turned aside quickly out of the way which I commanded them: they have made them a molten calf, and have worshipped it, and have sacrificed thereunto, and said, These be thy gods, O Israel, which have brought thee up out of the land of Egypt.

9 And the LORD said unto Moses, I have seen this people, and, behold, it is a stiff-necked people:

10 Now therefore let me alone, that my wrath may wax hot against them, and that I may consume them: and I will make of thee a great nation.

11 And Moses besought the LORD his God, and said, LORD, why doth thy wrath wax hot against thy people, which thou hast brought forth out of the land of Egypt with great power, and with a mighty hand?

12 Wherefore should the Egyptians speak, and say, For mischief did he bring them out, to slay them in the mountains, and to consume them from the face of the earth? Turn from thy fierce wrath, and repent of this evil against thy people.

13 Remember Abraham, Isaac, and Israel, thy servants, to whom thou didst swear by thine own self, and saidst unto them, I will multiply you as the stars of heaven, and all this land that I have spoken of will I give unto your children, and they shall inherit it for ever.

14 And the LORD repented of the evil which he thought to do unto his people.

15 And Moses turned, and went down from the mount, and the two tables of the testimony were in his hand: the tables were written on both their sides; on the one side and on the other were they written.

16 And the tables were the work of God, and the writing was the writing of God, graven upon the tables.

17 And when Joshua heard the noise of the people as they shouted, he said unto Moses, There is a noise of war in the camp.

18 And he said, It is not the voice of them that shout for mastery, neither is it the voice of them that cry for being overcome; but the noise of them that sing do I hear.

19 And it came to pass, as soon as he came nigh unto the camp, that he saw the calf, and the dancing: and Moses' anger waxed hot, and he cast the tables out of his hands, and broke them beneath the mount.

20 And he took the calf which they had made, and burnt it in the fire, and ground it to powder, and strewed it upon the water, and made the children of Israel drink of it.

21 And Moses said unto Aaron, What did this people unto thee, that thou hast brought so great a sin upon them?

22 And Aaron said, Let not the anger of my lord wax hot: thou knowest the people, that they are set on mischief.

23 For they said unto me, Make us gods, which shall go before us: for as for this Moses, the man that brought us up out of the land of Egypt, we know not what is become of him.

24 And I said unto them, Whosoever hath any gold, let them break it off. So they gave it me: then I cast it into the fire, and there came out this calf.

25 And when Moses saw that the people were disorganized, for Aaron had made them unbridled to their shame among their enemies;

26 Then Moses stood in the gate of the camp, and said, Who is on the LORD's side? let him come unto me. And all the sons of Levi gathered themselves together unto him.

27 And he said unto them, Thus saith the LORD God of Israel, Put every man his sword by his side, and go in and out from gate to gate throughout the camp, and slay every man his brother, and every man his companion, and every man his neighbour that is rebellious.

28 And the children of Levi did according to the word of Moses: and there fell of the people that day about three thousand men.

29 And Moses said, Consecrate yourselves to-day to the LORD, even every man upon his son, and upon his brother; that he may bestow upon you a blessing this day.

30 And it came to pass on the morrow, that Moses said unto the people, Ye have sinned a great sin: and now I will go up unto the LORD; peradventure I shall make an atonement for your sin.

31 And Moses returned unto the LORD, and said, Oh, this people have sinned a great sin, and have made them gods of gold.

32 Yet now, if thou wilt forgive their sin—; and if not, blot me, I pray thee, out of thy book which thou hast written.

33 And the LORD said unto Moses, Whosoever hath sinned against me, him will I blot out of my book.

34 Therefore now go, lead the people unto the place of which I have spoken unto thee: behold, my presence shall go before thee: nevertheless, in the day when I visit, I will visit their sin upon them.

35 And the LORD plagued the people, because of the calf, which Aaron made.

CHAPTER XXVII.

AND the LORD said unto Moses, Depart and go up hence, thou and the people which thou hast brought up out of the land of Egypt, unto the land which I sware unto Abraham, to Isaac, and to Jacob, saying, Unto thy children will I give it: unto a land flowing with milk and honey.

2 And the LORD said unto Moses, Say unto the children of Israel, Ye are a stiff-necked people: I will come up into the midst of thee in a moment, and consume thee: therefore now put off thy ornaments from thee, that I may know what to do unto thee.

3 And the children of Israel stripped themselves of their ornaments by the mount Horeb.

4 And Moses took the tabernacle, and pitched it without the camp, afar off from the camp, and called it the Tabernacle of the congregation. And it came to pass, that every one which sought the LORD went out unto the tabernacle of the congregation, which was without the camp.

5 And it came to pass, when Moses went out unto the tabernacle, that all the people rose up, and stood every man at his tent door, and looked after Moses, until he was gone into the tabernacle.

6 And it came to pass, as Moses entered into the tabernacle, the cloudy pillar descended, and stood at the door of the tabernacle, and the LORD talked with Moses.

7 And all the people saw the cloudy pillar stand at the tabernacle door: and all the people rose up and worshipped, every man in his tent door.

8 And the LORD spake unto Moses face to face, as a man speaketh unto his friend. And he turned again into the camp; but his servant Joshua, the son of Nun, a young man, departed not out of the tabernacle.

9 And Moses said unto the LORD, See, thou sayest unto me, Bring up this people: and thou hast not let me know whom thou wilt send with me. Yet thou hast said, I know thee by name, and thou hast also found grace in my sight.

10 Now therefore, I pray thee, if I have found grace in thy sight, shew me now thy way, that I may know thee, that I may find grace in thy sight: and consider that this nation is thy people.

11 And he said, My presence shall go with thee, and I will give thee rest.

12 And he said unto him, If thy presence go not with me, carry us not up hence.

13 For wherein shall it be known here that I and thy people have found grace in thy sight? is it not in that thou goest with us? So shall we be distinguished, I and thy people, from all the nations that are upon the face of the earth.

14 And the LORD said unto Moses, I will do this thing also that thou hast spoken: for thou hast found grace in my sight, and I know thee by name.

15 And he said, I beseech thee, shew me thy glory.

16 And he said, I will make all my goodness pass before thee, and I will proclaim the name of the LORD before thee; and will be gracious to whom I will be gracious, and will shew mercy on whom I will shew mercy.

17 And he said, Thou canst not see my presence: for no man can see me, and live.

18 And the LORD said, Behold, there is a place by me, and thou shalt stand upon a rock:

19 And it shall come to pass, while my glory passeth by, that I will put thee in a cleft of the rock, and will cover thee with my hand while I pass by:

20 And I will take away mine hand, and thou shalt see my following; but my face can not be seen.

CHAPTER XXVIII.

AND the LORD said unto Moses, Hew thee two tables of stone like unto the first: and I will write upon these tables the words that were in the first tables, which thou brakest.

2 And be ready in the morning, and come up in the morning unto mount Sinai, and present thyself there to me in the top of the mount.

3 And no man shall come up with thee, neither let any man be seen throughout all the mount; neither let the flocks nor herds feed before that mount.

4 And he hewed two tables of stone like unto the first, and Moses rose up early in the morning, and went up unto mount Sinai, as the LORD had commanded him, and took in his hand the two tables of stone.

5 And the LORD descended in the cloud, and stood with him there, and proclaimed the name of the LORD.

6 And the LORD passèd by before him, and proclaimed, The LORD, The LORD, is a merciful and gracious God, longsuffering, and abundant in goodness and truth,

7 Keeping mercy for thousands, forgiving iniquity and transgression and sin, and that will by no means clear the guilty; visiting the iniquity of the fathers upon the children, and upon the children's children, unto the third and to the fourth generation.

8 And Moses made haste, and bowed his head toward the earth, and worshipped.

9 And he said, If now I have found grace in thy sight, O Lord, let my Lord, I pray thee, go among us; for it is a stiff-necked people; and thou wilt pardon our iniquity and our sin, and take us for thine inheritance.

10 And he said, Behold, I make a covenant: before all thy people I will do marvels, such as have not been done in all the earth, nor in any nation: and all the people among which thou art shall see the work of the LORD: for it is a wonderful thing that I will do with thee.

11 Observe thou that which I command thee this day: behold, I drive out before thee -the Amorite, and the Canaanite, and the Hittite, and the Perizzite, and the Hivite, and the Jebusite.

12 Take heed to thyself, lest thou make a covenant with the inhabitants of the land whither thou goest, lest it be for a snare in the midst of thee:

13 But ye shall destroy their altars, break their images, and cut down their groves:

14 For thou shalt worship no other god: for the LORD, whose name is Jealous, is a jealous God.

15 Lest thou make a covenant with the inhabitants of the land, and they go worshipping their gods, and do sacrifice unto their gods, and will call thee, and thou eat of their sacrifice;

16 And thou take of their daughters unto thy sons, and their daughters go worshipping their gods, and make thy sons go after their gods.

17 Thou shalt make thee no molten images to worship them.

18 The feast of unleavened bread shalt thou keep. Seven days thou shalt eat unleavened bread, as I commanded thee, in the time of the month Abib: for in the month Abib thou camest out from Egypt.

19 Every firstborn is mine; and every firstling among thy cattle, whether ox or sheep, that is male.

20 But the firstling of an ass thou shalt redeem with a lamb. All the firstborn of thy sons thou shalt redeem. And none shall appear before me empty.

21 Six days thou shalt work, but on the seventh day thou shalt rest: in earing time and in harvest thou shalt rest.

22 And thou shalt observe the feast of weeks, of the firstfruits of wheat

harvest, and the feast of ingathering at the year's end.

23 Thrice in the year shall all your men appear before the Lord GOD, the God of Israel.

24 For I will cast out the nations before thee, and enlarge thy borders: neither shall any man desire thy land, when thou shalt go up to appear before the LORD thy God thrice in the year.

25 Thou shalt not offer the blood of my sacrifice with leaven; neither shall the sacrifice of the feast of the passover be left unto the morning.

26 The first of the firstfruits of thy land thou shalt bring unto the house of the LORD thy God. Thou shalt not seethe a kid in his mother's milk.

27 And the LORD said unto Moses, Write thou these words: for after the tenor of these words I have made a covenant with thee and with Israel.

28 And he was there with the LORD forty days and forty nights; he did neither eat bread, nor drink water. And he wrote upon the tables the words of the covenant, the ten commandments.

29 And it came to pass, when Moses came down from mount Sinai with the two tables of testimony in Moses' hand, when he came down from the mount, that Moses knew not that the skin of his face shone while one talked with him.

30 And when Aaron and all the children of Israel saw Moses, behold, the skin of his face shone; and they were afraid to come nigh him.

31 And Moses called unto them; and Aaron and all the rulers of the congregation returned unto him: and Moses talked with them.

32 And afterward all the children of Israel came nigh: and he gave them in commandment all th[at] the LORD had spoken with him in[mou]nt Sinai.

33 And till Moses h[ad] [do]ne speaking with them, he pu[t a v]eil on his face.

34 But when Moses went in before the LORD to speak with him, he took the veil off, until he came out. And he came out, and spoke unto the children of Israel that which he was commanded.

35 And the children of Israel saw the face of Moses, that the skin of Moses' face shone: and Moses put the veil upon his face again, until he went in to speak with God.

CHAPTER XXIX.

AND Moses gathered all the congregation of the children of Israel together, and said unto them, These are the words which the LORD hath commanded, that ye should do them.

2 Six days shall work be done, but on the seventh day there shall be to you a holy day, a Sabbath of rest to the LORD: whosoever doeth work therein shall be put to death.

3 Ye shall kindle no fire throughout your habitations upon the Sabbath day.

4 And Moses spoke unto all the congregation of the children of Israel, saying, This is the thing which the LORD commanded, saying,

5 Take ye from among you an offering unto the LORD: whosoever is of a willing heart, let him bring it, an offering of the LORD; gold, and silver, and brass,

6 And blue, and purple, and scarlet, and fine linen, and goats' hair,

7 And rams' skins dyed red, and badgers' skins, and cedar wood,

8 And oil for the light, and spices

for anointing oil, and for the sweet incense,

9 And onyx stones, and stones to be set for the ephod, and for the breastplate.

10 And every wise hearted among you shall come, and make all that the LORD hath commanded ;

11 The tabernacle, his tent, and his covering, his taches, and his boards, his bars, his pillars, and his sockets ;

12 The ark, and the staves thereof, with the mercy seat, and the veil of the covering ;

13 The table, and his staves, and all his vessels, and the shewbread ;

14 The candlestick also for the light, and his furniture, and his lamps, with the oil for the light ;

15 And the incense altar, and his staves, and the anointing oil, and the sweet incense, and the hanging for the door at the entering in of the tabernacle ;

16 The altar of burnt offering, with his brazen grate, his staves, and all his vessels, the laver and his foot ;

17 The hangings of the court, his pillars, and their sockets, and the hanging for the door of the court ;

18 The pins of the tabernacle, and the pins of the court, and their cords :

19 The clothes of service, to do service in the holy place, the holy garments for Aaron the priest, and the garments of his sons, to minister in the priest's office.

20 And all the congregation of the children of Israel departed from the presence of Moses.

21 And they came, every one whose heart stirred him up, and every one whom his spirit made willing, and they brought the LORD'S offering to the work of the tabernacle of the congre-gation, and for all his service, and for the holy garments.

22 And they came, both men and women, as many as were willing hearted, and brought bracelets, and earrings, and rings, and tablets, all jewels of gold : and every man that offered, offered an offering of gold unto the LORD.

23 And every man, with whom was found blue, and purple, and scarlet, and fine linen, and goats' hair, and red skins of rams, and badgers' skins, brought them.

24 Every one that did offer an offering of silver and brass brought the LORD'S offering : and every man, with whom was found cedar wood for any work of the service, brought it.

25 And all the women that were wise hearted did spin with their hands, and brought that which they had spun, both of blue, and of purple, and of scarlet, and of fine linen.

26 And all the women whose heart stirred them up in wisdom spun goats' hair.

27 And the rulers brought onyx stones, and stones to be set, for the ephod, and for the breastplate ;

28 And spice, and oil for the light, and for the anointing oil, and for the sweet incense.

29 The children of Israel brought a willing offering unto the LORD, every man and woman, whose heart made them willing to bring for all manner of work, which the LORD had commanded to be made by the hand of Moses.

30 And Moses said unto the children of Israel, See, the LORD hath called by name Bezaleel the son of Uri, the son of Hur, of the tribe of Judah ;

31 And he hath filled him with the

spirit of God, in wisdom, in understanding, and in knowledge, and in all manner of workmanship ;

*32 And to devise curious works, to work in gold, and in silver, and in brass,

33 And in the cutting of stones, to set them, and in carving of wood, to make any manner of cunning work.

34 And he hath put in his heart that he may teach, both he, and Aholiab, the son of Ahisamach, of the tribe of Dan.

35 Them hath he filled with wisdom of heart, to work all manner of work, of the engraver, and of the cunning workman, and of the embroiderer, in blue, and in purple, in scarlet, and in fine linen, and of the weaver, even of them that do any work, and of those that devise cunning work.

36 Then wrought Bezaleel and Aholiab, and every wise hearted man, in whom the LORD put wisdom and understanding to know how to work all manner of work for the service of the sanctuary, according to all that the LORD had commanded.

37 And Moses called Bezaleel and Aholiab, and every wise hearted man, in whose heart the LORD had put wisdom, even every one whose heart stirred him up to come unto the work to do it :

38 And they received of Moses all the offering, which the children of Israel had brought for the work of the service of the sanctuary, to make it withal. And they brought yet unto him free offerings every morning.

39 And all the wise men, that wrought all the work of the sanctuary, came every man from his work which they made ;

40 And they spake unto Moses, say-ing, The people bring much more than enough for the service of the work, which the LORD commanded to make.

41 And Moses gave commandment, and they caused it to be proclaimed throughout the camp, saying, Let neither man nor woman make any more work for the offering of the sanctuary. So the people were restrained from bringing.

42 For the stuff they had was suffi-cient for all the work to make it, and too much.

43 And every wise hearted man among them wrought the work of the tabernacle of fine twined linen, and blue, and purple, and scarlet: with cherubim of cunning work made he them.

CHAPTER XXX.

AND Bezaleel made the ark of cedar wood : two cubits and a half was the length of it, and a cubit and a half the breadth of it, and a cubit and a half the height of it :

2 And he overlaid it with pure gold within and without, and made a crown of gold to it round about.

3 And he cast for it four rings of gold, to be set by the four corners of it : even two rings upon the one side of it, and two rings upon the other side of it.

4 And he made staves of cedar wood, and overlaid them with gold.

5 And he put the staves into the rings by the sides of the ark, to bear the ark.

6 And he made the mercy seat of pure gold : two cubits and a half was the length thereof, and one cubit and a half the breadth thereof.

7 And he made two cherubim of gold, beaten out of one piece made he

them, on the two ends of the mercy seat;

·8 One cherub on the end on this side, and another cherub on the other end on that side: out of the mercy seat made he the cherubim on the two ends thereof.

9 And the cherubim spread out their wings on high, and covered with their wings over the mercy seat, their faces turned one to another; even toward the mercy seat were the faces of the cherubim.

10 And he made the table of cedar wood: two cubits was the length thereof, and a cubit the breadth thereof, and a cubit and a half the height thereof:

11 And he overlaid it with pure gold, and made thereunto a crown of gold round about.

12 Also he made thereunto a border of a handbreadth round about; and made a crown of gold for the border thereof round about.

13 And he cast for it four rings of gold, and put the rings upon the four corners that were in the four feet thereof.

14 Over against the border were the rings, the places for the staves to bear the table.

15 And he made the staves of cedar wood, and overlaid them with gold, to bear the table.

16 And he made the vessels which were upon the table, his dishes, and spoons, and his bowls, and his covers to cover withal, of pure gold.

17 And he made the candlestick of pure gold: of beaten work made he the candlestick; his shaft, and his branches, his bowls, his knops, and his flowers, were of the same:

18 And six branches going out of the sides thereof; three branches of the candlestick out of the one side thereof, and three branches of the candlestick out of the other side thereof:

19 Three bowls made after the fashion of almonds in one branch, a knop and a flower; and three bowls made like almonds in another branch, a knop and a flower: so throughout the six branches going out of the candlestick.

20 And in the candlestick were four bowls made like almonds, his knops, and his flowers:

21 And a knop under two branches of the same, and a knop under two branches of the same, and a knop under two branches of the same, according to the six branches going out of it.

22 Their knops and their branches were of the same: all of it was one beaten work of pure gold.

23 And he made his seven lamps, and his snuffers, and his snuffdishes, of pure gold.

24 Of a talent of pure gold made he it, and all the vessels thereof.

25 And he made the incense altar of cedar wood: the length of it was a cubit, and the breadth of it a cubit; it was four-square; and two cubits was the height of it; the horns thereof were of the same.

26 And he overlaid it with pure gold, both the top of it, and the sides thereof round about, and the horns of it: also he made unto it a crown of gold round about.

27 And he made two rings of gold for it under the crown thereof, by the two corners of it, upon the two sides thereof, to be places for the staves to bear it withal.

28 And he made the staves of cedar wood, and overlaid them with gold.

29 And he made the holy anointing oil, and the pure incense of sweet spices, according to the work of the apothecary.

30 And he made the altar of burnt offering of cedar wood: five cubits was the length thereof, and five cubits the breadth thereof; it was four-square; and three cubits the height thereof.

31 And he made the horns thereof on the four corners of it; the horns thereof were of the same: and he overlaid it with brass.

32 And he made all the vessels of the altar, the pots, and the shovels, and the basins, and the fleshhooks, and the firepans: all the vessels thereof made he of brass.

33 And of the blue, and purple, and scarlet, they made clothes of service, to do service in the holy place, and made the holy garments for Aaron; as the LORD commanded Moses.

34 And he made the ephod of gold, blue, and purple, and scarlet, and fine twined linen.

35 And they did beat the gold into thin plates, and cut it into wires, to work it in the blue, and in the purple, and in the scarlet, and in the fine linen; with cunning work.

36 And they made coats of fine linen of woven work for Aaron, and for his sons,

37 And a mitre of fine linen, and goodly bonnets of fine linen, and linen breeches of fine twined linen,

38 And a girdle of fine twined linen, and blue, and purple, and scarlet, of needlework; as the LORD commanded Moses.

39 And they made the plate of the holy crown of pure gold, and wrote upon it a writing, like to the engravings of a signet, HOLY TO THE LORD.

40 And they tied unto it a lace of blue, to fasten it on high upon the mitre; as the LORD commanded Moses.

41 Thus was all the work of the tabernacle of the tent of the congregation finished: and the children of Israel did according to all that the LORD commanded Moses, so did they.

42 And they brought the tabernacle unto Moses, and he did look upon all the work, and, behold, they had done it as the LORD had commanded, even so had they done it: and Moses blessed them.

CHAPTER XXXI.

AND the LORD spake unto Moses, saying,

2 On the first day of the first month shalt thou set up the tabernacle of the tent of the congregation.

3 And thou shalt bring Aaron and his sons unto the door of the tabernacle of the congregation, and wash them with water.

4 And thou shalt put upon Aaron the holy garments, and anoint him, and sanctify him; that he may minister unto me in the priest's office.

5 And thou shalt bring his sons, and clothe them with coats:

6 And thou shalt anoint them, as thou didst anoint their father, that they may minister unto me in the priest's office: for their anointing shall surely be an everlasting priesthood throughout the generations.

7 Thus did Moses: according to all that the LORD commanded him, so did he.

8 And it came to pass in the first

month in the second year, on the first day of the month, that the tabernacle was reared up.

9 And Moses reared up the tabernacle, and fastened his sockets, and set up the boards thereof, and put in the bars thereof, and reared up his pillars.

10 And he spread abroad the tent over the tabernacle, and put the covering of the tent above upon it; as the LORD commanded Moses.

11 And he took and put the testimony into the ark, and set the staves on the ark, and put the mercy seat above upon the ark:

12 And he brought the ark into the tabernacle, and set up the veil of the covering, and covered the ark of the testimony; as the LORD commanded Moses.

13 And he put the table in the tent of the congregation, upon the side of the tabernacle northward, without the veil.

14 And he set the bread in order upon it before the LORD; as the LORD had commanded Moses.

15 And he put the candlestick in the tent of the congregation, over against the table, on the side of the tabernacle southward.

16 And he lighted the lamps before the LORD; as the LORD commanded Moses.

17 And he put the golden altar in the tent of the congregation before the veil:

18 And he burnt sweet incense thereon; as the LORD commanded Moses.

19 And he set up the hanging at the door of the tabernacle.

20 And he put the altar of burnt offering by the door of the tabernacle of the tent of the congregation, and offered upon it the burnt offering and the meat offering; as the LORD commanded Moses.

21 And he set the laver between the tent of the congregation and the altar, and put water there, to wash withal.

22 And Moses and Aaron and his sons washed their hands and their feet thereat:

23 When they went into the tent of the congregation, and when they came near unto the altar, they washed; as the LORD commanded Moses.

24 And he reared up the court round about the tabernacle and the altar, and set up the hanging of the court gate. So Moses finished the work.

25 Then a cloud covered the tent of the congregation, and the glory of the LORD filled the tabernacle.

26 And Moses was not able to enter into the tent of the congregation, because the cloud abode thereon, and the glory of the LORD filled the tabernacle.

27 And when the cloud was taken up from over the tabernacle, the children of Israel went onward in all their journeys:

28 But if the cloud were not taken up, then they journeyed not till the day that it was taken up.

29 For the cloud of the LORD was upon the tabernacle by day, and a pillar of fire was on it by night, in the sight of all the house of Israel, throughout all their journeys.

LEVITICUS,

CALLED THE THIRD BOOK OF MOSES.

CHAPTER I.

AND the LORD called unto Moses, and spake unto him out of the tabernacle of the congregation, saying,

2 Take Aaron and his sons with him, and the garments, and the anointing oil, and a bullock for the sin offering, and two rams, and a basket of unleavened bread ;

3 And gather thou all the congregation together unto the door of the tabernacle of the congregation.

4 And Moses did as the LORD commanded him; and the assembly was gathered together unto the door of the tabernacle of the congregation.

5 And Moses said unto the congregation, This is the thing which the LORD commanded to be done.

6 And Moses brought Aaron and his sons, and washed them with water.

7 And he put upon him the coat, and girded him with the girdle, and clothed him with the robe, and put the ephod upon him, and he girded him with the curious girdle of the ephod, and bound it unto him therewith.

8 And he put the breastplate upon him: also he put in the breastplate the Urim and the Thummim.

9 And he put the mitre upon his head; also upon the mitre, even upon his forefront, did he put the golden plate, the holy crown; as the LORD commanded Moses.

10 And Moses took the anointing oil, and anointed the tabernacle and all that was therein, and sanctified them.

11 And he sprinkled thereof upon the altar seven times, and anointed the altar and all his vessels, both the laver and his foot, to sanctify them.

12 And he poured of the anointing oil upon Aaron's head, and anointed him, to sanctify him.

13 And Moses brought Aaron's sons, and put coats upon them, and girded them with girdles, and put bonnets upon them; as the LORD commanded Moses.

14 And he brought the bullock for the sin offering: and Aaron and his sons laid their hands upon the head of the bullock for the sin offering.

15 And he brought the ram for the burnt offering: and Aaron and his sons laid their hands upon the head of the ram.

16 And he slew it, and Moses burnt the whole upon the altar: it was a burnt sacrifice for a sweet savour, and an offering made by fire unto the LORD; as the LORD commanded Moses.

17 And he brought the other ram, the ram of consecration: and Aaron and his sons laid their hands upon the head of the ram, and he killed it, and Moses sprinkled the blood round about the altar.

18 And out of the basket of unleav-

ened bread, that was before the LORD, he took one unleavened cake, and a cake of oiled bread, and one wafer, and put them all upon Aaron's hands, and upon his sons' hands, and waved them for a wave offering before the LORD.

19 And Moses took them from off their hands, and burnt them on the altar upon the burnt offering: they were consecrations for a sweet savour: it is an offering made by fire unto the LORD.

20 And Moses took of the anointing oil, and sprinkled it upon Aaron, and upon his garments, and upon his sons, and upon his sons' garments, with him; and sanctified Aaron, and his garments, and his sons, and his sons' garments with him.

21 And Moses said unto Aaron and to his sons, Boil the flesh at the door of the tabernacle of the congregation; and there eat it with the bread that is in the basket of consecrations, as I commanded, saying, Aaron and his sons shall eat it.

22 And that which remaineth of the flesh and of the bread shall ye burn with fire.

23 And ye shall not go out of the door of the tabernacle of the congregation in seven days, until the days of your consecration be at an end: for seven days shall he consecrate you.

24 As he hath done this day, so the LORD hath commanded to do, to make an atonement for you.

25 Therefore shall ye abide at the door of the tabernacle of the congregation day and night seven days, and keep the charge of the LORD, that ye die not: for so I am commanded.

26 So Aaron and his sons did all things which the LORD commanded by the hand of Moses.

CHAPTER II.

AND it came to pass on the eighth day, that Moses called Aaron and his sons, and the elders of Israel;

2 And Moses said unto Aaron, Go unto the altar, and offer thy sin offering, and thy burnt offering, and make an atonement for thyself, and for the people: and offer the offering of the people, and make an atonement for them; as the LORD commanded.

3 Aaron therefore went unto the altar, and slew the calf of the sin offering, which was for himself.

4 And he brought the people's offering, and took the goat, which was the sin offering for the people, and slew it, and offered it for sin, as the first.

5 And he brought the burnt offering, and offered it according to the manner.

6 And he brought the meat offering, and took a handful thereof, and burnt it upon the altar, besides the burnt sacrifice of the morning.

7 He slew also the bullock and the ram for a sacrifice of peace offerings, which was for the people: and Aaron's sons presented unto him the blood, which he sprinkled upon the altar round about.

8 And Aaron lifted up his hand toward the people, and blessed them; and came down from offering of the sin offering, and the burnt offering, and peace offerings.

9 And Moses and Aaron went into the tabernacle of the congregation, and came out, and blessed the people: and the glory of the LORD appeared unto all the people.

10 And there came a fire out from before the LORD, and consumed upon the altar the burnt offering and the

fat: which when all the people saw, they shouted, and fell on their faces.

11 And Nadab and Abihu, the sons of Aaron, took each of them his censer, and put fire therein, and put incense thereon, and offered strange fire before the LORD, which he commanded them not.

12 And there went out fire from the LORD, and devoured them, and they died before the LORD.

13 Then Moses said unto Aaron, This is it that the LORD spake, saying, I will be sanctified in them that are near me, and before all the people I will be glorified. And Aaron held his peace.

14 And Moses called Mishael and Elzaphan, the sons of Uzziel the uncle of Aaron, and said unto them, Come near, carry your brethren from before the sanctuary out of the camp.

15 So they went near, and carried them in their coats out of the camp; as Moses had said.

16 And Moses said unto Aaron, and unto Eleazar and unto Ithamar, his sons, Uncover not your heads, neither rend your clothes; lest ye die, and lest wrath come upon all the people: but let your brethren, the whole house of Israel, bewail the burning which the LORD hath kindled.

17 And ye shall not go out from the door of the tabernacle of the congregation, lest ye die: for the anointing oil of the LORD is upon you. And they did according to the word of Moses.

18 And the LORD spake unto Aaron, saying,

19 Do not drink wine nor strong drink, thou, nor thy sons with thee, when ye go into the tabernacle of the congregation: it shall be a statute for ever throughout your generations:

20 And that ye may put difference between holy and unholy, and between unclean and clean;

21 And that ye may teach the children of Israel all the statutes which the LORD hath spoken unto them by the mouth of Moses.

22 And Moses spake unto Aaron, and unto Eleazar and unto Ithamar, his sons, that were left, Take the meat offering that remaineth of the offerings of the LORD made by fire, and eat it without leaven beside the altar: for it is most holy.

23 And ye shall eat it in the holy place, because it is thy due, and thy sons' due, of the sacrifices of the LORD made by fire: for so I am commanded.

24 And Moses diligently sought the goat of the sin offering, and, behold, it was burnt: and he was angry with Eleazar and Ithamar, the sons of Aaron which were left alive, saying,

25 Wherefore have ye not eaten the sin offering in the holy place, seeing it is most holy, and God hath given it you to bear the iniquity of the congregation, to make atonement for them before the LORD?

26 Behold, the blood of it was not brought in within the holy place: ye should indeed have eaten it in the holy place, as I commanded.

27 And Aaron said unto Moses, Behold, this day have they offered their sin offering and their burnt offering before the LORD; and such things have befallen me: and if I had eaten the sin offering to day, should it have been accepted in the sight of the LORD?

28 And when Moses heard that, he was content.

CHAPTER III.

AND the LORD spake unto Moses and to Aaron; saying unto them,

2 Speak unto the children of Israel, saying, These are the beasts which ye shall eat among all the beasts that are on the earth.

3 Whatsoever parteth the hoof, and is clovenfooted, and cheweth the cud, among the beasts, that shall ye eat.

4 Nevertheless, these shall ye not eat of them that chew the cud, or of them that divide the hoof: as the camel, because he cheweth the cud, but divideth not the hoof; he is unclean unto you.

5 And the coney, because he cheweth the cud, but divideth not the hoof; he is unclean unto you.

6 And the hare, because he cheweth the cud, but divideth not the hoof; he is unclean unto you.

7 And the swine, though he divide the hoof, and be clovenfooted, yet he cheweth not the cud; he is unclean to you.

8 Of their flesh shall ye not eat, and their carcass shall ye not touch; they are unclean to you.

9 These shall ye eat of all that are in the waters: whatsoever hath fins and scales in the waters, in the seas, and in the rivers, them shall ye eat.

10 And all that have not fins and scales in the seas, and in the rivers, of all that move in the waters, and of any living thing which is in the waters, they shall be an abomination unto you:

11 They shall be even an abomination unto you; ye shall not eat of their flesh, and ye shall have their carcasses in abomination.

12 Whatsoever hath no fins nor scales in the waters, that shall be an abomination unto you.

13 And these are they which ye shall have in abomination among the fowls; they shall not be eaten, they are an abomination: the eagle, and the ossifrage, and the ospray,

14 And the vulture, and the kite after his kind;

15 Every raven after his kind;

16 And the owl, and the nighthawk, and the cuckoo, and the hawk after his kind,

17 And the little owl, and the cormorant, and the great owl,

18 And the swan, and the pelican, and the gier eagle,

19 And the stork, the heron after her kind, and the lapwing, and the bat.

20 All fowls that kreep, going upon all four, shall be an abomination unto you.

21 Yet these may ye eat of every flying creeping thing that goeth upon all four, which have legs above their feet, to leap withal upon the earth;

22 Even these of them ye may eat; the locust after his kind, and the bald locust after his kind, and the beetle after his kind, and the grasshopper after his kind.

23 But all other flying creeping things, which have four feet, shall be an abomination unto you.

24 And every creeping thing that creepeth upon the earth shall be an abomination; it shall not be eaten.

25 Whatsoever goeth upon the belly, and whatsoever goeth upon all four, or whatsoever hath more feet among all creeping things that creep upon the earth, them ye shall not eat; for they are an abomination.

26 Ye shall not make yourselves

abominable with any creeping thing that creepeth, neither shall ye make yourselves unclean with them, that ye should be defiled thereby.

27 For I am the LORD your God: ye shall therefore sanctify yourselves, and ye shall be holy; for I am holy: neither shall ye defile yourselves with any manner of creeping thing that creepeth upon the earth.

28 For I am the LORD that brought you up out of the land of Egypt, to be your God : ye shall therefore be holy, for I am holy.

29 This is the law of the beasts, and of the fowl, and of every living creature that moveth in the waters, and of every creature that creepeth upon the earth :

30 To make a difference between the unclean and the clean, and between the beast that may be eaten and the beast that may not be eaten.

CHAPTER IV.

AND the LORD spake unto Moses after the death of the two sons of Aaron, when they offered before the LORD, and died ;

2 And the LORD said unto Moses, Speak unto Aaron thy brother, that he come not at all times into the holy place within the veil before the mercy seat, which is upon the ark; that he die not: for I will appear in the cloud upon the mercy seat.

3 Thus shall Aaron come into the holy place; with a young bullock for a sin offering, and a ram for a burnt offering.

4 He shall put on the holy linen coat, and he shall have the linen breeches upon his flesh, and shall be girded with a linen girdle, and with the linen mitre shall he be attired: these are the holy garments ; therefore shall he wash his flesh in water, and so put them on.

5 And he shall take of the congregation of the children of Israel two kids of the goats for a sin offering, and one ram for a burnt offering.

6 And Aaron shall offer his bullock of the sin offering, which is for himself, and make an atonement for himself, and for his house.

7 And he shall take the two goats, and present them before the LORD at the door of the tabernacle of the congregation.

8 And Aaron shall cast lots upon the two goats: one lot for the LORD, and the other lot for the scapegoat

9 And Aaron shall bring the goat upon which the LORD's lot fell, and offer him for a sin offering.

10 But the goat, on which the lot fell to be the scapegoat, shall be presented alive before the LORD, to make an atonement with him, and to let him go for a scapegoat into the wilderness.

11 And Aaron shall bring the bullock of his sin offering, and shall make an atonement for himself, and for his house, and shall kill the bullock of his sin offering:

12 And he shall take a censer full of burning coals of fire from off the altar before the LORD, and his hands full of sweet incense beaten small, and bring it within the veil:

13 And he shall put the incense upon the fire before the LORD, that the cloud of the incense may cover the mercy seat that is upon the testimony, that he die not:

14 And he shall take of the blood of the bullock, and sprinkle it with his finger upon the mercy seat eastward; and before the mercy seat shall he

sprinkle of the blood with his finger seven times.

15 Then shall he kill the goat of the sin offering, that is for the people, and bring his blood within the veil, and do with that blood as he did with the blood of the bullock, and sprinkle. it upon the mercy seat, and before the mercy seat :

16 And he shall make an atonement for the holy place, because of the uncleanness of the children of Israel, and because of their transgressions in all their sins: and so shall he do for the tabernacle of the congregation, that remaineth among them in the midst of their uncleanness.

17 And there shall be no man in the tabernacle of the congregation when he goeth in to make an atonement in the holy place, until he come out, and have made an atonement for himself, and for his household, and for all the congregation of Israel.

18 And he shall go out unto the altar that is before the LORD, and make an atonement for it ;. and shall take of the blood of the bullock, and of the blood of the' goat, and put it upon the horns of. the altar round about,

19 And he shall sprinkle of the blood upon it with his finger seven. times, and cleanse it, and hallow it from the uncleanness of the children of Israel.

20 And when he hath made an end of reconciling the holy place, and the tabernacle of the congregation, and the altar, he shall bring the live goat:

21 And Aaron shall lay both his hands upon the head of the live goat, and confess over him all the iniquities of the children of Israel, and all their transgressions in all their sins, putting them upon the head of .the goat, and shall send him away by the hand of a fit man into the wilderness:

22 And the goat shall bear upon him all their iniquities unto a land not inhabited: and he shall let go the goat in the wilderness.

23 And Aaron shall come into the tabernacle of the congregation, and shall put off the linen garments, which he put on when he went into the holy place, and shall leave them there :

24 And he shall wash his flesh with water in the holy place, and put on his garments, and come forth, and offer his burnt offering, and the burnt offering of the people, and make an atonement for himself, and for the people.

25 And the fat of the sin offering shall he burn upon the altar.

26 And he that bringeth the scapegoat into the wilderness shall wash his clothes, and bathe his flesh in water, and afterward come into the camp.

27 And the bullock for the sin offering, and the goat for the sin offering, whose blood was brought in to make atonement in the holy place, shall one carry forth without the camp ; and they shall burn in the fire their skins, and their flesh, and their appurtenance.

28 And he that burneth them shall wash his clothes, and bathe his flesh in water, and afterward he shall come into the camp.

29 And this shall. be a statute for ever unto· you: that in the seventh month, on the tenth day of the month, ye shall humble your souls, and do no work at all, whether it be one that is homeborn, or a stranger that sojourneth among you:

30 For on that day he shall make an atonement for you, to cleanse your-

selves from all your sins, that ye may be pure before the LORD. ·

31 It shall be a sabbath of rest unto you, and ye shall afflict your souls: this be a statute for ever.·

32 And the priest, whom he shall anoint, and whom he shall consecrate to minister in the priest's office in his father's stead, shall make the atonement, and shall put on the linen clothes, even the holy garments: ·

.33 And he shall make an atonement for the holy sanctuary, and he shall make an atonement for the tabernacle of the congregation, and for the altar: and he shall make an atonement for the priests, and for all the people of the congregation.

34 And this shall be an everlasting statute unto you, to make an atonement for the children of Israel for all their sins once a year. And he did as the LORD commanded Moses.

CHAPTER V. ·   ˈˈˈˈˈˈ.

AND the LORD spake unto Moses, saying,

2 Speak unto the children of Israel, and say unto them, I am the LORD your God.

3 After the doings of the land of Egypt, wherein ye dwelt, shall ye not do: and after the doings of the land of Canaan, whither I bring you, shall ye not do: neither shall ye walk in their ordinances.

4 Ye shall do my judgments, and keep mine ordinances, to walk therein: I am the LORD your God.

5 Ye shall therefore keep my statutes, and my judgments: which if a man do, he shall live in them: I am the LORD.

6 And the LORD spake unto Moses, saying,

7 Speak unto all the congregation of the children of Israel, and say unto them, Ye shall be holy: for I the LORD your God am holy.

8 Ye shall fear every man his mother, and his father, and keep my sabbath: I am the LORD your God.

9 Turn ye not unto idols, nor make to yourselves molten gods: I am the LORD your God.

10 And if ye offer a sacrifice of peace offerings unto the LORD, ye shall offer it at your own will.

11 It shall be eaten the same day ye offer it, and on the morrow: and if aught remain until the third day, it shall be burnt in the fire.

12 And if it be eaten at all on the third day, it is abominable; it shall not be accepted.

13 And when ye reap the harvest of your land, thou shalt not wholly reap the corners of thy field, neither shalt thou gather the gleanings of thy harvest.

14 And thou shalt not glean thy vineyard, neither shalt thou gather every grape of thy vineyard; thou shalt leave them for the poor and stranger: I am the LORD your God.

15 Ye shall not steal, neither deal falsely, neither lie one to another.

16 And ye shall not swear by my name falsely, neither shalt thou profane the name of thy God: I am the LORD.

17 Thou shalt not defraud thy neighbour, neither rob him: the wages of him that is hired shall not abide with thee all night until the morning.

18 Thou shalt not curse the deaf, nor put a stumblingblock before the blind, but shalt fear thy God: I am the LORD. ·

19 Ye shall do no unrighteousness in judgment; thou shalt not respect

the person of the poor, nor honour the person of the mighty: but in righteousness shalt thou judge thy neighbour.

20 Thou shalt not go about as a talebearer among thy people; neither shalt thou stand against the blood of thy neighbour: I am the LORD.

21 Thou shalt not hate thy brother in thine heart: but thou shalt reprove thy neighbour, and not suffer sin upon him.

22 Thou shalt not avenge, nor bear any grudge against the children of thy people, but thou shalt love thy neighbour as thyself: I am the LORD.

23 Ye shall keep my statutes. Thou shalt not sow thy field with mingled seed: neither shall a garment mingled of linen and woolen come upon thee.

24 If a soul sin, and commit a trespass against the LORD, and lie unto his neighbour in that which was delivered him to keep, or in fellowship, or in a thing taken away by violence, or hath deceived his neighbour;

25 Or have found that which was lost, and lieth concerning it, and sweareth falsely; in any of all these that a man doeth, sinning therein:

26 Then it shall be, when he hath sinned, and is guilty, that he shall restore that which he took violently away, or the thing which he hath deceitfully gotten, or that which was delivered him to keep, or the lost thing which he found,

27 Or all that about which he hath sworn falsely; he shall even restore it in the principal, and shall add the fifth part more thereto, and give it unto him to whom it appertaineth, in the day of his trespass offering.

28 And when ye shall come into the land, and shall have planted all manner of trees for food, then ye shall count the fruit thereof as uncircumcised unto you: it shall not be eaten of.

29 But in the fourth year all the fruit thereof shall be holy to praise the LORD withal.

30 And in the fifth year shall ye eat of the fruit thereof, that it may yield unto you the increase thereof: I am the LORD your God.

31 Ye shall not eat any thing with the blood: neither shall ye use enchantment, nor observe times.

32 Ye shall not round the corners of your heads, neither shalt thou mar the corners of thy beard.

33 Ye shall not make any cuttings in your flesh for the dead, nor print any marks upon you: I am the LORD.

34 Ye shall keep my sabbaths, and reverence my sanctuary: I am the LORD.

35 Regard not them that have familiar spirits, neither seek after wizards, to be defiled by them: I am the LORD your God.

36 Thou shalt rise up before the hoary head, and honour the face of an old man, and fear thy God: I am the LORD.

37 And if a stranger sojourn with thee in your land, ye shall not vex him.

38 But the stranger that dwelleth with you shall be unto you as one born among you, and thou shalt love him as thyself; for ye were strangers in the land of Egypt: I am the LORD your God.

39 Ye shall do no unrighteousness in judgment, in dealing, in weight, or in measure.

40 Just balances, just weights, a just ephah, and a just hin, shall ye have: I am the LORD your God, which brought you out of the land of Egypt.

41 Therefore shall ye observe all my statutes, and all my judgments, and do them: I am the LORD.

CHAPTER VI.

AND the LORD spake unto Moses, saying,

2 Thou shalt say to the children of Israel, Whosoever he be of the children of Israel, or of the strangers that sojourn in Israel, that giveth any of his children unto Molech; he shall surely be put to death: the people of the land shall stone him with stones.

3 And I will set my face against that man, and will cut him off from among his people; because he hath given of his children unto Molech, to defile my sanctuary, and to profane my holy name.

4 And if the people of the land do any ways hide their eyes from the man, when he giveth of his children unto Molech, and kill him not; '

5 Then I will set my face against that man, and against his family, and will cut him off, and all that do like unto him, to sacrifice unto Molech, from among their people.

6 And the soul that turneth after conjurers of spirits, and after wizards, to go after them, I will even set my face against that soul, and will cut him off from among his people.

7 Sanctify yourselves therefore, and be ye holy: for I am the LORD your God.

8 And ye shall keep my statutes, and do them: I am the LORD which sanctify you.

9 For every one that curseth his father or his mother shall be surely put to death: he hath cursed his father or his mother; his blood shall be upon him.

10 Ye shall therefore keep all my statutes, and all my judgments, and do them: that the land, whither I bring you to dwell therein, spew you not out.

11 And ye shall not walk in the manners of the nation, which I cast out before you: for they committed all these things, and therefore I abhorred them.

12 But I have said unto you, Ye shall inherit their land, and I will give it unto you to possess it, a land that floweth with milk and honey: I am the LORD your God, which have separated you from other people.

13 Ye shall therefore put difference between clean beasts and unclean, and between unclean fowls and clean: and ye shall not make your souls abominable by beast, or by fowl, or by any manner of living thing that creepeth on the ground, which I have separated from you as unclean.

14 And ye shall be holy unto me: for I the LORD am holy, and have severed you from other nations, that ye should be mine.

CHAPTER VII.

AND the LORD said unto Moses, Speak unto the priests the sons of Aaron, and say unto them, There shall none be defiled for the dead among his people:

2 But for his kin, that is near unto him, that is, for his mother, and for his father, and for his son, and for his daughter, and for his brother,

3 And for his sister a virgin, that is nigh unto him, for her may he be defiled.

4 But he shall not defile himself otherwise, being a chief man among his people, to profane himself.

5 They shall not make baldness upon their head, neither shall they shave off the corner of their beard, nor make any cuttings in their flesh.

6 They shall be holy unto their God, and not profane the name of their God: for the offerings of the LORD, and the bread of their God, they do offer: therefore they shall be holy.

7 Thou shalt sanctify him therefore; for he offereth the bread of thy God: he shall be holy unto thee: for I the LORD, which sanctify you, am holy.

8 And Moses told it unto Aaron, and to his sons, and unto all the children of Israel.

CHAPTER VIII.

AND the LORD spake unto Moses, saying,

2 Speak unto the children of Israel, and say unto them, Concerning the feasts of the LORD, which ye shall proclaim to be holy convocation, even these are my feasts:

3 Six days shall work be done: but the seventh day is the Sabbath of rest, a holy convocation; ye shall do no work therein: it is the Sabbath of the LORD in all your dwellings.

4 These are the feasts of the LORD, even holy convocations, which ye shall proclaim in their seasons.

5 In the fourteenth day of the first month at even is the LORD'S passover.

6 And on the fifteenth day of the same month is the feast of unleavened bread unto the LORD: seven days ye must eat unleavened bread.

7 In the first day ye shall have a holy convocation: ye shall do no servile work therein.

8 But ye shall offer an offering made by fire unto the LORD seven days: in the seventh day is a holy convocation; ye shall do no servile work therein.

9 And the LORD spake unto Moses, saying,

10 Speak unto the children of Israel, and say unto them, When ye be come into the land which I give unto you, and shall reap the harvest thereof, then ye shall bring a sheaf of the firstfruits of your harvest unto the priest:

11 And ye shall wave the sheaf before the LORD, to be accepted for you: on the morrow after the Sabbath the priest shall wave it.

12 And ye shall offer that day when ye wave the sheaf a lamb without blemish of the first year for a burnt offering unto the LORD.

13 And the meat offering thereof shall be two tenth deals of fine flour mingled with oil, an offering made by fire unto the LORD for a sweet savour: and the drink offering thereof shall be of wine, the fourth part of a hin.

14 And ye shall eat neither bread, nor parched corn, nor green ears, until the selfsame day that ye have brought an offering unto your God; it shall be a statute for ever throughout your generations in all your dwellings.

15 And ye shall count unto you from the morrow after the Sabbath, from the day that ye brought the sheaf of the wave offering; seven Sabbaths shall be complete:

16 Even unto the morrow after the seventh Sabbath shall ye number fifty days; and ye shall offer a new meat offering unto the LORD.

17 Ye shall bring out of your habitations two wave loaves of two tenth deals: they shall be of fine flour; they

shall be baken with leaven : they are the firstfruits unto the LORD.

18 And ye shall offer with the bread seven lambs without blemish of the first year, and one young bullock, and two rams : they shall be for a burnt offering unto the LORD, with their meat offering, and their drink offerings, even an offering made by fire, of sweet savour unto the LORD.

19 Then ye shall sacrifice one kid of the goats for a sin offering, and two lambs of the first year for a sacrifice of peace offerings.

20 And the priest shall wave them with the bread of the firstfruits for a wave offering before the LORD, with the two lambs : they shall be holy to the LORD for the priest.

21 And ye shall proclaim on the selfsame day, that it may be a holy convocation unto you : ye shall do no servile work therein : it shall be a statute for ever in all your dwellings throughout your generations.

22 And when ye reap the harvest of your land, thou shalt not make clean riddance of the corners of thy field when thou reapest, neither shalt thou gather any gleaning of thy harvest : thou shalt leave them unto the poor, and to the stranger : I am the LORD your God.

23 And the LORD spake unto Moses, saying,

24 Speak unto the children of Israel, saying, In the seventh month, in the first day of the month, shall ye have a Sabbath, a memorial of blowing of trumpets, a holy convocation.

25 Ye shall do no servile work therein : but ye shall offer an offering made by fire unto the LORD.

26 And the LORD spake unto Moses, saying,

27 Also on the tenth day of this seventh month there shall be a day of atonement : it shall be a holy convocation unto you : and ye shall afflict your souls, and offer an offering made by fire unto the LORD.

28 And ye shall do no work in that same day : for it is a day of atonement, to make an atonement for you before the LORD your God.

29 For whatsoever soul it be that shall not afflict himself in that same day, he shall be cut off from among his people.

30 And whatsoever soul it be that doeth any work in that same day, the same soul will I destroy from among his people.

31 Ye shall do no manner of work : it shall be a statute for ever throughout your generations in all your dwellings.

32 It shall be unto you a Sabbath of rest, and ye shall afflict your souls; in the ninth day of the month at even, from even unto even, shall ye celebrate your Sabbath.

33 And the LORD spake unto Moses, saying,

34 Speak unto the children of Israel, saying, The fifteenth day of this seventh month shall be the feast of tabernacles for seven days unto the LORD.

35 On the first day shall be a holy convocation : ye shall do no servile work therein.

36 Seven days ye shall offer an offering made by fire unto the LORD ; on the eighth day shall be a holy convocation unto you, and ye shall offer an offering made by fire unto the LORD : it is a solemn assembly ; and ye shall do no servile work therein.

37 These are the feasts of the LORD, which ye shall proclaim to be holy

convocations, to offer the offerings unto the LORD, a burnt offering, and a meat offering, a sacrifice, and drink offerings, every thing upon his day:

38 Beside the Sabbaths of the LORD, and beside your gifts, and beside all your vows, and beside all your freewill offerings, which ye give unto the LORD.

39 Also in the fifteenth day of the seventh month, when ye have gathered in the fruit of the land, ye shall keep a feast unto the LORD seven days: on the first day shall be a Sabbath, and on the eighth day shall be a Sabbath.

40 And ye shall take you on the first day the fruit of the hadar tree, branches of palm trees, and the branches of the myrtle tree, and willows of the brook; and ye shall rejoice before the LORD your God seven days.

41 And ye shall keep it a feast unto the LORD seven days in the year: it shall be a statute for ever in your generations; ye shall celebrate it in the seventh month.

42 Ye shall dwell in booths seven days; all that are born Israelites shall dwell in booths:

43 That your generations may know that I made the children of Israel to dwell in booths, when I brought them out of the land of Egypt: I am the LORD your God.

44 And Moses declared unto the children of Israel the feasts of the LORD.

CHAPTER IX.

AND the LORD spake unto Moses, saying,

2 Command the children of Israel, that they bring unto thee pure oil olive beaten for the light, to cause the lamps to burn continually.

3 Without the veil of the testimony, in the tabernacle of the congregation, shall Aaron order it from the evening unto the morning before the LORD continually: it shall be a statute for ever in your generations.

4 He shall order the lamps upon the pure candlestick before the LORD continually.

5 And thou shalt take fine flour, and bake twelve cakes thereof: two tenth deals shall be in one cake.

6 And thou shalt set them in two rows, six on a row, upon the pure table before the LORD.

7 And thou shalt put pure frankincense upon each row, that it may be on the bread for a memorial, even an offering made by fire unto the LORD.

8 Every Sabbath he shall set it in order before the LORD continually, being taken from the children of Israel by an everlasting covenant.

9 And it shall be Aaron's and his sons'; and they shall eat in the holy place: for it is most holy unto him of the offerings of the LORD made by fire by a perpetual statute.

10 And the son of an Israelitish woman, whose father was an Egyptian, went out among the children of Israel: and this son of the Israelitish woman and a man of Israel strove together in the camp;

11 And the Israelitish woman's son blasphemed the name of the LORD, and cursed. And they brought him unto Moses: (and his mother's name was Shelomith, the daughter of Dibri, of the tribe of Dan:).

12 And they put him in ward, that the mind of the LORD might be shewed them.

13 And the LORD spake unto Moses, saying,

14 Bring forth him that hath cursed without the camp; and let all that heard him lay their hands upon his head, and let all the congregation stone him.

15 And thou shalt speak unto the children of Israel, saying, Whosoever curseth his God shall bear his sin.

16 And he that blasphemeth the name of the LORD, he shall surely be put to death, and all the congregation shall certainly stone him: as well the stranger, as he that is born in the land, when he blasphemeth the name of the LORD, shall be put to death.

17 And he that killeth any man shall surely be put to death.

18 And he that killeth a beast shall make it good; beast for beast.

19 And if a man cause a blemish in his neighbour; as he hath done, so shall it be done to him;

20 Breach for breach, eye for eye, tooth for tooth: as he hath caused a blemish in a man, so shall it be done to him again.

21 And he that killeth a beast, he shall restore it: and he that killeth a man, he shall be put to death.

22 Ye shall have one manner of law, as well for the stranger, as for one of your own country: for I am the LORD your God.

23 And Moses spake to the children of Israel, that they should bring forth him that had cursed out of the camp, and stone him with stones: and the children of Israel did as the LORD commanded Moses.

CHAPTER X.

AND the LORD spake unto Moses in mount Sinai, saying,

2 Speak unto the children of Israel, and say unto them, When ye come into the land which I give you, then shall the land keep a Sabbath unto the LORD.

3 Six years thou shalt sow thy field, and six years thou shalt prune thy vineyard, and gather in the fruit thereof;

4 But in the seventh year shall be a Sabbath of rest unto the land, a Sabbath for the LORD: thou shalt neither sow thy field, nor prune thy vineyard.

5 That which groweth of its own accord of thy harvest thou shalt not reap, neither gather the grapes of thy vine undressed: for it is a year of rest unto the land.

6 And the Sabbath of the land shall be meat for you; for thee, and for thy servant, and for thy maid, and for thy hired servant, and for thy stranger that sojourneth with thee,

7 And for thy cattle, and for the beast that are in thy land, shall all the increase thereof be meat.

8 And thou shalt number seven Sabbaths of years unto thee, seven times seven years; and the space of the seven Sabbaths of years shall be unto thee forty and nine years.

9 Then shalt thou cause the trumpet of the jubilee to sound on the tenth day of the seventh month, on the day of atonement shall ye make the trumpet sound throughout all your land.

10 And ye shall hallow the fiftieth year, and proclaim liberty throughout all the land unto all the inhabitants thereof: it shall be a jubilee unto you; and ye shall return every man unto his possession, and ye shall return every man unto his family.

11 A jubilee shall that fiftieth year be unto you: ye shall not sow, neither

reap that which groweth of itself in it, nor gather the grapes in it of thy vine undressed.

12 For it is the jubilee; it shall be holy unto you: ye shall eat the increase thereof out of the field.

13 In the year of this jubilee ye shall return every man unto his possession.

14 And if thou sell aught unto thy neighbour, or buyest aught of thy neighbour's hand, ye shall not oppress one another:

15 According to the number of years after the jubilee, thou shalt buy of thy neighbour, and according unto the number of years of the fruits he shall sell unto thee:

16 According to the multitude of years thou shalt increase the price thereof, and according to the fewness of years thou shalt diminish the price of it: for according to the number of the years of the fruits doth he sell unto thee.

17 Ye shall not therefore oppress one another; but thou shalt fear thy God: for I am the LORD your God.

18 Wherefore ye shall do my statutes, and keep my judgments, and do them; and ye shall dwell in the land in safety.

19 And the land shall yield her fruit, and ye shall eat your fill, and dwell therein in safety.

20 And if ye shall say, What shall we eat the seventh year? behold, we shall not sow, nor gather in our increase:

21 Then I will command my blessing upon you in the sixth year, and it shall bring forth fruit for three years.

22 And ye shall sow the eighth year, and eat yet of old fruit until the ninth year; until her fruits come in ye shall eat of the old store.

23 The land shall not be sold for ever: for the land is mine; for ye are strangers and sojourners with me.

24 And in all the land of your possession ye shall grant a redemption for the land.

25 If thy brother be waxen poor, and hath sold away some of his possession, and if any of his kin come to redeem it, then shall he redeem that which his brother sold.

26 And if the man have none to redeem it, and himself be able to redeem it;

27 Then let him count the years of the sale thereof, and restore the overplus unto the man, to whom he sold it; that he may return unto his possession.

28 But if he be not able to restore it to him, then that which is sold shall remain in the hand of him that hath bought it until the year of jubilee: and in the year of jubilee it shall go out, and he shall return unto his possession.

29 And if a man sell a dwelling-house in a walled city, then he may redeem it within a whole year after it is sold; within a full year may he redeem it.

30 And if it be not redeemed within the space of a full year, then the house that is in the walled city shall be established for ever to him that bought it throughout his generations: it shall not go out in the jubilee.

31 But the houses of the villages which have no wall round about them shall be counted as the fields of the country: they may be redeemed, and they shall go out in the jubilee.

32 Notwithstanding the cities of the Levites, and the houses of the cities

of their possession, may the Levites redeem at any time.

33 And if a man purchase of the Levites, then the house that was sold, and the city of his possession, shall go out in the year of jubilee: for the houses of the cities of the Levites are their possession among the children of Israel.

34 But the field of the suburbs of their cities may not be sold; for it is their perpetual possession.

35 And if thy brother is waxen poor, and fallen in decay with thee; then thou shalt relieve him: yea, though he be a stranger, or a sojourner; that he may live with thee.

36 Take thou no usury of him, or increase: but fear thy God; that thy brother may live with thee.

37 Thou shalt not give him thy money upon usury, nor lend him thy victuals for increase.

38 I am the LORD your God, which brought you forth out of the land of Egypt, to give you the land of Canaan, and to be your God.

39 And if thy brother that dwelleth by thee be waxen poor, and be sold unto thee; thou shalt not compel him to serve as a bondservant:

40 But as a hired servant, and as a sojourner, he shall be with thee, and shall serve thee unto the year of jubilee:

41 And then shall he depart from thee, both he and his children with him, and shall return unto his own family, and unto the possession of his fathers shall he return.

42 For they are my servants, which I brought forth out of the land of Egypt: they shall not be sold as bondmen.

43 Thou shalt not rule over him with rigour; but shalt fear thy God.

44 And if a sojourner or stranger wax rich by thee, and thy brother that dwelleth by him wax poor, and sell himself unto the stranger or sojourner by thee, or to the stock of the stranger's family:

45 After that he is sold he may be redeemed again; one of his brethren may redeem him:

46 Either his uncle, or his uncle's son, may redeem him, or any that is nigh of kin unto him of his family may redeem him; or if he be able, he may redeem himself.

47 And he shall reckon with him that bought him from the year that he was sold to him unto the year of jubilee: and the price of his sale shall be according unto the number of years, according to the time of a hired servant shall it be with him.

48 If there be yet many years behind, according unto them he shall give again the price of his redemption out of the money that he was bought for.

49 And if there remain but few years unto the year of jubilee, then he shall count with him, and according unto his years shall he give him again the price of his redemption.

50 And as a yearly hired servant shall he be with him: and the other shall not rule with rigour over him in thy sight.

51 And if he be not redeemed in these years, then he shall go out in the year of jubilee, both he, and his children with him.

52 For unto me the children of Israel are servants; they are my servants whom I brought forth out of the land of Egypt: I am the LORD your God.

CHAPTER XI.

YE shall make you no idols nor graven image, neither rear you up a standing image, neither shall ye set up any image of stone in your land, to bow down unto it: for I am the LORD your God.

2 Ye shall keep my Sabbaths, and reverence my sanctuary: I am the LORD.

3 If ye walk in my statutes, and keep my commandments, and do them;

4 Then I will give you rain in due season, and the land shall yield her increase, and the trees of the field shall yield their fruit.

5 And your threshing shall reach unto the vintage, and the vintage shall reach unto the sowing time: and ye shall eat your bread to the full, and dwell in your land safely.

6 And I will give peace in the land, and ye shall lie down, and none shall make you afraid: and I will rid evil beasts out of the land, neither shall the sword go through your land.

7 And ye shall chase your enemies, and they shall fall before you by the sword.

8 And five of you shall chase a hundred, and a hundred of you shall put ten thousand to flight: and your enemies shall fall before you by the sword.

9 For I will have respect unto you, and make you fruitful, and multiply you, and establish my covenant with you.

10 And ye shall eat old store, and bring forth the old because of the new.

11 And I will set my tabernacle among you: and my spirit shall not abhor you.

12 And I will walk among you, and will be your God, and ye shall be my people.

13 I am the LORD your God, which brought you forth out of the land of Egypt, that ye should not be their bondmen; and I have broken the bands of your yoke, and made you go upright.

14 But if ye will not hearken unto me, and will not do all these commandments;

15 And if ye shall despise my statutes, or if your soul abhor my judgments, so that ye will not do all my commandments, but that ye break my covenant:

16 I also will do this unto you; I will set my face against you, and ye shall be slain before your enemies: they that hate you shall reign over you; and ye shall flee when none pursueth you.

17 And I will scatter you among the heathen, and will draw out a sword after you: and your land shall be desolate, and your cities waste.

18 Then shall the land enjoy her sabbaths, as long as it lieth desolate, and ye be in your enemies' land; even then shall the land rest, and enjoy her sabbaths.

19 And yet for all that, when they be in the land of their enemies, I will not cast them away, neither will I abhor them, to destroy them utterly, and to break my covenant with them: for I am the LORD their God.

20 But I will for their sakes remember the covenant of their ancestors, whom I brought forth out of the land of Egypt in the sight of the heathen, that I might be their God: I am the LORD.

21 These are the statutes and judgments and laws, which the LORD made between him and the children of Israel in mount Sinai by the hand of Moses.

NUMBERS,

CHAPTER I.

AND the LORD spake unto Moses in the wilderness of Sinai, in the tabernacle of the congregation, on the first day of the second month, in the second year after they were come out of the land of Egypt, saying,

2 Take ye the sum of all the congregation of the children of Israel, after their families, by the house of their fathers, with the number of their names, every male by their polls;

3 From twenty years old and upward, all that are able to go forth to war in Israel: thou and Aaron shall number them by their armies.

4 And with you there shall be a man of every tribe; every one head of the house of his fathers.

5 And these are the names of the men that shall stand with you: Of the tribe of Reuben: Elizur the son of Shedeur; of Simeon: Shelumiel the son of Zuri-shaddai; of Judah: Nahashon the son of Amminadab; of Issachar: Nethaneel the son of Zuar; of Zebulun: Eliab the son of Helon.

6 Of the children of Joseph: of Ephraim: Elishama the son of Ammihud; of Manasseh: Gamaliel the son of Pedahzur; of Benjamin: Abidan the son of Gideoni; of Dan: Ahiezer the son of Ammishaddai; of Asher: Pagiel the son of Ocran; of Gad: Eliasaph the son of Deuel; of Naphtali: Ahira the son of Enan.

7 These were the renowned of the congregation, princes of the tribes of their fathers, heads of thousands in Israel.

8 And Moses and Aaron took these men which are expressed by their names:

9 And they assembled all the congregation together on the first day of the second month, and they declared their pedigrees after their families, by the house of their fathers, according to the number of the names, from twenty years old and upward, by their polls.

10 As the LORD commanded Moses, so he numbered them in the wilderness of Sinai.

11 And all they that were numbered were six hundred thousand and three thousand and five hundred and fifty.

12 But the Levites after the tribe of their fathers were not numbered among them, for the LORD had spoken unto Moses, saying,

13 Thou shalt not number the tribe of Levi, neither take the sum of them among the children of Israel:

14 But thou shalt appoint the Levites over the tabernacle of testimony, and over all the vessels thereof, and over all things that belong to it: they shall bear the tabernacle, and all the vessels thereof; and they shall minister unto it, and shall encamp round about the tabernacle.

15 And when the tabernacle setteth forward, the Levites shall take it down; and when the tabernacle is to be pitched, the Levites shall set it up: and the stranger that cometh nigh shall be put to death.

16 And the children of Israel shall pitch their tents, every man by his own camp, and every man by his own standard, throughout their hosts.

17 But the Levites shall pitch round about the tabernacle of testimony, that there be no wrath upon the congregation of the children of Israel: and the Levites shall keep the charge of the tabernacle of testimony.

18 And the children of Israel did according to all that the LORD commanded Moses, so did they.

CHAPTER II.

AND the LORD spake unto Moses and unto Aaron, saying,

2 Every man of the children of Israel shall pitch by his own standard, with the ensign of their fathers' house: round about the tabernacle of the congregation shall they pitch.

3 And the children of Israel did according to all that the LORD commanded Moses: so they pitched by their standards, and so they set forward, every one after their families, according to the house of their fathers.

4 And the LORD spake unto Moses, saying,

5 And I, behold, I have taken the Levites from among the children of Israel instead of all the firstborn among the children of Israel; therefore the Levites shall be mine ;

6 Because all the firstborn are mine ; for on the day that I smote all the firstborn in the land of Egypt I hallowed unto me all the firstborn in Israel, both man and beast: mine they shall be: I am the LORD.

7 And the LORD spake unto Moses in the wilderness of Sinai, saying,

8 Number the children of Levi after the house of their fathers, by their families: every male from a month old and upward shalt thou number them.

9 And Moses numbered them according to the word of the LORD, as he was commanded.

10 All that were numbered of the Levites, which Moses and Aaron numbered at the commandment of the LORD, throughout their families, all the males from a month old and upward, were twenty and two thousand.

11 And the LORD spake unto Moses, saying,

12 Speak unto the children of Israel, When a man or woman shall commit any sin that men commit, to do a trespass against the LORD, and that person be guilty;

13 Then they shall confess their sin which they have done: and he shall recompense his trespass with the principal thereof, and add unto it the fifth part thereof, and give it unto him against whom he hath trespassed.

14 But if the man have no one to recompense the trespass unto, let the trespass be recompensed unto the LORD, even to the priest; beside the ram of the atonement, whereby an atonement shall be made for him.

15 And every offering of all the holy things of the children of Israel, which they bring unto the priest, shall be his.

16 And every man's hallowed things shall be his: whatsoever any man giveth the priest, it shall be his.

17 And the LORD spake unto Moses, saying,

18 Speak unto the children of Israel,

and say unto them, When either man or woman shall separate themselves to vow a vow of a Nazarite, to separate themselves unto the LORD ;

19 He shall separate himself from wine and strong drink, and shall drink no vinegar of wine, or vinegar of strong drink, neither shall he drink any liquor of grapes, nor eat moist grapes, or dried.

20 All the days of his separation shall he eat nothing that is made of the vine tree, from the kernels even to the husk.

21 All the days of the vow of his separation there shall no razor come upon his head: until the days be fulfilled, in the which he separateth himself unto the LORD, he shall be holy, and shall let the locks of the hair of his head grow.

22 All the days that he separateth himself unto the LORD he shall come at no dead body.

23 He shall not make himself unclean for his father, or for his mother, for his brother, or for his sister, when they die: because the consecration of his God is upon his head.

24 All the days of his separation he is holy unto the LORD.

25 And the LORD spake unto Moses, saying,

26 Speak unto Aaron and unto his sons, saying, On this wise ye shall bless the children of Israel, saying unto them,

27 The LORD bless thee, and keep thee:

28 The LORD make his face shine upon thee, and be gracious unto thee:

29 The LORD lift up his countenance upon thee, and give thee peace.

30 And they shall put my name upon the children of Israel, and I will bless them.

31 And the LORD spake unto Moses, saying,

32 Speak unto Aaron, and say unto him, When thou lightest the lamps, the seven lamps shall give light over against the candlestick.

33 And Aaron did so; he lighted the lamps thereof over against the candlestick, as the LORD commanded Moses.

34 And the work of the candlestick was of beaten gold ; unto the shaft thereof, unto the flowers thereof, was beaten work: according unto the pattern which the LORD had shewed Moses, so he made the candlestick.

CHAPTER III.

AND the LORD spake unto Moses in the wilderness of Sinai, in the first month of the second year after they were come out of the land of Egypt, saying,

2 Let the children of Israel also keep the passover at his appointed season.

3 In the fourteenth day of this month, at even, ye shall keep it in his appointed season: according to all the rites of it, and according to all the ceremonies thereof, shall ye keep it.

4 And Moses spake unto the children of Israel, that they should keep the passover.

5 And they kept the passover on the fourteenth day of the first month at even in the wilderness of Sinai: according to all that the LORD commanded Moses, so did the children of Israel.

6 And there were certain men, who were defiled by the dead body of a man, that they could not keep the passover on that day: and they came

before Moses and before Aaron on that day.

7 And those men said unto him, We are defiled by the dead body of a man: wherefore are we kept back, that we may not offer an offering of the LORD in his appointed season among the children of Israel ?

8 And Moses said unto them, Stand still, and I will hear what the LORD will command concerning you.

9 And the LORD spake unto Moses, saying,

10 Speak unto the children of Israel, saying, If any man of you or of your posterity shall be unclean by reason of a dead body, or be in a journey afar off, yet he would keep the passover unto the LORD.

11 The fourteenth day of the second month at even they shall keep it, and eat it with unleavened bread and bitter herbs.

12 They shall leave none of it unto the morning, nor break any bone of it: according to all the ordinances of the passover they shall keep it.

13 But the man that is clean, and is not in a journey, and forbeareth to keep the passover, even the same soul shall be cut off from among his people: because he brought not the offering of the LORD in his appointed season, that man shall bear his sin.

14 And if a stranger shall sojourn among you, and will keep the passover unto the LORD ; according to the ordinance of the passover, and according to the manner thereof, so shall he do: ye shall have one law, both for the stranger, and for him that was born in the land.

15 And if a stranger sojourn with you, or whosoever be among you in your generations, and will offer an offering unto the LORD, as ye do so shall he do.

16 One ordinance shall be both for you of the congregation, and also for the stranger, that sojourneth with you, an ordinance for ever unto your generations: as ye are, so shall the stranger be before the LORD.

17 One law and one right shall be for you, and for the stranger that sojourneth with you.

18 And on the day that the tabernacle was reared up the cloud covered the tabernacle, namely, the tent of the testimony: and at even there was upon the tabernacle as it were the appearance of fire, until the morning.

19 So it was alway: the cloud covered it by day, and the appearance of fire by night.

20 And when the cloud was taken up from the tabernacle, then after that the children of Israel journeyed: and in the place where the cloud abode, there the children of Israel pitched their tents.

21 At the commandment of the LORD the children of Israel journeyed, and at the commandment of the LORD they pitched: as long as the cloud abode upon the tabernacle they rested in their tents.

22 And when the cloud tarried long upon the tabernacle many days, then the children of Israel kept the charge of the LORD, and journeyed not.

23 And so it was, when the cloud was a few days upon the tabernacle; according to the commandment of the LORD they abode in their tents, and according to the commandment of the LORD they journeyed.

24 And so it was, when the cloud abode from even unto the morning, and that the cloud was taken up in the

morning, then they journeyed: whether it was by day or by night that the cloud was taken up, they journeyed.

25 Or whether it were two days, or a month, or a year, that the cloud tarried upon the tabernacle, remaining thereon, the children of Israel abode in their tents, and journeyed not: but when it was taken up, they journeyed.

26 At the commandment of the LORD they rested in their tents, and at the commandment of the LORD they journeyed: they kept the charge of the LORD, at the commandment of the LORD by the hand of Moses.

CHAPTER IV.

AND the LORD spake unto Moses, saying,

2 Make thee two trumpets of silver; of a whole piece shalt thou make them: that thou mayest use them for the calling of the assembly, and for the journeying of the camps.

3 And when they shall blow with them, all the assembly shall assemble to thee at the door of the tabernacle of the congregation.

4 And if they blow but with one trumpet, then the princes, which are heads of the thousands of Israel, shall gather themselves unto thee.

5 When ye blow an alarm, then the camps that lie on the east parts shall go forward.

6 When ye blow an alarm the second time, then the camps that lie on the south side shall take their journey: they shall blow an alarm for their journeys.

7 But when the congregation is to be gathered together, ye shall blow, but ye shall not sound an alarm.

8 And the sons of Aaron, the priests, shall blow with the trumpets; and they shall be to you for an ordinance for ever throughout your generations.

9 And if ye go to war in your land against the enemy that oppresseth you, then ye shall blow an alarm with the trumpets; and ye shall be remembered before the LORD your God, and ye shall be saved from your enemies.

10 Also in the day of your gladness, and in your solemn days, and in the beginnings of your months, ye shall blow with the trumpets over your burnt offerings, and over the sacrifices of your peace offerings; that they may be to you for a memorial before your God: I am the LORD your God.

11 And it came to pass on the twentieth day of the second month, in the second year, that the cloud was taken up from off the tabernacle of the testimony.

12 And the children of Israel took their journeys out of the wilderness of Sinai; and the cloud rested in the wilderness of Paran.

13 And they first took their journey according to the commandment of the LORD by the hand of Moses.

14 And they departed from the mount of the LORD three days' journey: and the ark of the covenant of the LORD went before them in the three days' journey, to search out a resting place for them.

15 And the cloud of the LORD was upon them by day, when they went out of the camp.

16 And it came to pass, when the ark set forward, that Moses said, Rise up, LORD, and let thine enemies be scattered; and let them that hate thee flee before thee.

17 And when it rested, he said, Return, O LORD, unto the many thousands of Israel.

18 And Moses said unto Hobab, the son of Raguel the Midianite, Moses' father in law, We are journeying unto the place of which the LORD said; I will give it you: come thou with us, and we will do thee good: for the LORD hath spoken good concerning Israel.

19 And he said unto him, I will not go; but I will depart to mine own land, and to my kindred.

20 And he said, Leave us not, I pray thee; forasmuch as thou knowest how we are to encamp in the wilderness, and thou mayest be to us instead of eyes.

21 And it shall be, if thou go with us, yea, it shall be, that what goodness the LORD shall do unto us, the same will we do unto thee.

CHAPTER V.

A ND it came to pass that the mixed multitude that was among Israel, fell a lusting: and the children of Israel also wept again, and said, Who shall give us flesh to eat?

2 We remember the fish, which we did eat in Egypt freely; the cucumbers, and the melons, and the leeks, and the onions, and the garlic:

3 But now our soul is dried away: there is nothing at all, besides this manna, before our eyes.

4 And the manna was as coriander seed, and the colour thereof as the colour of bdellium.

5 And the people went about, and gathered it, and ground it in mills, or beat it in a mortar, and baked it in pans, and made cakes of it: and the taste of it was as the taste of fresh oil.

6 And when the dew fell upon the camp in the night, the manna fell upon it.

7 Then Moses heard the people weep throughout their families, every man in the door of his tent: and the anger of the LORD was kindled greatly; Moses also was displeased.

8 And Moses said unto the LORD, Wherefore hast thou afflicted thy servant? and wherefore have I not found favour in thy sight, that thou layest the burden of all this people upon me?

9 Have I born all this people? or have I raised them, that thou shouldest say unto me, Carry them in thy bosom, as a nursing father beareth the sucking child, unto the land which thou swarest unto their fathers?

10 Whence should I have flesh to give unto all this people? for they weep unto me, saying, Give us flesh, that we may eat.

11 I am not able to bear all this people alone; because it is to heavy for me.

12 And if thou deal thus with me, kill me, I pray thee, out of hand, if I have found favour in thy sight; and let me not see my wretchedness.

13 And the LORD said unto Moses, Gather unto me seventy men of the elders of Israel, whom thou knowest to be the elders of the people, and officers over them; and bring them unto the tabernacle of the congregation, that they may stand there with thee.

14 And I will come down and talk with thee there: and I will take of the spirit which is upon thee, and will put it upon them; and they shall bear the burden of the people with thee, that thou bear it not thyself alone.

15 And say thou unto the people, Sanctify yourselves against to morrow, and ye shall eat flesh: for ye have

wept in the ears of the LORD, saying, Who shall give us flesh to eat? for it was well with us in Egypt: therefore the LORD will give you flesh, and ye shall eat.

16 Ye shall not eat one day, nor two days, nor five days, neither ten days, nor twenty days;

17 But even a whole month, until it come out at your nostrils, and it be loathsome unto you: because that ye have despised the LORD which is among you, and have wept before him, saying, Why came we forth out of Egypt?

18 And Moses said, The people, among whom I am, are six hundred thousand men on foot; and thou hast said, I will give them flesh, that they may eat a whole month.

19 Shall all the flocks and the herds be slain for them, to suffice them? or shall all the fish of the sea be gathered together for them, to suffice them?

20 And the LORD said unto Moses, Is the LORD'S hand waxed short? thou shalt see now whether my word shall come to pass unto thee or not.

21 And Moses went out, and told the people the words of the LORD, and gathered the seventy men of the elders of the people, and set them round about the tabernacle.

22 And the LORD came down in a cloud, and spake unto him, and took of the spirit that was upon him, and gave it unto the seventy elders: and it came to pass, that, when the spirit rested upon them, they prophesied, and did not cease.

23 But there remained two of the men in the camp, the name of the one was Eldad, and the name of the other Medad: and the spirit rested upon them; and they were of them that were written, but went not out unto the tabernacle: and they prophesied in the camp.

24 And there ran a young man, and told Moses, and said, Eldad and Medad do prophesy in the camp.

25 And Joshua the son of Nun, the servant of Moses, one of his young men, answered and said, My lord Moses, forbid them.

26 And Moses said unto him, Enviest thou for my sake? would God that all the LORD'S people were prophets, and that the LORD would put his spirit upon them.

27 And Moses returned into the camp, he and the elders of Israel.

28 And there went forth a wind from the LORD, and brought quails from the sea, and let them fall by the camp, as it were a day's journey on this side, and as it were a day's journey on the other side, round about the camp, and as it were two cubits high upon the face of the earth.

29 And the people stood up all that day, and all that night, and all the next day, and they gathered the quails: he that gathered least gathered ten homers: and they spread them all abroad for themselves round about the camp.

30 And while the flesh was yet between their teeth, ere it was chewed, the wrath of the LORD was kindled against the people, and the LORD smote the people with a very great plague.

31 And he called the name of that place Kibroth-hattaavah: because there they buried the people that lusted.

32 And the people journeyed from Kibroth-hattaavah unto Hazeroth; and abode at Hazeroth.

CHAPTER VI.

AND Miriam and Aaron spoke against Moses because of the Ethiopian woman whom he had married: for he had married an Ethiopian woman.

2 And they said, Hath the LORD indeed spoken only by Moses? hath he not spoken also by us? And the LORD heard it.

3 Now the man Moses was very meek, above all the men which were upon the face of the earth,

4 And the LORD spake suddenly unto Moses, and unto Aaron, and unto Miriam, Come out ye three unto the tabernacle of the congregation. And they three came out.

5 And the LORD came down in the pillar of the cloud, and stood in the door of the tabernacle, and called Aaron and Miriam: and they both came forth.

6 And he said, Hear now my words: If there be a prophet among you, I the LORD will make myself known unto him in a vision, and will speak unto him in a dream.

7 Not so with my servant Moses, who is faithful in all mine house.

8 With him will I speak mouth to mouth, even apparently, and not in dark speeches; and the similitude of the LORD shall he behold: wherefore then were ye not afraid to speak against my servant Moses?

9 And the anger of the LORD was kindled against them; and he departed.

10 And the cloud departed from off the tabernacle: and behold, Miriam became leprous, white as snow: and Aaron looked upon Miriam, and, behold, she was leprous.

11 And Aaron said unto Moses, Alas, my lord, I beseech thee, lay not the sin upon us, wherein we have done foolishly, and wherein we have sinned.

12 Let her not be as one dead, of whom the flesh is half consumed when he cometh out into the world.

13 And Moses cried unto the LORD, saying, O God, I beseech thee, heal her now.

14 And the LORD said unto Moses, If her father had but spit in her face, should she not be ashamed seven days? let her be shut out from the camp seven days, and after that let her be received in again.

15 And Miriam was shut out from the camp seven days: and the people journeyed not till Miriam was brought in again.

16 And afterward the people removed from Hazeroth, and pitched in the wilderness of Paran.

CHAPTER VII.

AND the LORD spake unto Moses, saying,

2 Send thou men, that they may search the land of Canaan, which I give unto the children of Israel: of every tribe of their fathers shall ye send a man, every one a ruler among them.

3 And Moses by the commandment of the LORD sent them from the wilderness of Parau: all those men were heads of the children of Israel.

4 And Moses sent them to spy out the land of Canaan, and said unto them, Get you up this way southward, and go up into the mountain:

5 And see the land, what it is; and the people that dwelleth therein, whether they be strong or weak, few or many;

6 And what the land is that they

dwell in, whether it be good or bad; and what the cities be that they dwell in, whether in tents, or in strong holds;

7 And what the land is, whether it be fat or lean, whether there be wood therein, or not. And be ye of good courage, and bring of the fruit of the land. Now the time was the time of the first ripe grapes.

8 So they went up, and searched the land from the wilderness of Zin unto Rehob, as one cometh to Hamath.

9 And they ascended by the south, and came unto Hebron; where Ahiman, Shehai, and Talmai, the children of Anak, were. (Now Hebron was built seven years before Zoan in Egypt.)

10 And they came unto the brook of Eshcol, and cut down from thence a branch with one cluster of grapes, and they bare it between two upon a staff; and they brought of the pomegranates, and of the figs.

11 The place was called the brook Eshcol, because of the cluster of grapes which the children of Israel cut down from thence.

12 And they returned from searching of the land after forty days.

13 And they went and came to Moses, and to Aaron, and to all the congregation of the children of Israel, unto the wilderness of Paran, to Kadesh; and brought back word unto them, and unto all the congregation, and shewed them the fruit of the land.

14 And they told him, and said, We came unto the land whither thou sendest us, and surely it floweth with milk and honey; and this is the fruit of it.

15 Nevertheless the people are strong that dwell in the land, and the cities are walled, and very great: and moreover we saw the children of Anak there.

16 The Amalekites dwell in the land of the south: and the Hittites, and the Jebusites, aud the Amorites, dwell in the mountains: and the Canaanites dwell by the sea, and by the coast of Jordan.

17 And Caleb stilled the people before Moses, and said, Let us go up at once, and possess it; for we are well able to overcome it.

18 But the men that went up with him, said, We are not able to go up against the people; for they are stronger than we.

19 And they brought up an evil report of the land which they had searched unto the children of Israel, saying, The land, through which we have gone to search it, is a land that eateth up the inhabitants thereof; and all the people that we saw in it are men of a great stature.

20 And there we saw the giants, the sons of Anak, which come of the giants: and we were in our own sight as grasshoppers, and so we were in their sight.

CHAPTER VIII.

AND all the congregation lifted up their voice, and cried; and the people wept that night.

2 And all the children of Israel murmured against Moses and against Aaron: and the whole congregation said unto them, Would God that we had died in the land of Egypt! or would God we had died in this wilderness!

3 And wherefore hath the LORD brought us unto this land, to fall by the sword, that our wives and our

children should be a prey? were it not better for us to return into Egypt?

4 And they said one to another, Let us make a captain, and let us return into Egypt.

5 Then Moses and Aaron fell on their faces before all the assembly of the congregation of the children of Israel.

6 And Joshua the son of Nun, and Caleb the son of Jephunneh, which were of them that searched the land, rent their clothes:

7 And they spoke unto all the company of the children of Israel, saying, The land, which we passed through to search it, is an exceeding good land.

8 If the LORD delight in us, then he will bring us into this land, and give it us: a land which floweth with milk and honey.

9 Only rebel not ye against the LORD, neither fear ye the people of the land; for they are bread for us: their defence is departed from them, and the LORD is with us: fear them not.

10 But all the congregation bade stone them with stones. And the glory of the LORD appeared in the tabernacle of the congregation before all the children of Israel.

11 And the LORD said unto Moses, How long will this people provoke me? and how long will it be ere they believe me, for all the signs which I have shewed among them?

12 I will smite them with the pestilence, and disinherit them, and will make of thee a greater nation and mightier than they.

13 And Moses said unto the LORD, Then the Egyptians shall hear it, (for thou broughtest up this people in thy might from among them;)

14 And they will tell it to the inhabitants of this land: for they have heard that thou LORD art among this people, that thou LORD art seen face to face, and that thy cloud standeth over them, and that thou goest before them, by daytime in a pillar of a cloud, and in a pillar of fire by night.

15 Now if thou shalt kill all this people as one man, then the nations which have heard the fame of thee will speak, saying,

16 Because the LORD was not able to bring this people into the land which he sware unto them, therefore he hath slain them in the wilderness.

17 And now, I beseech thee, let the power of my LORD be great, according as thou hast spoken, saying,

18 The LORD is longsuffering, and of great mercy, forgiving iniquity and transgression, and by no means clearing the guilty, visiting the iniquity of the fathers upon the children unto the third and fourth generation.

19 Pardon, I beseech thee, the iniquity of this people according unto the greatness of thy mercy, and as thou hast forgiven this people, from Egypt even until now.

20 And the LORD said, I have pardoned according to thy word:

21 But as truly as I live, and as all the earth is filled with the glory of the LORD:

22 Because all those men which have seen my glory, and my miracles, which I did in Egypt and in the wilderness, and have tempted me now these ten times, and have not hearkened to my voice;

23 Surely they shall not see the land which I sware unto their fathers, neither shall any of them that provoked me see it:

24 But my servant Caleb, because he had another spirit with him, and hath followed me fully, him will I bring into the land whereinto he went; and his children shall possess it.

25 (Now the Amalekites and the Canaanites dwelt in the valley.) To morrow turn you, and get you into the wilderness by the way of the Red sea.

26 And the LORD spake unto Moses and unto Aaron, saying,

27 How long shall I bear with this evil congregation, which murmur against me? I have heard the murmurings of the children of Israel, which they murmur against me.

28 Say unto them, As truly as I live, saith the LORD, as ye have spoken in mine ears, so will I do to you:

29 Your bodies shall fall in this wilderness, and all that were numbered of you, according to your whole number, from twenty years old and upward, which have murmured against me.

30 Doubtless ye shall not come into the land, concerning which I sware to make you dwell therein, save Caleb son of Jephunneh, and Joshua the son of Nun.

31 But your little ones, which ye said should be a prey, them will I bring in, and they shall know the land which ye have despised.

32 But as for you, your bodies, they shall fall in this wilderness.

33 And your children shall wander in the wilderness forty years, and bear your sins, until your bodies be wasted in the wilderness.

34 After the number of the days in which ye searched the land, even forty days, each day for a year, shall ye bear your iniquities, even forty years, and ye shall know my recompense.

35 I the LORD have said, I will surely do it unto all this evil congregation, that are gathered together against me: in this wilderness they shall be consumed, and there they shall die.

36 And the men which Moses sent to search the land, who returned, and made all the congregation to murmur against him, by bringing up a slander upon the land, died by the plague before the LORD.

37 But Joshua the son of Nun, and Caleb the son of Jephunneh, which were of the men that went to search the land, remained alive.

38 And Moses told these sayings unto all the children of Israel: and the people mourned greatly.

39 And they rose up early in the morning, and went up into the top of the mountain, saying, Lo, we are here, and will go up unto the place which the LORD hath promised : for we have sinned.

40 And Moses said, Wherefore now do ye transgress the commandment of the LORD? but it shall not prosper.

41 Go not up, for the LORD is not with you ; that ye be not smitten before your enemies.

42 For the Amalekites and the Canaanites are there before you, and ye shall fall by the sword: because ye are turned away from the LORD, therefore the LORD will not be with you.

43 But they presumed to go up unto the hill top: nevertheless the ark of the covenant of the LORD, and Moses, departed not out of the camp.

44 Then the Amalekites came down, and the Canaanites which dwelt in that hill, and smote them, and discomfited them, even unto Hormah.

CHAPTER IX.

NOW Korah, the son of Jizhar, the son of Kohath, the son of Levi, and Dathan and Abiram, the sons of Eliab, and On, the son of Peleth, sons of Reuben, conspired.

2 And they rose up before Moses, with certain men of the children of Israel, two hundred and fifty leaders of the assembly, famous in the congregation, men of renown:

3 And they gathered themselves together against Moses and against Aaron, and said unto them, Ye take too much upon you, seeing all the congregation are holy, every one of them, and the LORD is among them: wherefore then lift ye up yourselves above the congregation of the LORD?

4 And when Moses heard it, he fell upon his face:

5 And he spake unto Korah and unto all his company, saying, Even to morrow the LORD will shew who are his, and who is holy; and will cause him to come near unto him: even him whom he hath chosen will he cause to come near unto him.

6 This do; Take you censers, Korah, and all his company;

7. And put fire therein, and put incense in them before the LORD to morrow: and it shall be that the man whom the LORD doth choose, he shall be holy: ye take too much upon you, ye sons of Levi.

8 And Moses said unto Korah, Hear, I pray you, ye sons of Levi:

9 Seemeth it but a small thing unto you, that the God of Israel hath separated you from the congregation of Israel, to bring you near to himself to do the service of the tabernacle of the LORD, and to stand before the congregation to minister unto them?

10 And he hath brought thee near to him, and all thy brethren the sons of Levi with thee: and seek ye the priesthood also?

11 For which cause both thou and all thy company are gathered together against the LORD: and what is Aaron, that ye murmur against him?

12 And Moses sent to call Dathan and Abiram, the sons of Eliab; but they said, We will not come up:

13 Is it a small thing that thou hast brought us up out of a land that floweth with milk and honey, to kill us in the wilderness, and now thou make thyself altogether a prince over us?

14 Moreover, thou hast not brought us into a land that floweth with milk and honey, or given us inheritance of fields and vineyards: wilt thou put out the eyes of these men? we will not come up.

15 And Moses said unto Korah, Be thou and all thy company before the LORD, thou, and they, and Aaron, to morrow:

16 And take every man his censer, and put incense in them, and bring ye before the LORD every man his censer, two hundred an fifty censers; thou also, and Aaron, each of you his censer.

17 And they took every man his censer, and put fire in them, and laid incense thereon, and stood in the door of the tabernacle of the congregation with Moses and Aaron.

18 And Korah gathered all the congregation against them unto the door of the tabernacle of the congregation: and the glory of the LORD appeared unto all the congregation.

19 And the LORD spake unto Moses and unto Aaron, saying,   .

20 Separate yourselves from among this congregation, that I may consume them in a moment.

21 And they fell upon their faces, and said, O God, the God of the spirits of all flesh, shall one man sin, and wilt thou be wroth with all the congregation?

22 And the LORD spake unto Moses, saying,   '

23 Speak unto the congregation, saying, Get you up from about the tabernacle of Korah, Dathan, and Abiram.

24 And Moses rose up and went unto Dathan and Abiram; and the elders of Israel followed him.

25 And he spake unto the congregation, saying, Depart, I pray you, from the tents of these wicked men, and touch nothing of theirs, lest ye be consumed in all their sins.

26 So they got up from the tabernacle of Korah, Dathan, and Abiram, on every side: and Dathan and Abiram came out, and stood in the door of their tents, and their wives, and their sons, and their little children.

27 And Moses said, Hereby ye shall know that the LORD hath sent me to do all these works; for I have not done them of mine own mind.

28 If these men die the common death of all men, or if they be visited after the visitation of all men; then the LORD hath not sent me.

29 But if the LORD make a new thing, and the earth open her mouth, and swallow them up, with all that appertain unto them, and they go down quick into the pit; then ye shall understand that these men have provoked the LORD.

30 And it came to pass, as he had made an end of speaking all these words, that the ground clave asunder that was under them:

31 And the earth opened her mouth, and swallowed them up, and their houses, and all the men that appertained unto Korah, and all their goods.

32 They, and all that appertained to them, went down alive into the pit, and the earth closed upon them: and they perished from among the congregation.

33 And all Israel that were round about them fled at the cry of them: for they said, Lest the earth swallow us up also.

34 And there came out a fire from the LORD, and consumed the two hundred and fifty men that offered incense.

35 And the LORD spake unto Moses, saying,

36 Speak unto Eleazar the son of Aaron the priest, that he take up the censers out of the burning, and scatter thou the fire yonder; for they are hallowed.

37 The censers of these sinners against their own souls, let them make them broad plates for a covering of the altar: for they offered them before the LORD, therefore they are hallowed: and they shall be a sign unto the children of Israel.   .

38 And Eleazar the priest took the brazen censers, wherewith they that were burnt had offered; and they were made broad plates for a covering of the altar:

39 To be a memorial unto the children of Israel, that no stranger, which is not of the seed of Aaron, come near to offer incense before the LORD; that he be not as Korah, and as his

company: as the LORD said to him by the hand of Moses.

40 But on the morrow all the congregation of the children of Israel murmured against Moses and against Aaron, saying, Ye have killed the people of the LORD.

41 And it came to pass, when the congregation was gathered against Moses and against Aaron, that they looked toward the tabernacle of the congregation: and, behold, the cloud covered it, and the glory of the LORD appeared.

42 And Moses and Aaron came before the tabernacle of the congregation.

43 And the LORD spake unto Moses, saying, Get up from among this congregation, that I may consume them as in a moment. And they fell upon their faces.

44 And Moses said unto Aaron, Take a censer, and put fire therein from off the altar, and put on incense, and go quickly unto the congregation, and make an atonement for them: for there is wrath gone out from the LORD; the plague is begun.

45 And Aaron took as Moses commanded, and ran into the midst of the congregation; and, behold, the plague was begun among the people: and he put on incense, and made an atonement for the people.

46 And he stood between the dead and the living; and the plague was stayed.

47 Now they that died in the plague were fourteen thousand and seven hundred, besides them that died about the matter of Korah.

48 And Aaron returned unto Moses unto the door of the tabernacle of the congregation: and the plague was stayed.

CHAPTER X.

AND the LORD spake unto Moses, saying,

2 Speak unto the children of Israel, and take of every one of them a rod according to the house of their fathers, of all their princes according to the house of their fathers, twelve rods: write thou every man's name upon his rod.

3 And thou shalt write Aaron's name upon the rod of Levi: for one rod shall be for the head of the house of their fathers.

4 And thou shalt lay them up in the tabernacle of the congregation before the testimony, where I will meet with you.

5 And it shall come to pass, that the man's rod, whom I shall choose, shall blossom: and I will make to cease from me the murmurings of the children of Israel, whereby they murmur against you.

6 And Moses spoke unto the children of Israel, and every one of their princes gave him a rod apiece, for each prince one, according to their fathers' houses, even twelve rods: and the rod of Aaron was among their rods.

7 And Moses laid up the rods before the LORD in the tabernacle of witness.

8 And it came to pass, that on the morrow Moses went into the tabernacle of witness; and, behold, the rod of Aaron for the house of Levi was budded, and brought forth buds, and bloomed blossoms, and yielded almonds.

9 And Moses brought out all the rods from before the LORD unto all the children of Israel: and they looked, and took every man his rod.

10 And the LORD said unto Moses, Bring Aaron's rod again before the testimony, to be kept for a token against the rebels; and thou shalt take away their murmurings from me, that they die not.

11 And Moses did so: as the LORD commanded him, so did he.

CHAPTER XI.

AND the LORD spake unto Moses and unto Aaron, saying,

2 This is the ordinance of the law which the LORD hath commanded, saying, Speak unto the children of Israel, that they bring thee a red heifer without spot, wherein is no blemish, and upon which never came a yoke.

3 And ye shall give her unto Eleazar the priest, that he may bring her forth without the camp, and one shall slay her before his face:

4 And Eleazar the priest shall take of her blood with his finger, and sprinkle of her blood directly before the tabernacle of the congregation seven times.

5 And one shall burn the heifer in his sight; her skin, and her flesh, and her blood, with her appurtenance, shall he burn:

6 And the priest shall take cedar wood, and hyssop, and scarlet, and cast it into the midst of the burning of the heifer.

7 Then the priest shall wash his clothes, and he shall bathe his flesh in water, and afterward he shall come into the camp, and the priest shall be unclean until the even.

8 And he that burneth her shall wash his clothes in water, and bathe his flesh in water, and shall be unclean until the even.

9 And a man that is clean shall gather up the ashes of the heifer, and lay them up without the camp in a clean place, and it shall be kept for the congregation of the children of Israel for a water of separation: it is purification for sin.

10 And he that gathereth the ashes of the heifer shall wash his clothes, and be unclean until the even: and it shall be unto the children of Israel, and unto the stranger that sojourneth among them, for a statute for ever.

11 He that toucheth the dead body of any man shall be unclean seven days.

12 He shall purify himself with it on the third day, and on the seventh day he shall be clean: but if he purify not himself the third day, then the seventh day he shall not be clean.

13 Whosoever toucheth the body of any man that is dead, and purifieth not himself, defileth the tabernacle of the LORD; and that soul shall be cut off from Israel: because the water of separation was not sprinkled upon him, he shall be unclean; his uncleanness is yet upon him.

14 This is the law, when a man dieth in a tent: all that come into the tent, and all that is in the tent, shall be unclean seven days.

15 And every open vessel, which hath no covering bound upon it, is unclean.

16 And whosoever toucheth one that is slain with a sword in the open fields, or a dead body, or a bone of a man, or a grave, shall be unclean seven days.

17 And for an unclean person they shall take of the ashes of the burnt heifer of purification for sin, and running water shall be put in a vessel:

18 And a clean person shall take hyssop, and dip it in the water, and sprinkle it upon the tent, and upon the persons that were there, and upon him that touched a bone, or one slain, or one dead, or a grave:

19 And the clean person shall sprinkle upon the unclean on the third day, and on the seventh day: and on the seventh day he shall purify himself, and wash his clothes, and bathe himself in water, and shall be clean at even.

20 And it shall be a perpetual statute unto them; he that sprinkleth the water of separation shall wash his clothes; and he that toucheth the water of separation shall be unclean until even.

21 And whatsoever the unclean person toucheth shall be unclean; and the soul that toucheth it shall be unclean until even.

CHAPTER XII.

THEN came the children of Israel, even the whole congregation, into the desert of Zin in the first month: and the people abode in Kadesh; and Miriam died there, and was buried there.

2 And there was no water for the congregation: and they gathered themselves together against Moses and against Aaron.

3 And the people chode with Moses, and spoke, saying, Would God that we had died when our brethren died before the LORD!

4 And why have ye brought up the congregation of the LORD into this wilderness, that we and our cattle should die there?

5 And wherefore have ye made us to come up out of Egypt, to bring us in unto this evil place? it is no place of seed, or of figs, or of vines, or of pomegranates; neither is there even any water to drink.

6 And Moses and Aaron went from the presence of the assembly unto the door of the tabernacle of the congregation, and they fell upon their faces: and the glory of the LORD appeared unto them.

7 And the LORD spake unto Moses, saying,

8 Take the rod, and gather thou the assembly together, thou and Aaron thy brother, and speak ye unto the rock before their eyes; and it shall give forth water, and thou shalt bring forth to them water out of the rock: so thou shalt give the congregation and their beasts drink.

9 And Moses took the rod from before the LORD, as he commanded him.

10 And Moses and Aaron gathered the congregation together before the rock, and he said unto them, Hear now, ye rebels; must we fetch you water out of this rock?

11 And Moses lifted up his hand, and with his rod he smote the rock twice: and the water came out abundantly, and the congregation drank, and their beasts also.

12 And the LORD spake unto Moses and Aaron, Because ye believed me not, to sanctify me in the eyes of the children of Israel, therefore ye shall not bring this congregation into the land which I have given them.

13 This is the water of Meribah; because the children of Israel strove with the LORD, and he was sanctified in them.

14 And Moses sent messengers from Kadesh unto the king of Edom, Thus saith thy brother Israel, Thou know-

est all the travail that hath befallen us:

15 How our fathers went down into Egypt, and we have dwelt in Egypt a long time ; and the Egyptians vexed us, and our fathers:

16 And when we cried unto the LORD, he heard our voice, and sent an angel, and hath brought us forth out of Egypt: and, behold, we are in Kadesh, a city in the uttermost of thy border.

17 Let us pass, I pray thee, through thy country: we will not pass through the fields, or through the vineyards, neither will we drink of the water of the wells: we will go by the king's high way, we will not turn to the right hand nor to the left, until we have passed thy borders.

18 And Edom said unto him, Thou shalt not pass by me, lest I come out against thee with the sword.

19 And the children of Israel said unto him, We will go by the high way: and if I and my cattle drink of thy water, then I will pay for it: I will only, without doing any thing else, go through on my feet. ·

20 And he said, Thou shalt not go through. And Edom came out against him with much people, and with a strong hand.

21 Thus Edom refused to give Israel passage through his border: wherefore Israel turned away from him.

22 And the children of Israel, even the whole congregation, journeyed from Kadesh, and came unto mount Hor.

23 And the LORD spake unto Moses and Aaron in mount Hor, by the coast of the land of Edom, saying,

24 Aaron shall be gathered unto his people: for he shall not enter into the land which I have given unto the children of Israel, because ye rebelled against my word at the water of Meribah.

25 Take Aaron and Eleazar his son, and bring them up unto mount Hor :

26 And strip Aaron of his garments, and put them upon Eleazar his son: and Aaron shall be gathered unto his people, and shall die there.

27 And Moses did as the LORD commanded: and they went up into mount Hor in the sight of all the congregation.

28 And Moses stripped Aaron of his garments, and put them upon Eleazar his son; and Aaron died there in the top of the mount: and Moses and Eleazar came down from the mount.

29 And when all the congregation saw that Aaron was dead, they mourned for Aaron thirty days, even all the house of Israel.

CHAPTER XIII.

AND when king Arad the Canaanite, which dwelt in the south, heard tell that Israel came by the way of the spies; then he fought against Israel, and took some of them prisoners.

2 And Israel vowed a vow unto the LORD, and said, if thou wilt indeed deliver this people into my hand, then I will utterly destroy their cities.

3 And the LORD hearkened to the voice of Israel, and delivered up the Canaanites; and they utterly destroyed them and their cities: and he called the name of the place Hormah.

4 And they journeyed from mount Hor by the way of the Red sea, to compass the land of Edom: and the soul of the people was much discouraged because of the way.

5 And the people spoke against God,

and against Moses, Wherefore have ye brought us up out of Egypt to die in the wilderness? for there is no bread, neither is there any water; and our soul loatheth this light bread.

6 And the LORD sent fiery serpents among the people, and they bit the people; and much people of Israel died.

7 Therefore the people came to Moses, and said, We have sinned, for we have spoken against the LORD, and against thee; pray unto the LORD, that he take away the serpent from us. And Moses prayed for the people.

8 And the LORD said unto Moses, Make thee a fiery serpent, and set it upon a pole: and it shall come to pass, that every one that is bitten, when he looketh upon it, shall live.

9 And Moses made a serpent of brass, and put it upon a pole; and it came to pass, that if a serpent had bitten any man, when he beheld the serpent of brass, he lived.

10 And the children of Israel set forward, and pitched in Oboth.

. 11 And they journeyed from Oboth, and pitched at Ije-abarim, in the wilderness which is before Moab, toward the sunrising.

12 From thence they removed, and pitched in the valley of Zared.

13 From thence they removed, and pitched on the other side of Arnon, which is in the wilderness that cometh out of the coasts of the Amorites: for Arnon is the border of Moab, between Moab and the Amorites.

14 Wherefore it is said in the 'Book of the wars of the LORD':

15 Vaheb in Suphah,
   and the streams of Arnon,
   and the slope of the streams,
   which sinks toward the seat of Ar,
   and leans on the border of Moab.

16 And from thence they went to Be-er, that is the well whereof the LORD spake unto Moses, Gather the people together and I will give them water.

17 Then Israel sang this song:
   Spring up, O well—
   Sing ye to it—
18 O well, which princes dug,
   the nobles of the nation hollowed,
   with sceptre and staff.

19 And from the wilderness they went to Mattanah, and from Mattanah to Nahaliel, and from Nahaliel to Bamoth;

20 From Bamoth in the valley, which is in Moab's field, to Pisgah's summit, which looks out upon the desert.

21 And Israel sent messengers unto Sihon king of the Amorites, saying,

22 Let me pass through thy land: we will not turn into the fields, or into the vineyards; we will not drink of the waters of the well: but we will go along by the king's high way, until we are past thy borders.

23 And Sihon would not suffer Israel to pass through his border: but Sihon gathered all his people together, and went out against Israel into the wilderness: and he came to Jahaz, and fought against Israel.

24 And Israel smote him with the edge of the sword, and possessed his land from Arnon unto Jabbok, even unto the children of Ammon: for the border of the children of Ammon was strong.

25 And Israel took all these cities: and Israel dwelt in all the cities of the Amorites, in Heshbon, and in all the villages thereof.

26 For Heshbon was the city of Sihon the king of the Amorites, who

had fought against the former king of Moab, and taken all his land out of his hand, even unto Arnon.

27 Wherefore the poets sing:
Come ye into Heshbon:
let Sihon's city be built and erected.
28 Lo, a fire has sprung from Heshbon,
a flame from Sihon's capital;
it has consumed Moab's Ar,
the lords of Arnon-Heights.
29 Woe to thee, Moab;
thou art lost, Chemosh's people—
he has rendered his sons fugitives,
and his daughters captives
of the Amorite king, Sihon.
30 And we triumphed:
Heshbon is destroyed, as far as Dibon;
we have wasted as far as Nophah,
which extends to Medeba.

31 Thus Israel dwelt in the land of the Amorites.

32 And Moses sent to spy out Jaazer, and they took the villages thereof, and drove out the Amorites that were there.

33 And they turned and went up by the way of Bashan: and Og the king of Bashan went out against them, he, and all his people, to the battle at Edrei.

34 And the LORD said unto Moses, Fear him not: for I have delivered him into thy hand, and all his people, and his land; and thou shalt do to him as thou didst unto Sihon king of the Amorites, which dwelt at Heshbon.

35 So they smote him, and his sons, and all his people, until there was none left him alive: and they possessed his land.

CHAPTER XIV.

AND the children of Israel set forward, and pitched in the plains of Moab on this side Jordan by Jericho.

2 And Balak the son of Zippor saw all that Israel had done to the Amorites.

3 And Moab was sore afraid of the people, because they were many: and Moab was distressed because of the children of Israel.

4 And Moab said unto the elders of Midian, Now shall this company lick up all that are round about us, as the ox licketh up the grass of the field. And Balak the son of Zippor was king of the Moabites at that time.

5 He sent messengers therefore unto Balaam the son of Beor to Pethor, which is by the river of the land of the children of his people, to call him, saying, Behold, there is a people come out from Egypt: behold, they cover the face of the earth, and they abide over against me:

6 Come now therefore, I pray thee, curse me this people; for they are too mighty for me: peradventure I shall prevail, that we may smite them, and that I may drive them out of the land: for I know that he whom thou blessest is blessed, and he whom thou cursest is cursed.

7 And the elders of Moab and the elders of Midian departed with the rewards of divination in their hand; and they came unto Balaam, and spoke unto him the words of Balak.

8 And he said unto them, Lodge here this night, and I will bring you word again, as the LORD shall speak unto me: and the princes of Moab abode with Balaam.

9 And God came unto Balaam, and said, What men are these with thee?

10 And Balaam said unto God, Balak the son of Zippor, king of Moab, hath sent unto me, saying,

11 Behold, there is a people come out of Egypt, which covereth the face

of the earth: come now, curse me them; peradventure I shall be able to overcome them, and drive them out.

12 And God said unto Balaam, Thou shalt not go with them; thou shalt not curse the people: for they are blessed.

13 And Balaam rose up in the morning, and said unto the princes of Balak, Get you into your land: for the LORD refuseth to give me leave to go with you.

14 And the princes of Moab rose up, and they went unto Balak, and said, Balaam refuseth to come with us.

15 And Balak sent yet again princes, more, and more honourable than they.

16 And they came to Balaam, and said to him, Thus saith Balak the son of Zippor, Let nothing, I pray thee, hinder thee from coming unto me:

17 For I will promote thee unto very great honour, and I will do whatsoever thou sayest unto me: come therefore, I pray thee, curse me this people.

18 And Balaam answered and said, unto the servants of Balak, If Balak would give me his house full of silver and gold, I cannot go beyond the word of the LORD my God, to do less or more.

19 Now therefore, I pray you, tarry ye also here this night, that I may know what the LORD will say unto me more.

20 And God came unto Balaam at night, and said unto him, If the men came to call thee, rise up, and go with them; but yet the word which I shall say unto thee, that shalt thou do.

21 And Balaam rose up in the morning, and saddled his ass, and went with the princes of Moab.

22 And God's anger was kindled because he went: and the angel of the LORD stood in the way for an adversary against him. Now he was riding upon his ass, and his two servants were with him.

23 And the ass saw the angel of the LORD standing in the way, and his sword drawn in his hand: and the ass turned aside out of the way, and went into the field: and Balaam smote the ass, to turn her into the way.

24 But the angel of the LORD stood in a path of the vineyards, a wall being on this side, and a wall on that side.

25 And when the ass saw the angel of the LORD, she thrust herself unto the wall, and crushed Balaam's foot against the wall: and he smote her again.

26 And the angel of the LORD went further, and stood in a narrow place, where was no way to turn either to the right or to the left.

27 And when the ass saw the angel of the LORD, she fell down under Balaam: and Balaam's anger was kindled, and he smote the ass with a staff.

28 And the LORD opened the mouth of the ass, and she said unto Balaam, What have I done unto thee, that thou hast smitten me these three times?

29 And Balaam said unto the ass, Because thou hast mocked me: I would there were a sword in mine hand, for now would I kill thee.

30 And the ass said unto Balaam, Am not I thine ass, upon which thou hast ridden ever since I was thine unto this day? was I ever wont to do so unto thee? And he said, Nay.

31 Then the LORD opened the eyes of Balaam, and he saw the angel of the LORD standing in the way, and his sword drawn in his hand: and he

bowed down his head, and fell flat on his face.

32 And the angel of the LORD said unto him, Wherefore hast thou smitten thine ass these three times? Behold, I went out to withstand thee, because thy way is perverse before me:

33 And the ass saw me, and turned from me these three times: unless she had turned from me, surely now also I had slain thee, and saved her alive.

34 And Balaam said unto the angel of the LORD, I have sinned; for I knew not that thou stoodest in the way against me: now therefore, if it displease thee, I will get me back again.

35 And the angel of the LORD said unto Balaam, Go with the men: but only the word that I shall speak unto thee, that thou shalt speak. So Balaam went with the princes of Balak.

36 And when Balak heard that Balaam was come, he went out to meet him unto a city of Moab, which is in the border of Arnon, which is in the utmost coast.

37 And Balak said unto Balaam, Did I not earnestly send unto thee to call thee? wherefore camest thou not unto me? am I not able indeed to promote thee to honour?

38 And Balaam said unto Balak, Lo, I am come unto thee: have I now any power at all to say any thing? the word that God putteth in my mouth, that shall I speak.

39 And Balaam went with Balak, and they came unto Kirjath-huzoth.

40 And Balak offered oxen and sheep, and sent to Balaam, and to the princes that were with him.

41 And it came to pass on the morrow, that Balak took Balaam, and brought him up into the high places of Baal, that thence he might see the utmost part of the people.

CHAPTER XV.

AND Balaam said unto Balak, Build me here seven altars, and prepare me here seven oxen and seven rams.

2 And Balak did as Balaam had spoken; and Balak and Balaam offered on every altar a bullock and a ram.

3 And Balaam said unto Balak, Stand by the burnt offering, and I will go: peradventure the LORD will come to meet me; and whatsoever he sheweth me I will tell thee. And he went to a high place.

4 And God met Balaam: and he said unto him, I have prepared seven altars, and I have offered upon every altar a bullock and a ram.

5 And the LORD put a word in Balaam's mouth, and said, Return unto Balak, and thus thou shalt speak.

6 And he returned unto him, and, lo, he stood by his burnt sacrifice, he, and all the princes of Moab.

7 And he took up his parable, and said,

'From Aram Balak, Moab's king,
    bringeth me;
from the mountains of the East:
"Come, curse for me Jacob;
come, execrate Israel."

8 How shall I curse whom God curseth not?
how shall I execrate whom the LORD execrateth not?

9 For from the summit of rocks I see him,
from hilltops I behold him:
lo, a people dwelling apart,
nor reckoning itself among the nations.

10 Who counteth the dust of Jacob?
who numbereth the fourth part of Israel?
May I die the death of the righteous,
and may my end be like theirs.'

11 And Balak said unto Balaam, What hast thou done unto me? I took thee to curse mine enemies, and, behold, thou hast blessed them altogether.

12 And he answered and said, Must I not take heed to speak that which the LORD hath put in my mouth?

13 And Balak said unto him, Come, I pray thee, with me unto another place,- from whence thou mayest see them, thou shalt see but the utmost part of them, and shalt not see them all: and curse me them from thence.

14 And he brought him into the field of Zophim, to the top of Pisgah, and built seven altars, and offered a bullock and a ram on every altar.

15 And he said unto Balak, Stand here by thy burnt offering, while I meet the LORD yonder.

16 And the LORD met Balaam, and put a word in his mouth, and said, Go again unto Balak, and say thus.

17 And when he came to him, behold, he stood by his burnt offering, and the princes of Moab with him. And Balak said unto him, What hath the LORD spoken?

18 And he took up his parable, and said,

'Rise, Balak, and hear;
listen to me, O son of Zippor:
19 God is not a man, that he should lie;
not the son of a man, that he should repent;
if he has said, will he not do?
if he has spoken, will he not fulfill?
20 Lo, a blessing I have heard;
. he has blessed—I cannot reverse it.
21 He beholdeth no iniquity in Jacob,
he seeth no evil in Israel.
Jehovah, his God, is with him,
shouts for a king resound in his midst.
22 God leading him out of Egypt,
the wild buffalo's rush is his.

23 Yea, there is no enchantment in Jacob,
no divination in Israel;
in due time Jacob, Israel, is told what God is working.
24 Behold, a people that riseth like a lioness,
lifteth itself up like a lion;
it lieth not down before devouring prey,
before drinking the blood 'of the slain.'

25 And Balak said unto Balaam, Neither curse them at all, nor bless them at all.

26 But Balaam answered and said unto Balak, Did I not tell thee, saying, All that the LORD speaketh, that I must do?

27 And Balak said unto Balaam, Come, I pray thee, I will bring thee unto another place: peradventure it will please God that thou mayest curse me them from thence.

28 And Balak brought Balaam unto the top of Peor, that looketh toward the desert.

29 And Balaam said unto Balak, Build me here seven altars, and prepare me here seven bullocks and seven rams.

30 And Balak did as Balaam had said, and offered a bullock and a ram on every altar.

CHAPTER XVI.

AND when Balaam saw that it pleased the LORD to bless Israel, he went not, as at other times, to seek for enchantments, but he set his face toward the wilderness.

2 And Balaam lifted up his eyes, and he saw Israel abiding in his tents according to their tribes; and the spirit of God came upon him.

3 And he took up his parable, and said,

'This is the oracle of Balaam, Beor's
    son,
the oracle of the man whose eye is
    locked;
the oracle of him who heareth the
    sayings of God,
and seeth the vision of the Al-
    mighty—
prostrate, yet with eyes unlocked:
4 How beautiful are thy tents, O Jacob!
    thy tabernacles, O Israel!
like vales spread out,
like gardens on river banks,
like aloe-trees planted by the LORD,
like cedars by streams.
5 Water runeth from his buckets,
    where his seed lieth abundant waters
        flow.
His king is higher than Agag,
    his kingdom exalted.
6 God leading him out of Egypt,
    the wild buffalo's rush is his.
7 He devoureth nations, his foes,
    and gnaweth their bones—
    crusheth with his arrows.
8 He coucheth, lieth down, like a lion,
    like a lioness —who shall rouse him?
9 ·Blessed is whoever blesseth thee,
    Cursed whoever curseth thee.'

10 And Balak's anger was kindled against Balaam, and he smote · his hands together: and Balak said unto Balaam, ·I called thee to curse mine enemies, and, behold, thou hast altogether blessed them these three times.

11 Therefore now flee thou to thy place: I thought to promote thee unto great honour ; but, lo, the LORD hath kept thee back from honour.

12 And Balaam said unto Balak, Spake I not also to thy messengers which thou sentest unto me, saying,

13 If Balak would give me his house full of silver and gold, I cannot go beyond the commandment of the LORD, to do either good or bad of mine own mind ; but what the LORD saith, that will I speak?

14 And now, behold, I go unto my people : ·come therefore, and · I will advise thee of what this people shall do to thy people in the latter days. ·

15 And he took up his parable, and said,

'This is the oracle of Balaam, Beor's
    son,
the oracle of the man whose eye is
    locked;
the oracle of him who heareth the
    sayings of God,
knoweth the knowledge of the Most
    High,
and seeth the vision of the Al-
    mighty—
prostrate, yet with eyes unlocked:
16 I see him—not now;
    I behold him—not nigh.
17 A star breaketh forth from Jacob,
    a sceptre ariseth from Israel;
    it crusheth the sides of Moab,
    overthroweth all the men of tumult;
18 Edom becometh a conquest,
    Seir a conquest of its foes;
    Israel doeth valiantly.
19 He from Jacob is master, ·
    and destroyeth the remnant in the
        cities.

20 And when he looked on Amalek, he took up his parable, and said,

'Foremost among nations was Amalek;
    his end tendeth to perdition.'

21 And he looked on the Kenites, and he took up his parable, and said,

'Firm is thy seat,
    upon a rock is set thy nest;
22 Yet Qayin will be wasted.
    Till when ? — Asshur carrieth thee
        away captive.'

23 And he took up his parable, and said,

'Alas! who can live after God's ap-
    pointing him ?
24 Yet, ships come from Chittim's
    shores,
    and afflict Asshur, and afflict Eber—
    and he, too, perisheth.'

25 And Balaam rose up, and went and returned to his place: and Balak also went his way.

CHAPTER XVII.

AND when Israel abode in the plains of Moab, the people made acquaintance with the daughters of Moab.

2 And they called the people unto the sacrifices of their gods: and the people did eat, and bowed down to their gods.

3 And Israel joined himself unto Baal-peor: and the anger of the LORD was kindled against Israel.

4 And the LORD said unto Moses, Take all the leaders of the people, and hang them up before the LORD against the sun, that the fierce anger of the LORD may be turned away from Israel.

5 And Moses said unto the judges of Israel, Slay ye every one his men that were joined unto Baal-peor.

6 And, behold, one of the children of Israel came and brought unto his brethren a Midianitish woman in the sight of Moses, and in the sight of all the congregation of the children of Israel, who were weeping before the door of the tabernacle of the congregation.

7 And when Phinehas, the son of Eleazar, the son of Aaron the priest, saw it, he rose up from among the congregation, and took a javalin in his hand;

8 And he went after the man of Issael, and thrust both of them through, the man of Israel, and the woman. So the plague was stayed from the children of Israel.

9 And those that died in the plague were twenty and four thousand.

10 And the LORD spake unto Moses, saying,

11 Phinehas, the son of Eleazar, the son of Aaron the priest, hath turned my wrath away from the children of Israel, while he was zealous for my sake among them, that I consumed not the children of Israel in my jealousy;

12 Wherefore say, Behold, I give unto him my covenant of peace:

13 And he shall have it, and his children after him, even the covenant of an everlasting priesthood; because he was zealous for his God, and made an atomement for the children of Israel.

14 And the LORD spake unto Moses, saying,

15 Make war upon the Midianites, and smite them:

16 For they vexed you with their wiles, wherewith they have beguiled you in the matter of Peor, in the day of the plague for Peor's sake.

17 And Moses spake unto the people, saying, Arm some of yourselves unto the war, and let them go against the Midianites, and avenge the LORD of Midian.

18 Of every tribe a thousand, throughout all the tribes of Israel, shall ye send to the war.

19 So there were delivered out of the thousands of Israel, a thousand of every tribe, twelve thousand armed for war.

20 And Moses sent them to the war, a thousand of every tribe, them and Phinehas the son of Eleazar the priest, to the war, with the holy instruments, and the trumpets to blow in his hand.

21 And they warred against the Midianites, as the LORD commanded Moses; and they slew all the males.

22 And they slew the kings of Midian, beside the rest of them that were slain; namely, Evi, and Rekem, and

Zur, and Hur, and Reba, five kings of Midian: Balaam also the son of Beor they slew with the sword.

23 And they. burnt all their cities wherein they dwelt and all their strong castles with fire.

24 And they took all the spoil and all the prey, both of men and of beast.

25 And they brought all unto Moses and Eleazar the priest, and unto the congregation of the children of Israel, unto the camp at the plains of Moab by the Jordan near Jericho.

CHAPTER XVIII.

THEN came the daughters of Zelophehad, the son of Hepher, the son of Gilead, the son of Machir, the son of Manasseh, of the families of Manasseh the son of Joseph; and these are the names of his daughters; Mahlah, Noah, and Hoglah, and Milcah, and Tirzah.

2 And they stood before Moses, and before Eleazar the priest, and before the princes and all the congregation, by the door of the tabernacle of the congregation, saying,

3 Our father died in the wilderness, and he was not in the company of them that gathered themselves together against the LORD in the company of Korah; but died in his own sin, and had no sons.

4 Why should the name of our father perish from among his family because he hath no son? Give unto us therefore a possession among the brethren of our father.

5 And Moses brought their cause before the LORD.

6 And the LORD spake unto Moses, saying,

7 The daughters of Zelophehad speak right: thou shalt surely give them a possession of an inheritance among their father's brethren; and thou shalt cause the inheritance of their father to pass unto them.

8 And thou shalt speak unto the children of Israel, saying, If a man die, and have no son, then ye shall cause his inheritance to pass unto his daughter.

9 And if he have no daughter, then ye shall give his inheritance unto his brethren.

10 And if he have no brethren, then ye shall give his inheritance unto his father's brethren.

11 And if his father have no brethren, then ye shall give his inheritance unto his kinsman that is next to him of his family, and he shall possess it: and it shall be unto the children of Israel a statute of judgment, as the LORD commanded Moses.

12 And the LORD said unto Moses, Get thee up into this mount Abarim, and see the land which I have given unto the children of Israel.

13 And when thou hast seen it, thou also shalt be gathered unto thy people, as Aaron thy brother was gathered.

14 For ye rebelled against my commandment in the desert of Zin, in the strife of the congregation, to sanctify me at the water before their eyes: that is the water of Meribah in Kadesh in the wilderness of Zin.

15 And Moses spake unto the LORD, saying,

16 Let the LORD, the God of the spirits of all flesh, set a man over the congregation,

17 Which may go out before them, and which may go in before them, and which may lead them out, and which may bring them in; that the congre-

gation of the LORD be not as sheep which have no shepherd.

18 And the LORD said unto Moses, Take thee Joshua the son of Nun, a man in whom is the spirit, and lay thine hand upon him;

19 And set him before Eleazar the priest, and before all the congregation; and give him a charge in their sight.

20 And thou shalt put some of thine honour upon him, that all the congregation of the children of Israel may be obedient.

21 And he shall stand before Eleazar the priest, who shall ask counsel for him after the judgment of Urim before the LORD: at his word shall they go out, and at his word they shall come in, both he, and all the children of Israel with him, even all the congregation.

22 And Moses did as the LORD commanded him: and he took Joshua, and set him before Eleazar the priest, and before all the congregation:

23 And he laid his hands upon him, and gave him a charge, as the LORD commanded by the hand of Moses.

CHAPTER XIX.

AND Moses spake unto the heads of the tribes of the children of Israel, saying, This is the thing which the LORD hath commanded.

2 If a man vow a vow unto the LORD, or swear an oath to bind his soul with a bond; he shall not break his word, he shall do according to all that proceedeth out of his mouth.

3 If a woman also vow a vow unto the LORD, and bind herself by a bond, being in her father's house in her youth;

4 And her father hear her vow, and her bond wherewith she hath bound

her soul, and her father shall hold his peace at her; then all her vows shall stand, and every bond wherewith she hath bound her soul shall stand.

5 But if her father disallow her in the day that he heareth, not any of her vows, or of her bonds wherewith she hath bound her soul, shall stand; and the LORD shall forgive her, because her father disallowed her.

6 And if she had a husband, when she vowed, or uttered aught out of her lips, wherewith she bound her soul;

7 And her husband heard it, and held his peace at her in the day that he heard it: then her vows shall stand, and her bonds wherewith she bound her soul shall stand.

8 But if her husband disallowed her on the day that he heard it, then he shall make her vow which she vowed, and that which she uttered with her lips, wherewith she bound her soul, of none effect; and the LORD shall forgive her.

9 But every vow of a widow, and of her that is divorced, wherewith they have bound their souls, shall stand against her,

10 And if she vowed in her husband's house, or bound her soul by a bond with an oath;

11 And her husband heard it, and held his peace at her, and dissallowed her not: then all her vows shall stand, and every bond wherewith she bound her soul shall stand.

12 But if her husband hath utterly made them void on the day he heard them; then whatsoever proceeded out of her lips concerning her vows, or concerning the bond of her soul, shall not stand: her husband hath made

them void; and the LORD shall forgive her.

13 Every vow, and every binding oath to afflict the soul, her husband may establish it, or her husband may make it void.

14 But if her husband altogether hold his peace at her from day to day; then he establisheth all her vows, or all her bonds, which are upon her: he confirmeth them, because he held his peace at her in the day that he heard them.

15 But if he shall any ways make them void after that he hath heard them ; then he shall bear her iniquity.

16 These are the statutes, which the LORD commanded Moses, between a man and his wife, between the father and his daughter, being yet in her youth in her father's house.

CHAPTER XX.

NOW the children of Reuben and the children of Gad had a very great multitude of cattle: and when they saw the land of Jazer, and the land of Gilead, that, behold, the place was a place for cattle;

2 The children of Gad and the children of Reuben came and spake unto Moses, and to Eleazar the priest, and unto the princes of the congregation, saying,

3 Ataroth, and Dibon, and Jazer, and Nimrah, and Heshbon, and Elealeh, and Shebam, and Nebo, and Beon,

4 Even the country which the LORD smote before the congregation of Israel, is a land for cattle, and thy servants have cattle :

5 Wherefore, said they, if we have found grace in thy sight, let this land be given unto thy servants for a possession, and bring us not over Jordan.

6 And Moses said unto the children of Gad and to the children of Reuben, Shall your brethren go to war, and shall ye sit here ?

7 And wherefore discourage ye the heart of the children of Israel from going over into the land which the LORD hath given them ?

8 Thus did your fathers, when I sent them from Kadesh-barnea to see the land.

9 For when they went up unto the valley of Eshcol, and saw the land, they discouraged the heart of the children of Israel, that they should not go into the land which the LORD had given them.

10 And the LORD'S anger was kindled the same time, and he sware, saying,

11 Surely none of the men that came up out of Egypt, from twenty years old and upward, shall see the land which I sware unto Abraham, unto Isaac, and unto Jacob ; because they have not wholly followed me:

12 Save Caleb the son of Jephunneh the Kenezite, and Joshua the son of Nun : for they have wholly followed the LORD.

13 And the LORD'S anger was kindled against Israel, and he made them wander in the wilderness forty years, until all the generation, that had done evil in the sight of the LORD, was consumed.

14 And, behold, ye are risen up in your father's stead, an increase of sinful men, to augment yet the fierce anger of the LORD toward Israel.

15 For if ye turn away from after him, he will yet again leave them in the wilderness; and ye shall destroy all this people.

16 And they came near unto him,

and said, We will build sheepfolds here for our cattle, and cities for our little ones :

17 But we ourselves will go ready armed before the children of Israel, until we have brought them unto their place: and our little ones shall dwell in the fenced cities, because of the inhabitants of the land.

18 We will not return unto our houses, until the children of Israel have inherited every man his inheritance :

19 For we will not inherit with them on yonder side Jordan, or forward; because our inheritance is fallen to us on this side Jordan eastward.

20 And Moses said unto them, If ye will do this thing, if ye will go armed before the LORD to war,

21 And will go all of you armed over Jordan before the LORD, until he hath driven out his enemies from before him,

22 And the land be subdued before the LORD: then afterward ye shall return, and be guiltless before the LORD, and before Israel; and this land shall be your possession before the LORD.

23 But if ye will not do so, behold, ye have sinned against the LORD: and be sure your sin will find you out.

24 Build you cities for your little ones, and folds for your sheep; and do that which hath proceeded out of your mouth.

25 And the children of Gad and the children of Reuben spoke unto Moses, saying, Thy servants will do as my lord commandeth.

26 Our little ones, our wives, our flocks, and all our cattle, shall be there in the cities of Gilead:.

27 But thy servants will pass over,

every man armed for war, before the LORD to battle, as my lord saith.

28 So concerning them Moses commanded Eleazar the priest, and Joshua the son of Nun, and the chief fathers of the tribes of the children of Israel:

29 And Moses said unto them, If the children of Gad and the children of Reuben will pass with you over Jordan, every man armed to battle, before the LORD, and the land shall be subdued before you; then ye shall give them the land of Gilead for a possession :

30 But if they will not pass over with you armed, they shall have possessions among you in the land of Canaan.

31 And the children of Gad and the children of Reuben answered, saying, As the LORD hath said unto thy servants, so will we do.

32 We will pass over armed before the LORD into the land of Canaan, that the possession of our inheritance on this side Jordan may be ours.

33 And Moses gave unto them, even to the children of Gad, and to the children of Reuben, and unto half the tribe of Manasseh the son of Joseph, the kingdom of Sihon king of the Amorites, and the kingdom of Og king of Bashan, the land, with the cities thereof in the coasts, even the cities of the country round about.

34 And the children of Gad built Dibon, and Ataroth, and Aroer,

35 And Atroth, Shophan, and Jaazer, and Jogbehah,

36 And Beth-nimrah, and Bethharan, fenced cities; and. folds for sheep.

37 And the children of Reuben built Heshbon, and Elealeh, and Kirjathaim,

38 And Nebo, and Baal-meon, (their names being changed,) and Shibmah: and gave other names unto the cities which they builded.

39 And the children of Machir the son of Manasseh went to Gilead, and took it, and dispossessed the Amorite which was in it.

40 And Moses gave Gilead unto Machir the son of Manasseh; and he dwelt therein.

41 And Jair the son of Manasseh went and took the small towns thereof, and called them Havoth-jair.

42 And Nobah went and took Kenath, and the villages thereof, and called it Nobah, after his own name.

CHAPTER XXI.

THESE are the journeys of the children of Israel, which went forth out of the land of Egypt with their armies under the hand of Moses and Aaron.

2 And Moses wrote their goings out according to their journeys by the commandment of the LORD: and these are their journeys according to their goings out.

3 And they departed from Rameses in the first month, on the fifteenth day of the first month; on the morrow after the passover the children of Israel went out with a high hand in the sight of all the Egyptians:

4 And they departed from Succoth and pitched in Etham, and then turned again unto Pi-hahiroth.

5 And they departed from Pi-hahiroth, and passed through the midst of the sea into the wilderness, and came to Marah.

6 And they removed from Marah and came to Elim; and they removed from Elim and encamped by the Red sea; from thence they removed and encamped in the wilderness of Sin.

7 And they took up their journey from the wilderness of Sin and encamped at the following stations: Dophkah, Alush, Rephidim, Sinai, Kibroth-hattaavah, Hazeroth, Rithmah, Rimon-parez, Libnah, Rissah, Kehelathah, Shapher, Aaradah, Makheloth, Tahath, Tarah, Mithcah, Hashmonah, Moseroth, Bene-jaakan, Hor-hagidgad, Jotbathah, Ebronah, Ezion-gaber, Kadesh, Mount Hor, Zalmonah, Punon, Oboth, Iye-abarin, Dibon-Gad, Almon-diblothaim, Mount Nebo.

8 And they departed from the mountains of Abarim, near Nebo, and pitched in the plains of Moab by Jordan near Jericho.

9 And the LORD spake unto Moses in the plains of Moab by Jordan near Jericho, saying, Speak unto the children of Israel, and say unto them, When ye are passed over Jordan into the land of Canaan;

10 Then ye shall drive out all the inhabitants of the land from before you, and destroy all their pictures, and destroy all their molten images, and quite pluck down all their high places:

11 And ye shall possess the land, and dwell therein: for I have given you the land to possess it.

12 And ye shall divide the land by lot for an inheritance among your families;. and to the more ye shall give the more inheritance, and to the fewer ye shall give the less inheritance: every man's inheritance shall be in the place where his lot falleth; according to the tribes of your fathers ye shall inherit.

CHAPTER XXII.

A ND the LORD spake unto Moses, saying,

2 Command the children of Israel, and say unto them, When ye come into the land of Canaan; the land that shall fall unto you for an inheritance, even the land of Canaan with the coasts thereof:

3 Then your south quarter shall be from the wilderness of Zin along by the coast of Edom, and your south border shall be the outmost coast of the salt sea eastward:

4 And your border shall turn from the south to the ascent of Akrabbim, and pass on to Zin: and the going forth thereof shall be from the south to Kadesh-barnea, and shall go on to Hazar-addar, and pass on to Azmon:

5 And the border shall fetch a compass from Azmon unto the river of Egypt, and the goings out of it shall be at the sea.

6 And as for the western border, ye shall even have the great sea for a border: this shall be your west border.

7 And this shall be your north border: from the great sea ye shall point out for you mount Hor:

8 From mount Hor ye shall point out your border unto the entrance of Hamath; and the goings forth of the border shall be to Zedad:

9 And the border shall go on to Ziphron and the goings out of it shall be at Hazar-enan: this shall be your north border.

10 And ye shall point out your east border from Hazar-enan to Shepham:

11 And the coast shall go down from Shepham to Riblah, on the east side of Ain; and the border shall descend, and shall reach unto the side of the sea of Chinnereth eastward:

12 And the border shall go down to Jordan, and the goings out of it shall be at the salt sea: this shall be your land with the coasts thereof round about.

13 And Moses commanded the children of Israel, saying, This is the land which ye shall inherit by lot, which the LORD commanded to give unto the nine tribes, and to the half tribe:

14 For the tribe of the children of Reuben according to the house of their fathers, and the tribe of the children of Gad according to the house of their fathers, have received their inheritance; and half the tribe of Manasseh have received their inheritance:

15 The two tribes and the half tribe have received their inheritance on this side Jordan near Jericho eastward, toward the sunrising.

CHAPTER XXIII.

A ND the LORD spake unto Moses, saying,

2 Speak unto the children of Israel, and say unto them, When ye be come over Jordan into the land of Canaan,

3 Then ye shall appoint you cities to be cities of refuge for you; that the slayer may flee thither, which killeth any person at unawares.

4 And they shall be unto you cities for refuge from the avenger; that the manslayer die not, until he stand before the congregation in judgment.

5 And of these cities which ye shall give, six cities shall ye have for refuge.

6 Ye shall give three cities on this side Jordan, and three cities shall ye give in the land of Canaan, which shall be cities of refuge.

7 These six cities shall be a refuge,

both for the children of Israel, and for the stranger, and for the sojourner among them; that every one that killeth any person unawares may flee thither.

8 And if he smite him with an instrument of iron, so that he die, he is a murderer: the murderer shall surely be put to death.

9 And if he smite him with throwing a stone, wherewith he may die, and he die, he is a murderer: the murderer shall surely be put to death.

10 Or if he smite him with a hand weapon of wood, wherewith he may die, and he die, he is a murderer: the murderer shall surely be put to death.

11 The revenger of blood himself shall slay the murderer: when he meeteth him, he shall slay him.

12 And if he thrust him of hatred, or hurl at him by laying of wait, that he die;

13 Or in enmity smite him with his hand, that he die: he that smote him shall surely be put to death; for he is a murderer: the revenger of blood shall slay the murderer, when he meeteth him.

14 But if he thrust him suddenly without enmity, or have cast upon him any thing without laying of wait,

15 Or with any stone, wherewith a man may die, seeing him not, and cast it upon him, that he die, and was not his enemy, neither sought his harm:

16 Then the congregation shall judge between the slayer and the revenger of blood according to these judgments:

17 And the congregation shall deliver the slayer out of the hand of the revenger of blood, and the congregation shall restore him to the city of his refuge, whither he was fled: and

he shall abide in it unto the death of the high priest, which was anointed with the holy oil.

18 But if the slayer shall at any time come without the border of the city of his refuge, whither he was fled;

19 And the revenger of blood find him without the borders of the city of his refuge and the revenger of blood kill the slayer; he shall not be guilty of blood:

20 Because he should have remained in the city of his refuge until the death of the high priest: but after the death of the high priest the slayer shall return into the land of his possession

21 And these things shall be for a statute of judgment unto you throughout your generations in all your dwellings.

22 Whoso killeth any person, the murderer shall be put to death by the mouth of witnesses: but one witness shall not testify against any person to cause him to die.

23 Moreover ye shall take no satisfaction for the life of a murderer, which is guilty of death: but he shall be surely put to death.

24 And ye shall take no satisfaction for him that is fled to the city of his refuge, that he should come again to dwell in the land, until the death of the priest.

25 And ye shall not pollute the land wherein ye are; for blood defileth the land: and the land cannot be cleansed of the innocent blood that is shed therein, but by the blood of him that shed it.

26 Defile not therefore the land which ye shall inhabit, wherein I dwell: for I the LORD dwell among the children of Israel.

CHAPTER XXIV.

AND the chief fathers of the families of the children of Gilead, the son of Machir, the son of Manasseh, of the families of the sons of Joseph, came near, and spake before Moses, and before the princes, the chief fathers of the children of Israel:

2 And they said, The LORD commanded my lord to give the land for an inheritance by lot to the children of Israel: and my lord was commanded by the LORD to give the inheritance of Zelophehad our brother unto his daughters.

3 And if they be married to any of the sons of the other tribes of the children of Israel, then shall their inheritance be taken from the inheritance of our fathers, and shall be put to the inheritance of the tribe whereunto they are received: so shall it be taken from the lot of our inheritance.

4 And when the jubilee of the children of Israel shall be, then shall their inheritance be put unto the inheritance of the tribe whereunto they are received: so shall their inheritance be taken away from the inheritance of the tribe of our fathers.

5 And Moses commanded the children of Israel according to the word of the LORD, saying, The tribe of the sons of Joseph hath said well.

6 This is the thing which the LORD doth command concerning the daughters of Zelophehad, saying, Let them marry to whom they think best: only to the family of the tribe of their father shall they marry.

7 So shall not the inheritance of the children of Israel remove from tribe to tribe: for every one of the children of Israel shall keep himself to the inheritance of the tribe of his fathers.

8 And every daughter that possesseth an inheritance in any tribe of the children of Israel, shall be wife unto one of the family of the tribe of her father, that the children of Israel may enjoy every man the inheritance of his fathers.

9 Neither shall the inheritance remove from one tribe to another tribe; but every one of the tribes of the children of Israel shall keep himself to his own inheritance.

10 Even as the LORD commanded Moses, so did the daughters of Zelophehad;

11 For Mahlah, Tirzah, and Hoglah, and Milcah, and Noah, the daughters of Zelophehad, were married unto their father's brother's sons:

12 And they were married into the families of the sons of Manasseh the son of Joseph, and their inheritance remained in the tribe of the family of their father.

13 These are the commandments and the judgments, which the LORD commanded, by the hand of Moses, unto the children of Israel in the plains of Moab by Jordan near Jericho.

DEUTERONOMY,

CHAPTER I.

THESE are the words which Moses spake unto all Israel on this side Jordan in the wilderness, in the plain over against the Red sea, between Paran, and Tophel, and Laban, and Hazeroth, and Dizahab.

2 (There are eleven days' journey from Horeb by the way of mount Seir unto Kadesh-barnea.)

3 And it came to pass in the fortieth year, in the eleventh month, on the first day of the month, that Moses spake unto the children of Israel, according unto all that the LORD had commanded him unto them;

4 After he had slain Sihon the king of the Amorites, which dwelt in Heshbon, and Og the king of Bashan, which dwelt at Astaroth in Edrei:

5 On this side Jordan, in the land of Moab, began Moses to declare this law, saying,

6 The LORD our God spake unto us in Horeb, saying, Ye have dwelt long enough in this mount:

7 Turn you, and take your journey, and go to the mount of the Amorites, and unto all the places nigh thereunto, in the plain, in the hills, and in the vale, and in the south, and by the sea side, to the land of the Canaanites, and unto Lebanon, unto the great river, the river Euphrates.

8 Behold, I have set the land before you: go in and possess the land which the LORD sware unto your fathers, Abraham, Isaac, and Jacob, to give unto them and to their children after them.

9 And I spake unto you at that time, saying, I am not able to bear you myself alone:

10 The LORD your God hath multiplied you, and, behold, ye are this day as the stars of heaven for multitude.

11 The LORD God of your fathers make you a thousand times so many more as ye are, and bless you, as he hath promised you!

12 How can I myself alone bear your cumbrance, and your burden, and your strife?

13 Take you wise men, men of understanding, and known among your tribes, and I will make them rulers over you.

14 And ye answered me, and said, The thing which thou hast spoken is good for us to do.

15 So I took the chiefs of your tribes, wise men, and known, and made them heads over you, captains over thousands, and captains over hundreds, and captains over fifties, and captains over tens, and officers among your tribes.

16 And I charged your judges at that time, saying, Hear the causes between your brethren, and judge righteously between every man and his brother, and the stranger that is with him.

17 Ye shall not respect persons in judgment; but ye shall hear the small as well as the great; ye shall not be afraid of the face of man; for the judgment is. God's: and the cause that is too hard for you, bring it unto me, and I will hear it.

18 And I commanded you at that time all the things which ye should do.

19 And when we departed from Horeb, we went through all that great and terrible wilderness, which ye saw by the way of the mountain of the Amorites, as the LORD our God commanded us; and we came to Kadesh-barnea.

20 And I said unto you, Ye are come unto the mountain of the Amorites, which the LORD our God doth give unto us.

21 Behold, the LORD thy God hath set the land before thee: go up and possess it, as the LORD God of thy fathers hath said unto thee; fear not, neither be discouraged.

22 And ye came near unto me every one of you, and said, We will send men before us, and they shall search us out the land, and bring us word again by what way we must go up, and into what cities we shall come.

23 And the saying pleased me well; and I took twelve men of you, one of each tribe:

24 And they turned and went up into the mountain, and came unto the valley of Eshcol, and searched it out.

25 And they took of the fruit of the land in their hands, and brought it down unto us, and brought us word again, and said, It is a good land which the LORD our God doth give us.

26 Notwithstanding ye would not go up, but, rebelled against the commandment of the LORD your God:

27 And ye murmured in your tents, and said, Because the LORD hated us, he hath brought us forth out of the land of Egypt, to deliver us into the hand of the Amorites, to destroy us.

28 Whither shall we go up? our brethren have discouraged our heart, saying, The people are greater and taller than we; the cities are great and walled up to heaven; and moreover we have seen the sons of the Anakim there.

29 Then I said unto you, Dread not, neither be afraid of them.

30 The LORD your God which goeth before you, he shall fight for you, according to all that he did for you in Egypt before your eyes;

31 And in the wilderness, where thou hast seen how that the LORD thy God bare thee, as a man doth bear his son, in all the way that ye went, until ye came into this place.

32 Yet in this thing ye did not believe the LORD your God,

33 Who went in the way before you, to search you out a place to pitch your tents in, in fire by night, to show you by what way ye should go, and in a cloud by day.

34 And the LORD heard the voice of your words, and was wroth, and sware, saying,

35 Surely there shall not one of these men of this evil generation see that good land, which I sware to give unto your fathers,

36 Save Caleb the son of Jephunneh; he shall see it, and to him will I give the land that he hath trodden upon, and to his children, because he hath wholly followed the LORD.

37 Also the LORD was angry with me for your sakes, saying, Thou also shalt not go in thither.

38 But Joshua the son of Nun, which standeth before thee, he shall go in thither: encourage him: for he shall cause Israel to inherit it.

39 Moreover your little ones, which ye said should be a prey, and your children, which in that day had no knowledge between good and evil, they shall go in thither, and unto them will I give it, and they shall possess it.

40 But as for you, turn you, and take your journey into the wilderness by the way of the Red sea.

41 Then ye answered and said unto me, We have sinned against the LORD, we will go up and fight, according to all that the LORD our God commanded us. And when ye had girded on every man his weapons of war, ye were ready to go up into the hill.

42 And the LORD said unto me, Say unto them, Go not up, neither fight; for I am not among you; lest ye be smitten before your enemies.

43 So I spake unto you; and ye would not hear, but rebelled against the commandment of the LORD, and went presumptuously up into the hill.

44 And the Amorites, which dwelt in that mountain, came out against you, and chased you, as bees do, and destroyed you in Seir, even unto Hormah.

45 And ye returned and wept before the LORD; but the LORD would not hearken to your voice, nor give ear unto you.

46 So ye abode in Kadesh many days, according unto the days that ye abode there.

CHAPTER II.

THEN we turned, and took our journey into the wilderness by the way of the Red sea, as the LORD spake unto me: and we compassed mount Seir many days.

2 And the LORD spake unto me, saying,

3 Ye have compassed this mountain long enough: turn you northward.

4 And command thou the people, saying, Ye are to pass through the coast of your brethren the children of Esau, which dwell in Seir; and they shall be afraid of you: take ye good heed unto yourselves therefore:

5 Meddle not with them; for I will not give you of their land, no, not so much as a footbreadth; because I have given mount Seir unto Esau for a possession.

6 Ye shall buy meat of them for money, that ye may eat; and ye shall also buy water of them for money, that ye may drink.

7 For the LORD thy God hath blessed thee in all the works of thy hand: he knoweth thy walking through this great wilderness: these forty years the LORD thy God hath been with thee; thou hast lacked nothing.

8 And when we passed by from our brethren the children of Esau, which dwell in Seir, through the way of the plain from Elath, and from Eziongaber, we turned and passed by the way of the wilderness of Moab.

9 And the LORD said unto me, Distress not the Moabites, neither contend with them in battle: for I will not give thee of their land for a possession: because I have given Ar unto the children of Lot for a possession.

10 The Emim dwelt therein in times past, a people great, and many, and tall, as the Anakim;

11 Which also were accounted giants, as the Anakim; but the Moabites call them Emim.

12 The Horim also dwelt in Seir beforetime; but the children of Esau succeeded them, when they had destroyed them from before them, and dwelt in their stead; as Israel did unto the land of his possession, which the LORD gave unto them.

13 Now rise up, said I, and get you over the brook Zered. And we went over the brook Zered.

14 And the space in which we came from Kadesh-barnea, until we were come over the brook Zered, was thirty and eight years; until all the generation of the men of war were wasted out from among the host, as the LORD sware unto them.

15 For indeed the hand of the LORD was against them, to destroy them from among the host, until they were consumed.

16 So it came to pass, when all the men of war were consumed and dead from among the people, ·

17 That the LORD spake unto me, saying,

18 Thou art to pass over through Ar, the coast of Moab, this day:

19 And when thou comest nigh over against the children of Ammon, distress them not, nor meddle with them: for I will not give thee of the land of the children of Ammon any possession; because I have given it unto the children of Lot for a possession.

20 Rise ye up, take your journey, and pass over the river Arnon: behold, I have given into thine hand Sihon the Amorite, king of Heshbon, and his land: begin to possess it, and contend with him in battle.

21 This day will I begin to put the dread of thee and the fear of thee upon the nations that are under the whole heaven, who shall hear report of thee, and shall tremble, and be in awe because of thee.

22 And I sent messengers out of the wilderness of Kedemoth unto Sihon king of Heshbon with words of peace, saying,

23 Let me pass through thy land: I will go along by the high way, I will neither turn unto the right hand nor to the left.

24 Thou shalt sell me meat for money, that I may eat; and give me water for money, that I may drink: only I will pass through on my feet;

25 (As the children of Esau which dwell in Seir, and the Moabites which dwell in Ar, did unto me:) until I shall pass over Jordan into the land which the LORD our God giveth us.

26 But Sihon king of Heshbon would not let us pass by him.

27 And the LORD said unto me, Behold, I have begun to give Sihon and his land before thee: begin to possess, that thou mayest inherit his land.

28 Then Sihon came out against us, he and all his people, to fight at Jahaz.

29 And the LORD our God delivered him before us; and we smote him, and his sons, and all his people.

30 And we took all his cities at that time.

31 From Aroer, which is by the brink of the river of Arnon, and from the city that is by the river, even unto Gilead, there was not one city too strong for us: the LORD our God delivered all unto us:

32 Only unto the land of the children of Ammon thou camest not, nor unto any place of the river Jabbok, nor unto the cities in the mountains, nor unto whatsoever the LORD our God forbade us.

CHAPTER III.

THEN we turned, and went up the way to Bashan: and Og the king of Bashan came out against us, he and all his people, to battle at Edrei.

2 And the LORD said unto me, Fear him not: for I will deliver him, and all his people, and his land, into thy hand; and thou shalt do unto him as thou didst unto Sihon king of the Amorites, which dwelt at Heshbon.

3 So the LORD our God delivered into our hands Og also, the king of Bashan, and all his people: and we smote him until none was left to him remaining.

4 And we took all his cities at that time, there was not a city which we took not from them, threescore cities, all the region of Argob, the kingdom of Og in Bashan.

5 All these cities were fenced with high walls, gates, and bars; beside unwalled towns a great many.

6 For only Og king of Bashan remained of the remnant of giants: behold, his bedstead was a bedstead of iron; is it not in Rabbath of the children of Ammon? nine cubits was the length thereof, and four cubits the breadth of it, after the cubit of a man.

7 And this land, which we possessed at that time, from Aroer, which is by the river Arnon, and half mount Gilead, and the cities thereof, gave I unto the Reubenites and to the Gadites.

8 And the rest of Gilead, and all Bashan, being the kingdom of Og, gave I unto the half tribe of Manasseh; all the region of Argob, with all Bashan, which was called the land of giants.

9 Jair the son of Manasseh took all the country of Argob unto the coasts of Geshuri and Maachathi; and called them after his own name, Bashan-havoth-jair, unto this day.

10 And I gave Gilead unto Machir.

11 And unto the Reubenites and unto the Gadites I gave from Gilead even unto the river Arnon half the valley, and the border even unto the river Jabbok, which is the border of the children of Ammon;

12 The plain also, and Jordan, and the coast thereof, from Chinnereth even unto the sea of the plain, even the salt sea, under Ashdoth-pisgah eastward.

13 And I commanded you at that time, saying, The LORD your God hath given you this land to possess it: ye shall pass over armed before your brethren the children of Israel, all that are meet for the war.

14 But your wives, and your little ones, and your cattle, (for I know that ye have much cattle,) shall abide in your cities which I have given you;

15 Until the LORD have given rest unto your brethren, as well as unto you, and until they also possess the land which the LORD your God hath given them beyond Jordan: and then shall ye return every man unto his possession, which I have given you.

16 And I commanded Joshua at that time, saying, Thine eyes have seen all that the LORD your God hath done unto these two kings: so shall the LORD do unto all the kingdoms whither thou passest.

17 Ye shall not fear them: for the LORD your God he shall fight for you.

18 And I besought the LORD at that time, saying,

19 O LORD God, thou hast begun to shew thy servant thy greatness, and

thy mighty hand: for what God is there in heaven or in earth, that can do according to thy works, and according to thy might?

20 I pray thee, let me go over, and see the good land that is beyond Jordan, that goodly mountain, and Lebanon.

21 But the LORD was wroth with me for your sakes, and would not hear me: and the LORD said unto me, Let it suffice thee; speak no more unto me of this matter.

22 Get thee up into the top of Pisgah, and lift up thine eyes westward, and northward, and southward, and eastward, and behold it with thine eyes: for thou shalt not go over this Jordan.

23 But charge Joshua, and encourage him, and strengthen him: for he shall go over before this people, and he shall cause them to inherit the land which thou shalt see.

24 So we abode in the valley over against Beth-peor.

CHAPTER IV.

NOW therefore hearken, O Israel, unto the statutes and unto the judgments, which I teach you, for to do them, that ye may live, and go in and possess the land which the LORD God of your fathers giveth you.

2 Ye shall not add unto the word which I command you, neither shall ye diminish aught from it, that ye may keep the commandments of the LORD your God which I command you.

3 Your eyes have seen what the LORD did because of Baal-peor: for all the men that followed Baal-peor, the LORD thy God hath destroyed them from among you.

4 But ye that did cleave unto the LORD thy God are alive every one of you this day.

5 Behold, I have taught you statutes and judgments, even as the LORD my God commanded me, that ye should do so in the land whither ye go to possess it.

6 Keep therefore and do them; for this is your wisdom and your understanding in the sight of the nations, which shall hear all these statutes, and say, Surely this great nation is a wise and understanding people.

7 For what nation is there so great, who hath God so nigh unto them, as the LORD our God is in all things that we call upon him for?

8 And what nation is there so great, that hath statutes and judgments so righteous as all this law, which I set before you this day?

9 Only take heed to thyself, and keep thy soul diligently, lest thou forget the things which thine eyes have seen, and lest they depart from thy heart all the days of thy life: but teach them thy sons, and thy sons' sons;

10 Specially the day that thou stoodest before the LORD thy God in Horeb, when the LORD said unto me, Gather me the people together, and I will make them hear my words, that they may learn to fear me all the days that they shall live upon the earth, and that they may teach their children.

11 And ye came near and stood under the mountain; and the mountain burned with fire unto the midst of heaven, with darkness, clouds, and thick darkness.

12 And the LORD spake unto you out of the midst of the fire: ye heard the voice of the words, but saw no manner of form; only ye heard a voice.

.13 And he declared unto you his covenant, which he commanded you to perform, even ten commandments; and he wrote them upon two tables of stone.

14 And the LORD commanded me at that time to teach you statutes and judgments, that ye might do them in the land whither ye go over to possess it.

15 Take ye therefore good heed unto yourselves; for ye saw no manner of similitude on the day that the LORD spake unto you in Horeb out of the midst of the fire;

16 Lest ye corrupt yourselves, and make you a graven image, the likeness of any figure, the likeness of male or female,

17 The likeness of any beast that is on the earth, the likeness of any winged fowl that flieth in the air,

.18 The likeness of any thing that creepeth on the ground, the likeness of any fish that is in the waters beneath the earth:

19 And lest thou lift up thine eyes unto heaven, and when thou seest the sun, and the moon, and the stars, even all the host of heaven, shouldest be driven to worship them, and serve them, which the LORD thy God hath divided unto all nations under the whole heaven.

.20 But the LORD hath taken you, and brought you forth out of the iron furnace, even out of Egypt, to be unto him a people of inheritance, as ye are this day.

21 Furthermore the LORD was angry with me for your sakes, and sware that I should not go over Jordan, and that I should not go in unto that good land, which the LORD thy God giveth thee for an inheritance:

22 But I must die in this land, I must not go over Jordan: but ye shall go over, and possess that good land.

23 Take heed unto yourselves, lest ye forget the covenant of the LORD your God, which he made with you, and make you a graven image, or the likeness of any thing, which the LORD thy God hath forbidden thee.

24 For the LORD thy God is a consuming fire, even a jealous God.

25 When thou shalt have children, and children's children, and ye shall have remained long in the land, and shall corrupt yourselves, and make a graven image, or the likeness of any thing, and shall do evil in the sight of the LORD thy God, to provoke him to anger;

26 I call heaven and earth to witness against you this day, that ye shall soon utterly perish from off the land whereunto ye go over Jordan to possess it; ye shall not prolong your days upon it, but shall utterly be destroyed.

27 And the LORD shall scatter you among the nations, and ye shall be left few in number among the heathen, whither the LORD shall lead you.

28 And there ye shall serve gods, the work of men's hands, wood and stone, which neither see, nor hear, nor eat, nor smell.

29 But if from thence thou shalt seek the LORD thy God, thou shalt find him, if thou seek him with all thine heart and with all thy soul.

30 When thou art in tribulation, and all these things are come upon thee, even in the latter days, if thou turn to the LORD thy God, and shalt be obedient unto his voice;

31 (For the LORD thy God is a merciful God;) he will not forsake thee, neither destroy thee, nor forget the

covenant of thy fathers, which he sware unto them.

32 For ask now of the days that are past, which were before thee, since the day that God created man upon the earth, and ask from the one side of heaven unto the other, whether there hath been any such thing as this great thing is, or hath been heard like it?

33 Did ever people hear the voice of God speaking out of the midst of the fire, as thou hast heard, and live?

34 Or hath God assayed to go and take him a nation from the midst of another nation, by temptations, by signs, and by wonders, and by war, and by a mighty hand, and by a stretched out arm, and by great terrors, according to all that the LORD your God did for you in Egypt before your eyes?

35 Unto thee it was shewed, that thou mightest know that the LORD he is God; there is none else beside him.

36 Out of heaven he made thee to hear his voice, that he might instruct thee: and upon earth he shewed thee his great fire; and thou heardest his words out of the midst of the fire.

37 And because he loved thy fathers, therefore he chose their children after them, and brought thee out in his sight with his mighty power out of Egypt;

38 To drive out nations from before thee greater and mightier than thou art, to bring thee in, to give thee their land for an inheritance, as it is this day.

39 Know therefore this day, and consider it in thine heart, that the Eternal he is God in heaven above, and upon the earth beneath: there is none else.

40 Thou shalt keep therefore his statutes, and his commandments, which I command thee this day, that it may go well with thee, and with thy children after thee, and that thou mayest prolong thy days upon the earth, which the LORD thy God giveth thee, for ever.

41 Then Moses severed three cities on this side Jordan toward the sunrising;

42 That the slayer might flee thither, which should kill his neighbour unawares, and hated him not in times past; and that fleeing unto one of these cities he might live:

43 Namely, Bezer in the wilderness, in the plain country, of the Reubenites; and Ramoth in Gilead, of the Gadites; and Golan in Bashan, of the Manassites.

44 And this is the law which Moses set before the children of Israel:

45 These are the testimonies, and the statutes, and the judgments, which Moses spake unto the children of Israel, after they came forth out of Egypt.

CHAPTER V.

AND Moses called all Israel, and said unto them, Hear, O Israel, the statutes and judgments which I speak in your ears this day, that ye may learn them, and keep and do them.

2 The LORD our God made a covenant with us in Horeb.

3 The LORD made not this covenant with our fathers, but with us, even us, who are all of us here alive this day.

4 The LORD talked with you face to face in the mount out of the midst of the fire,

5 (I stood between the LORD and

you at that time, to shew you the word of the LORD: for ye were afraid by reason of the fire, and went not up into the mount,) saying,

6 I am the LORD thy God, which brought thee out of the land of Egypt, from the house of bondage.

7 Thou shalt have no other gods before me.

8 Thou shalt not make thee any graven image, or any likeness of any thing that is in heaven above, or that is in the earth beneath, or that is in the waters beneath the earth:

9 Thou shalt not bow down thyself unto them, nor serve them: for I the LORD thy God am a jealous God, visiting the iniquity of the fathers upon the children unto the third and fourth generation of them that hate me,

10 And shewing mercy unto thousands of them that love me and keep my commandments.

11 Thou shalt not take the name of the LORD thy God in vain: for the LORD will not hold him guiltless that taketh his name in vain.

12 Keep the sabbath day to sanctify it, as the LORD thy God hath commanded thee.

13 Six days thou shalt labour, and do all thy work:

14 But the seventh day is the sabbath of the LORD thy God: in it thou shalt not do any work, thou, nor thy son, nor thy daughter, nor thy manservant, nor thy maidservant, nor thine ox, nor thine ass, nor any of thy cattle, nor thy stranger that is within thy gates; that thy manservant and thy maidservant may rest as well as thou.

15 And remember that thou wast a servant in the land of Egypt, and that the LORD thy God brought thee out

thence through a mighty hand and by a stretched out arm: therefore the LORD thy God commanded thee to keep the sabbath day.

16 Honour thy father and thy mother, as the LORD thy God hath commanded thee; that thy days may be prolonged, and that it may go well with thee, in the land which the LORD thy God giveth thee.

17 Thou shalt not kill.

18 Thou shalt not commit adultery.

19 Thou shalt not steal.

20 Thou shalt not bear false witness against thy neighbour.

21 Thou shalt not desire thy neighbour's wife, neither shalt thou covet thy neighbour's house, his field, or his manservant, or his maidservant, his ox, or his ass, or any thing that is thy neighbour's.

22 These words the LORD spake unto all your assembly in the mount out of the midst of the fire, of the cloud, and of the thick darkness, with a great and unceasing voice. And he wrote them in two tables of stone, and delivered them unto me.

23 And it came to pass, when ye heard the voice out of the midst of the darkness, (for the mountain did burn with fire,) that ye came near unto me, even all the heads of your tribes, and your elders;

24 And ye said, Behold, the LORD our God hath shewed us his glory and his greatness, and we have heard his voice out of the midst of the fire: we have seen this day that God doth talk with man, and he liveth.

25 Now therefore why should we die? for this great fire will consume us: if we hear the voice of the LORD our God any more, then we shall die.

26 For who is there of all flesh, that

hath heard the voice of the living God speaking out of the midst of the fire, as we have, and lived?

27 Go thou near, and hear all that the LORD our God shall say; and speak thou unto us all that the LORD our God shall speak unto thee; and we will hear it, and do it.

'28 And the LORD heard the voice of your words, when ye spake unto me; and the LORD said unto me, I have heard the voice of the words of this people, which they have spoken unto thee: they have well said all that they have spoken.

29 Oh that there were such a heart in them, that they would fear me, and keep all my commandments always, that it might be well with them, and with their children for ever!

30 Go say to them, Get you into your tents again.

31 But as for thee, stand thou here by me, and I will speak unto thee all the commandments, and the statutes, and the judgments, which thou shalt teach them, that they may do them in the land which I give them to possess it.

32 Ye shall observe to do therefore as the LORD your God hath commanded you: ye shall not turn aside to the right hand or to the left.

33 Ye shall walk in all the ways which the LORD your God hath commanded you, that ye may live, and that it may be well with you, and that ye may prolong your days in the land which ye shall possess.

CHAPTER VI.

NOW these are the commandments, the statutes, and the judgments, which the LORD your God commanded to teach you, that ye might do them in the land whither ye go to possess it:

2 That thou mightest fear the LORD thy God, to keep all his statutes and his commandments, which I command thee, thou, and thy son, and thy son's son, all the days of thy life; and that thy days may be prolonged.

3 Hear therefore, O Israel, and observe to do it; that it may be well with thee, and that ye may increase mightily, as the LORD God of thy fathers hath promised thee, in the land that floweth with milk and honey.

4 HEAR, O ISRAEL: THE LORD OUR GOD, THE LORD IS ONE GOD.

5 And thou shalt love the LORD thy God with all thine heart, and with all thy soul, and with all thy might.

6 And these words, which I command thee this day, shall be in thine heart:

7 And thou shalt teach them diligently unto thy children, and shalt talk of them when thou sittest in thine house, and when thou walkest by the way, and when thou liest down, and when thou risest up.

8 And thou shalt bind them for a sign upon thine hand, and they shall be as frontlets between thine eyes.

9 And thou shalt write them upon the posts of thy house, and on thy gates.

10 And it shall be, when the LORD thy God shall have brought thee into the land which he sware unto thy fathers, to Abraham, to Isaac, and to Jacob, to give thee great and goodly cities, which thou hast not built,

11 And houses full of all good things, which thou didst not fill, and wells digged, which thou didst not dig, vineyards and olive trees, which thou hast not planted; when thou shalt have eaten and be full;

12 Then beware lest thou forget the LORD, which brought thee forth out of the land of Egypt, from the house of bondage,

13 Thou shalt fear the LORD thy God, and serve him, and shalt swear by his name.

14 Ye shall not go after other gods, of the gods of the people which are round about you;

15 For the LORD thy God is a jealous God among you; lest the anger of the LORD thy God be kindled against thee, and destroy thee from off the face of the earth.

16 Ye shall not tempt the LORD your God, as ye tempted him in Massah.

17 Ye shall diligently keep the commandments of the LORD your God, and his testimonies, and his statutes, which he hath commanded thee.

18 And thou shalt do that which is right and good in the sight of the LORD; that it may be well with thee, and that thou mayest go in and possess the good land which the LORD sware unto thy fathers,

19 To cast out all thine enemies from before thee, as the LORD hath spoken.

20 And when thy son asketh thee in time to come, saying, What mean the testimonies, and the statutes, and the judgments, which the LORD our God hath commanded you?

21 Then thou shalt say unto thy son, We were Pharaoh's bondmen in Egypt; and the LORD brought us out of Egypt with a mighty hand:

22 And the LORD shewed signs and wonders, great and sore, upon Egypt, upon Pharaoh, and upon all his household, before our eyes:

23 And he brought us out from thence, that he might bring us in, to give us the land which he sware unto our fathers.

24 And the LORD commanded us to do all these statutes, to fear the LORD our God, for our good always, that he might preserve us alive, as it is at this day.

25 And it shall be our righteousness, if we observe to do all these commandments before the LORD our God, as he hath commanded us.

CHAPTER VII.

WHEN the LORD thy God shall bring thee into the land whither thou goest to possess it, and hath cast out many nations before thee, the Hittites, and the Girgashites, and the Amorites, and the Canaanites, and the Perizzites, and the Hivites, and the Jebusites, seven nations greater and mightier than thou;

2 And when the LORD thy God shall deliver them before thee, thou shalt make no covenant with them; neither shalt thou make marriages with them; thy daughter thou shalt not give unto his son, nor his daughter shalt thou take unto thy son.

3 For they will turn away thy son from following me, that they may serve other gods: so will the anger of the LORD be kindled against you, and destroy thee suddenly.

4 But thus shall ye deal with them; ye shall destroy their altars, and break down their images, and cut down their groves, and burn their graven images with fire.

5 For thou art a holy people unto the LORD thy God: the LORD thy God hath chosen thee to be a special people unto himself, above all people that are upon the face of the earth.

6 The LORD did not set his love upon you, nor choose you, because ye were more in number than any people; for ye are the fewest of all people:

7 But because the LORD loved you, and because he would keep the oath which he had sworn unto your fathers, hath the LORD brought you out with a mighty hand, and redeemed you out of the house of bondage, from the hand of Pharaoh king of Egypt.

8 Know therefore that the Eternal thy God, he is God, the faithful God, which keepeth covenant and mercy with them that love him and keep his commandments to a thousand generations;

9 And repayeth them that hate him to their face, to destroy them: he will not be slack to him that hateth him, he will repay him to his face.

10 Thou shalt therefore keep the commandments, and the statutes, and the judgments, which I command thee this day, to do them.

11 Wherefore it shall come to pass, if ye hearken to these judgments, and keep and do them, that the LORD thy God shall keep unto thee the covenant and the mercy which he sware unto thy fathers:

12 And he will love thee, and bless thee, and multiply thee: he will also bless the fruit of thy land, thy corn, and thy wine, and thine oil, the increase of thy kine, and the flocks of thy sheep, in the land which he sware unto thy fathers to give thee.

13 Thou shalt be blessed above all people:

14 And the LORD will take away from thee all sickness, and will put none of the evil diseases of Egypt, which thou knowest, upon thee.

CHAPTER VIII.

ALL the commandments which I command thee this day shall ye observe to do, that ye may live, and multiply, and go in and possess the land which the LORD sware unto your fathers.

2 And thou shalt remember all the way which the LORD thy God led thee these forty years in the wilderness, to humble thee, and to prove thee, to know what was in thine heart, whether thou wouldest keep his commandments, or not.

3 And he humbled thee, and suffered thee to hunger, and fed thee with manna, which thou knewest not, neither did thy fathers know; that he might make thee know that man doth not live by bread only, but by every word that proceedeth out of the mouth of the LORD doth man live.

4 Thy raiment waxed not old upon thee, neither did thy foot swell, these forty years.

5 Thou shalt also consider in thine heart, that, as a man chasteneth his son, so the LORD thy God chastened thee.

6 Therefore thou shalt keep the commandments of the LORD thy God, to walk in his ways, and to fear him.

7 For the LORD thy God bringeth thee into a good land, a land of brooks of water, of fountains and depths that spring out of valleys and hills;

8 A land of wheat, and barley, and vines, and fig trees, and pomegranates; a land of oil olive, and honey;

9 A land wherein thou shalt eat bread without scarceness, thou shalt not lack any thing in it; a land whose stones are iron, and out of whose hills thou mayest dig brass.

10. When thou hast eaten and art satisfied then thou shalt bless the LORD thy God for the good land which he hath given thee.'

11 Beware that thou forget not the LORD thy God, in not keeping his commandments, and his judgments, and his statutes, which I command thee this day:

12 Lest when thou hast eaten and art satisfied, and hast built goodly houses, and dwelt therein;

13 And when thy herds and thy flocks multiply, and thy silver and thy gold is multiplied, and all that thou hast is multiplied;

14 Then thine heart be lifted up, and thou forget the LORD thy God, which brought thee forth out of the land of Egypt, from the house of bondage;

15 Who led thee through that great and terrible wilderness, wherein were fiery serpents, and scorpions, and drought, where there was no water; who brought thee forth water out of the rock of flint;

16 Who fed thee in the wilderness with manna, which thy fathers knew not, that he might humble thee, and that he might prove thee, to do thee good at thy latter end;

17 And thou say in thine heart, My power and the might of mine hand hath gotten me this wealth.

· 18 But thou shalt remember the LORD thy God: for it is he that giveth thee power to get wealth, that he may establish his covenant which he sware unto thy fathers, as it is this day.

19 And it shall be, if thou do at all forget the LORD thy God, and walk after other gods, and serve them, and worship them, I testify against you this day that ye shall surely perish.

20 As the nations which the LORD destroyeth before your face, so shall ye perish; because ye would not be obedient unto the voice of the LORD your God.

CHAPTER IX.

HEAR, O Israel: Thou art to pass over Jordan this day, to go in to possess nations greater and mightier than thyself, cities great and fenced up to heaven,

2 A people great and tall, the children of the Anakim, whom thou knowest, and of whom thou hast heard say, Who can stand before the children of Anak!

3 Understand therefore this day, that the LORD thy God is he which goeth over before thee; as a consuming fire he shall destroy them, and he shall bring them down before thy face: so shalt thou drive them out, and destroy them quickly, as the LORD hath said unto thee.

4 Speak not thou in thine heart, after that the LORD thy God hath cast them out from before thee, saying, For my righteousness the LORD hath brought me in to possess this land: but for the wickedness of these nations the LORD doth drive them out from before thee.

5 Not for thy righteousness, or for the uprightness of thine heart, dost thou go to possess their land: but for the wickedness of these nations the LORD thy God doth drive them out from before thee, and that he may perform the word which the LORD sware unto thy fathers, Abraham, Isaac, and Jacob.

6 Understand therefore, that the LORD thy God giveth thee not this good land to possess it for thy right-

eousness; for thou art a stiffnecked people.

7 Remember, and forget not, how thou provokedst the LORD thy God to wrath in the wilderness: from the day that thou didst depart out of the land of Egypt, until ye came unto this place, ye have been rebellious against the LORD.

8 Also in Horeb ye provoked the LORD to wrath, so that the LORD was angry with you to have destroyed you.

9 When I was gone up into the mount to receive the tables of stone, even the tables of the covenant which the LORD made with you, then I abode in the mount forty days and forty nights; I neither did eat bread nor drink water:

10 And the LORD delivered unto me two tables of stone written with the finger of God; and on them was written according to all the words which the LORD spake with you in the mount, out of the midst of the fire, in the day of the assembly.

11 And it came to pass at the end of forty days and forty nights, that the LORD gave me the two tables of stone, even the tables of the covenant.

12 And the LORD said unto me, Arise, get thee down quickly from hence; for thy people which thou hast brought forth out of Egypt have corrupted themselves; they are quickly turned aside out of the way which I commanded them; they have made them a molten image.

13 Furthermore the LORD spake unto me, saying, I have seen this people, and, behold, it is a stiffnecked people:

14 Let me alone, that I may destroy them, and blot out their name from under heaven: and I will make of thee a nation mightier and greater than they.

15 So I turned and came down from the mount, and the mount burned with fire: and the two tables of the covenant were in my two hands.

16 And I looked, and, behold, ye had sinned against the LORD your God, and had made you a molten calf: ye had turned aside quickly out of the way which the LORD had commanded you.

17 And I took the two tables, and cast them out of my two hands, and broke them before your eyes.

18 And I fell down before the LORD, as at the first, forty days and forty nights: I did neither eat bread nor drink water, because of all your sins which ye sinned, in doing wickedly in the sight of the LORD, to provoke him to anger.

19 For I was afraid of the anger and hot displeasure, wherewith the LORD was wroth against you to destroy you. But the LORD hearkened unto me at that time also.

20 And the LORD was very angry with Aaron to have destroyed him: and I prayed for Aaron also the same time.

21 And I took your sin, the calf which ye had made, and burnt it with fire, and stamped it, and ground it very small, even until it was as small as dust: and I cast the dust thereof into the brook that descended out of the mount.

22 And at Taberah, and at Massah, and at Kibroth-hataavah, ye provoked the LORD to wrath.

23 Likewise when the LORD sent you from Kadesh-barnea, saying, Go up and possess the land which I have given you; then ye rebelled against the commandment of the LORD your

God, and ye believed him not, nor hearkened to his voice.

24 Ye have been rebellious against the LORD from the day that I knew you.

25 Thus I fell down before the LORD forty days and forty nights, as I fell down at the first; because the LORD had said he would destroy you.

26 I prayed therefore unto the LORD, and said, O LORD God, destroy not thy people and thine inheritance, which thou hast redeemed through thy greatness, which thou hast brought forth out of Egypt with a mighty hand.

27 Remember thy servants, Abraham, Isaac, and Jacob; look not unto the stubbornness of this people, nor to their wickedness, nor to their sin:

28 Lest the land whence thou broughtest us out say, Because the LORD was not able to bring them into the land which he promised them, and because he hated them, he hath brought them out to slay them in the wilderness.

29 Yet they are thy people and thine inheritance, which thou broughtest out by thy mighty power and by thy stretched out arm.

CHAPTER X.

AT that time the LORD said unto me, Hew thee two tables of stone like unto the first, and come up unto me into the mount, and make thee an ark of wood.

2 And I will write on the tables the words that were in the first tables which thou brakest, and thou shalt put them in the ark.

3 And I made an ark of cedar wood, and hewed two tables of stone like unto the first, and went up into the mount, having the two tables in mine hand.

4 And he wrote on the tables, according to the first writing, the ten commandments, which the LORD spake unto you in the mount, out of the midst of the fire, in the day of the assembly: and the LORD gave them unto me.

5 And I turned myself and came down from the mount, and put the tables in the ark which I had made; and there they are, as the LORD commanded me.

6 And the children of Israel took their journey from Beeroth bene Jaakan to Mosera: there Aaron died, and there he was buried; and Eleazar his son ministered in the priest's office in his stead.

7 From thence they journeyed unto Gudgodah; and from Gudgodah to Jotbath, a land of rivers of waters.

8 At that time the LORD separated the tribe of Levi, to bear the ark of the covenant of the LORD to stand before the LORD to minister unto him, and to bless in his name, unto this day.

9 Wherefore Levi hath no part nor inheritance with his brethren; the LORD is his inheritance, according as the LORD thy God promised him.

10 And I stayed in the mount, according to the first time, forty days and forty nights; and the LORD hearkened unto me at that time also, and the LORD would not destroy thee.

11 And the LORD said unto me, Arise, take thy journey before the people, that they may go in and possess land, which I sware unto their fathers to give unto them.

12 And now, Israel, what doth the LORD thy God require of thee, but to fear the LORD thy God, to walk in all his ways, and to love him, and to

serve the LORD thy God with all thy heart and with all thy soul,·

13 To keep the commandments of the LORD, and his statutes, which I command thee this day for thy good?

14 Behold, the heaven and the heaven of heavens is the LORD's thy God, the earth also, with all that therein is.

15 Only the LORD had a delight in thy fathers to love them, and he chose their children after them, even you, above all people, as it is this day.

16 Circumcise therefore your heart, and be no more stiffnecked.

17 For the LORD your God is God of gods, and Lord of lords, a great God, a mighty, and a terrible, which regardeth not persons, nor taketh reward:

18 He doth execute the judgment of the fatherless and widow, and loveth the stranger, in giving him food and raiment.

19 Love ye therefore the stranger: for ye were strangers in the land of Egypt.

20 Thou shalt fear the LORD thy God; him shalt thou serve, and to him shalt thou cleave, and swear by his name.

21 He is thy glory, and he is thy God, that hath done for thee these great and terrible things, which thine eyes have seen.

22 With threescore and ten persons thy fathers went down into Egypt; and now the LORD thy God hath made thee as the stars of heaven for multitude.

CHAPTER XI.

THEREFORE thou shalt love the LORD thy God, and keep his charge, and his statutes, and his judgments, and his commandments, always.

•2 And know ye this day: for I speak not with your children which have not known, and which have not seen the chastisement of the LORD your God, his greatness, his mighty hand, and his stretched out arm.

3 And his miracles, and his acts, which he did in the midst of Egypt unto Pharaoh the king of Egypt, and unto all his land;

4 And what he did unto the army of Egypt, unto their horses, and to their chariots; how he made the water of the Red sea to overflow them as they pursued after you, and how the LORD hath destroyed them unto this day;

5 And what he did unto you in the wilderness, until ye came into this place;

6 And what he did unto Dathan and Abiram, the sons of Eliab, the son of Reuben: how the earth opened her mouth, and swallowed them up, and their households, and their tents, and all the substance that was in their possession, in the midst of all Israel:

7 But your eyes have seen all the great acts of the LORD which he did.

8 Therefore shall ye keep all the commandments which I command you this day, that ye may be strong, and go in and possess the land, whither ye go to possess it;

9 And that ye may prolong your days in the land, which the LORD sware unto your fathers to give unto them and to their posterity, a land that floweth with milk and honey.

10 For the land, whither thou goest in to possess it, is not as the land of Egypt, from whence ye came out, where thou sowedst thy seed, and wateredst it with thy foot, as a garden of herbs:

·11 But the land, whither ye go to possess it, is a land of hills and valleys, and drinketh water of the . rain of heaven: ·

12 A land which the LORD thy God careth for: the eyes of the LORD thy God are always upon it, from the beginning of the year even unto the end of the year.

13 And it shall come to pass if ye shall hearken diligently unto my commandments which I command you this day, to love the LORD your God, and to serve him with all your heart and with all your soul,

14 That I will give you the rain of your land in his due season, the first rain and the latter rain, that thou mayest gather·in thy corn, and thy wine, and thine oil.

15 And I will send grass in thy fields for thy cattle, that thou mayest eat and be full.

16 Take heed to yourselves, that your heart be not deceived, and ye turn aside, and serve other gods, and worship them ;

17 And then the LORD'S wrath be kindled against you, and he shut up the heaven, that there be no rain, and that the land yield not her fruit; and lest ye perish quickly from off the good land which the LORD giveth you.

18 Therefore shall ye lay up these my words in your heart and in your soul, and bind them for a sign upon your hand, that they may be as frontlets between your eyes.

19 And ye shall teach them your children, speaking of them when thou sittest in thine house, and when thou walkest by the way, when thou liest down, and when thou risest up.

20 And thou shalt write them upon the door posts of thine house, and upon thy gates:

21 That your days may be multiplied, and the days of your children, in the land which the LORD sware unto your fathers to give them, as the days of heaven upon the earth.

22 For if ye shall diligently keep all these commandments which I command you, to do them, to love the LORD your God, to walk in all his ways, and to cleave unto him ;

23 Then will the LORD drive out all these nations from before you, and ye shall possess greater nations and mightier than yourselves.

24 Every place whereon the soles of your feet shall tread shall be yours: from the wilderness and Lebanon, from the river, the river Euphrates, even unto the uttermost sea shall your coast be.

25 There shall no man be able to stand before you: for the LORD your God shall lay the fear of you and the dread of you upon all the land that ye shall tread upon, as he hath said unto you.

26 Behold, I set before you this day a blessing and a curse ;

27 A blessing, if ye obey the commandments of the LORD your God, which I command you this day:

28 And a curse, if ye will not obey the commandments of the LORD your God, but turn aside out of the way which I command you this day, to go after other gods, which ye have not known.

29 And it shall come to pass, when the LORD thy God hath brought thee in unto the land whither thou goest to possess it, that thou shalt put the blessing upon mount Gerizim, and the curse upon mount Ebal.

30 Are they not on the other side Jordan, by the way where the sun goeth down, in the land of the Canaanites, which dwell in the plains over against Gilgal, beside the groves of Moreh?

31 For ye shall pass over Jordan to go in to possess the land which the LORD your God giveth you, and ye shall possess it, and dwell therein.

32 And ye shall observe to do all the statutes and judgments which I set before you this day.

CHAPTER XII.

THESE are the statutes and judgments, which ye shall observe to do in the land, which the LORD God of thy fathers giveth thee to possess it, all the days that ye live upon the earth.

2 Ye shall utterly destroy all the places, wherein the nations which ye shall possess served their gods, upon the high mountains, and upon the hills, and under every green tree:

3 And ye shall overthrow their altars, and break their pillars, and burn their groves with fire; and ye shall hew down the graven images of their gods, and destroy the names of them out of that place.

4 Ye shall not do so unto the LORD your God.

5 But unto the place which the LORD your God shall choose out of all your tribes to put his name there, even unto his habitation shall ye seek, and thither thou shalt come:

6 And thither ye shall bring your burnt offerings, and your sacrifices, and your tithes, and heave offerings, of your hand, and your vows, and your freewill offerings, and the firstlings of your herds and of your flocks:

7 And there ye shall eat before the LORD your God, and ye shall rejoice in all that ye put your hand unto, ye and your households, wherein the LORD thy God hath blessed thee.

8 Ye shall not do after all the things that we do here this day, every man whatsoever is right in his own eyes.

9 For ye are not as yet come to the rest and to the inheritance, which the LORD your God giveth you.

10 But when ye go over Jordan, and dwell in the land which the LORD your God giveth you to inherit, and when he giveth you rest from all your enemies round about, so that ye dwell in safety;

11 Then there shall be a place which the LORD your God shall choose to cause his name to dwell there; thither shall ye bring all that I command you; your burnt offerings, and your sacrifices, your tithes, and the heave offering of your hand, and all your choice vows which ye vow unto the LORD:

12 And ye shall rejoice before the LORD your God, ye, and your sons, and your daughters, and your menservants and your maidservants, and the Levite that is within your gates; forasmuch as he hath no part nor inheritance with you.

13 Take heed to thyself that thou offer not thy burnt offerings in every place that thou seest:

14 But in the place which the LORD shall choose in one of thy tribes, there thou shalt offer thy burnt offerings, and there thou shalt do all that I command thee.

15 Notwithstanding, thou mayest kill and eat flesh in all thy gates, whatsoever thy soul lusteth after, according to the blessing of the LORD thy God which he hath given thee: the unclean

and the clean may eat thereof, as of the roebuck, and as of the hart.

16 Only ye shall not eat the blood; ye shall pour it upon the earth as water.

17 Thou mayest not eat within thy gates the tithe of thy corn, or of thy wine, or of thy oil, or the firstlings of thy herds or of thy flock, nor any of thy vows which thou vowest, nor thy freewill offerings, or heave offering of thine hand:

18 But thou must eat them before the LORD thy God in the place which the LORD thy God shall choose, thou, and thy son and thy daughter, and thy manservant, and thy maidservant, and the Levite that is within thy gates: and thou shalt rejoice before the LORD thy God in all that thou puttest thine hands unto.

19 Take heed to thyself that thou forsake not the Levite as long as thou livest upon the earth.

20 When the LORD thy God shall enlarge thy border, as he hath promised thee, and thou shalt say, I will eat flesh, because thy soul longeth to eat flesh; thou mayest eat flesh, whatsoever thy soul lusteth after.

21 If the place which the LORD thy God hath chosen to put his name there be too far from thee, then thou shalt kill of thy herd and of thy flock, which the LORD hath given thee, as I have commanded thee, and thou shalt eat in thy gates whatsoever thy soul lusteth after.

22 Even as the roebuck and the hart is eaten, so thou shalt eat them: the unclean and the clean shall eat of them alike.

23 Only be sure that thou eat not the blood: for the blood is the life; and thou mayest not eat the life with the flesh.

24 Thou shalt not eat it; thou shalt pour it upon the earth as water.

25 Thou shalt not eat it; that it may go well with thee, and with thy children after thee, when thou shalt do that which is right in the sight of the LORD.

26 Only thy holy things which thou hast, and thy vows, thou shalt take, and go unto the place which the LORD shall choose:

27 And thou shalt offer thy burnt offerings, the flesh and the blood, upon the altar of the LORD thy God: and the blood of thy sacrifices shall be poured out upon the altar of the LORD thy God, and thou shalt eat the flesh.

28 Observe and hear all these words which I command thee, that it may go well with thee, and with thy children after thee forever, when thou doest that which is good and right in the sight of the LORD thy God.

29 When the LORD thy God shall cut off the nations from before thee, whither thou goest to possess them, and thou succeedest them, and dwellest in their land;

30 Take heed to thyself that thou be not snared by following them, and that thou inquire not after their gods, saying, How did these nations serve their gods? even so will I do likewise.

31 Thou shalt not do so unto the LORD thy God: for every abomination to the LORD which he hateth have they done unto their gods; for even their sons and their daughters they have burnt in the fire to their gods.

32 What thing soever I command you, observe to do it: thou shalt not add thereto, nor diminish from it.

CHAPTER XIII.

IF there arise among you a prophet, or a dreamer of dreams, and giveth thee a sign or a wonder,

2 And the sign or the wonder come to pass, whereof he spake unto thee, saying, Let us go after other gods, which thou hast not known, and let us serve them;

3 Thou shalt not hearken unto the words of that prophet, or that dreamer of dreams: for the LORD your God proveth you, to know whether ye love the LORD your God with all your heart and with all your soul.

4 Ye shall walk after the LORD your God, and fear him, and keep his commandments, and obey his voice, and ye shall serve him, and cleave unto him.

5 And that prophet, or that dreamer of dreams, shall be put to death; because he hath spoken to turn you away from the LORD your God, which brought you out of the land of Egypt, and redeemed you out of the house of bondage, to thrust thee out of the way which the LORD thy God commanded thee to walk in. So shalt thou put the evil away from the midst of thee.

6 If thy brother, the son of thy mother, or thy son, or thy daughter, or thy wife, or thy friend, which is as thine own soul, entice thee secretly, saying, Let us go and serve other gods, which thou hast not known, thou, nor thy fathers;

7 Namely, of the gods of the people which are round about you, nigh unto thee, or far off from thee, from the one end of the earth even unto the other end of the earth;

8 Thou shalt not consent unto him, nor hearken unto him; neither shalt thou spare, neither shalt thou conceal him:

9 But thou shalt surely kill him; thine hand shall be first upon him to put him to death, and afterwards the hand of all the people.

10 And thou shalt stone him with stones, that he die; because he hath sought to thrust thee away from the LORD thy God, which brought thee out of the land of Egypt, from the house of bondage.

11 And all Israel shall hear, and fear, and shall do no more any such wickedness as this is among you.

12 If thou shalt hear say in one of thy cities, which the LORD thy God hath given thee to dwell there, saying,

13 Certain men, the sons of vileness, are gone out from among you, and have withdrawn the inhabitants of their city, saying, Let us go and serve other gods, which ye have not known;

14 Then shalt thou inquire, and make search, and ask diligently; and, behold, if it be truth, and the thing certain, that such abomination is wrought among you;

15 Thou shalt surely smite the inhabitants of that city with the edge of the sword, destroying it utterly, and all that is therein, and the cattle thereof, with the edge of the sword.

16 And thou shalt gather all the spoil of it into the midst of the street thereof, and shalt burn with fire the city, and all the spoil thereof every whit, for the LORD thy God: and it shall be a heap for ever; it shall not be built again.

17 And there shall cleave nought of the ban to thine hand: that the LORD may turn from his anger, and shew thee mercy, and have compassion upon

thee, and multiply thee, as he hath sworn unto thy fathers;

18 When thou shalt hearken to the voice of the LORD thy God, to keep all his commandments which I command thee this day, to do that which is right in the eyes of the LORD thy God.

CHAPTER XIV.

YE are the children of the LORD your God: ye shall not disfigure yourselves, nor make any baldness between your eyes for the dead.

2 For thou art a holy people unto the LORD thy God, and the LORD hath chosen thee to be a peculiar people unto himself, above all the nations that are upon the earth.

3 These are the beasts which ye shall eat: the ox, the sheep, and the goat,

4 The hart, and the roebuck, and the fallow deer, and the wild goat, and the pygarg, and the wild ox, and the chamois.

5 And every beast that parteth the hoof, and cleaveth the cleft into two claws and cheweth the cud among the beasts, that ye shall eat.

6 Nevertheless these ye shall not eat, of them that chew the cud, or of them that divide the cloven hoof; as the camel, and the hare, and the coney: for they chew the cud, but divide not the hoof; therefore they are unclean unto you.

7 And the swine, because it divideth the hoof, yet cheweth not the cud, it is unclean unto you: ye shall not eat of their flesh, nor touch their dead carcass.

8 These ye shall eat, of all that are in the waters: all that have fins and scales shall ye eat:

9 And whatsoever hath not fins and scales ye may not eat; it is unclean unto you.

10 Of all clean birds ye shall eat.

11 But these are they of which ye shall not eat: the eagle, and the ossifrage, and the ospray,

12 And the glede, and the kite, and the vulture after his kind,

13 And every raven after his kind,

14 And the owl, and the nighthawk, and the cuckoo, and the hawk after his kind,

15 The little owl, and the great owl, and the swan,

16 And the pelican, and the gier eagle, and the cormorant,

17 And the stork, and the heron after her kind, and the lapwing, and the bat.

18 And every creeping thing that flieth is unclean unto you: they shall not be eaten.

19 But of all clean fowls ye may eat.

20 Ye shall not eat of any thing that dieth of itself: for thou art a holy people unto the LORD thy God. Thou shalt not seethe a kid in his mother's milk.

21 Thou shalt truly tithe all the increase of thy seed, that the field bringeth forth year by year.

22 And thou shalt eat before the LORD thy God, in the place which he shall choose to place his name there, the tithe of thy corn, of thy wine, and of thine oil, and the firstlings of thy herds and of thy flocks; that thou mayest learn to fear the LORD thy God always.

23 And if the way be too long for thee, so that thou art not able to carry it; or if the place be too far from thee, which the LORD thy God shall choose to set his name there, when the LORD thy God hath blessed thee:

24 Then shalt thou turn it into money, and bind up the money in thine hand, and shalt go unto the place which the LORD thy God shall choose:

25 And thou shalt bestow that money for whatsoever thy soul lusteth after, for oxen, or for sheep, or for wine, or for strong drink, or for whatsoever thy soul desireth: and thou shalt eat there before the LORD thy God, and thou shalt rejoice, thou, and thine household,

26 And the Levite that is within thy gates; thou shalt not forsake him: for he hath no part nor inheritance with thee.

27 At the end of three years thou shalt bring forth all the tithe of thine increase the same year, and shalt lay it up within thy gates:

28 And the Levite, (because he hath no part nor inheritance with thee,) and the stranger, and the fatherless, and the widow, which are within thy gates, shall come, and shall eat and be satisfied; that the LORD thy God may bless thee in all the work of thine hand which thou doest.

CHAPTER XV.

AT the end of every seven years thou shalt make a release.

2 And this is the manner of the release: Every creditor that lendeth aught unto his neighbour shall release it; he shall not exact it of his neighbour, or of his brother; because it is called the LORD's release.

3. Of a foreigner thou mayest exact it again: but that which is thine with thy brother thine hand shall release;

4 But there ought to be no poor among you; for the LORD shall greatly bless thee in the land which the LORD thy God giveth thee for an inheritance to possess it:

5 Only if thou carefully hearken unto the voice of the LORD thy God, to observe to do all these commandments which I command thee this day.

6 For the LORD thy God blesseth thee, as he promised thee: and thou shalt lend unto many nations, but thou shalt not borrow; and thou shalt reign over many nations, but they shall not reign over thee.

7 If there be among you a poor man, one of thy brethren within any of thy gates in thy land which the LORD thy God giveth thee, thou shalt not harden thine heart, nor shut thine hand from thy poor brother:

8 But thou shalt open thine hand wide unto him, and shalt surely lend him sufficient for his need, in that which he wanteth.

9 Beware that there be not a thought in thy wicked heart, saying, The seventh year, the year of release, is at hand; and thine eye be evil against thy poor brother, and thou givest him nought; and he cry unto the LORD against thee, and it be sin unto thee.

10 Thou shalt surely give him, and thine heart shall not be grieved when thou givest unto him: because that for this thing the LORD thy God shall bless thee in all thy works, and in all that thou puttest thine hand unto.

11 For the poor will never cease out of the land: therefore I command thee, saying, Thou shalt open thine hand wide unto thy brother, to thy poor, and to thy needy, in thy land.

12 And if thy brother, a Hebrew man, or a Hebrew woman, be sold unto thee, and serve thee six years; then in the seventh year thou shalt let him go free from thee.

13 And when thou sendest him out free from thee, thou shalt not let him go away empty:

14 Thou shalt furnish him liberally out of thy flock, and out of thy floor, and out of thy winepress: of that wherewith the LORD thy God hath blessed thee thou shalt give unto him.

15 And thou shalt remember that thou wast a bondman in the land of Egypt, and the LORD thy God redeemed thee: therefore I command thee this thing to day.

16 And it shall be, if he say unto thee, I will not go away from thee; because he loveth thee and thine house, because he is well with thee;

17 Then thou shalt take an awl, and thrust through his ear unto the door, and he shall be thy servant for ever. And also unto thy maidservant thou shalt do likewise, (not to let her go away empty).

18 It shall not seem hard unto thee, when thou sendest him away free from thee; for he hath been worth double a hired servant to thee, in serving thee six years: and the LORD thy God shall bless thee in all that thou doest.

19 All the firstling males that come of thy herd and of thy flock thou shalt sanctify unto the LORD thy God: thou shalt do no work with the firstling of thy bullock, nor shear the firstling of thy sheep.

20 Thou shalt eat it before the LORD thy God year by year in the place which the LORD shall choose, thou and thy household.

21 And if there be any blemish therein, as if it be lame, or blind, or have any ill blemish, thou shalt not sacrifice it unto the*LORD thy God.

22 Thou shalt eat it within thy gates: the unclean and the clean person shall eat it alike, as the roebuck, and as the hart.

23 Only thou shalt not eat the blood thereof; thou shalt pour it upon the ground as water.

CHAPTER XVI.

OBSERVE the month of Abib, and keep the passover unto the LORD thy God: for in the month of Abib the LORD thy God brought thee forth out of Egypt by night.

2 Thou shalt therefore sacrifice the passover unto the LORD thy God, of the flock and the herd, in the place which the LORD shall choose to place his name there.

3 Thou shalt eat no leavened bread with it; seven days shalt thou eat unleavened bread therewith, even the bread of affliction; for thou camest forth out of the land of Egypt in haste: that thou mayest remember the day when thou camest forth out of the land of Egypt all the days of thy life.

4 And there shall be no leavened bread seen with thee in all thy coast seven days; neither shall there any thing of the flesh, which thou sacrificest the first day at even, remain all night until the morning.

5 Thou mayest not sacrifice the passover within any of thy gates, which the LORD thy God giveth thee:

6 But at the place which the LORD thy God shall choose to place his name in, there thou shalt sacrifice the passover at even, at the going down of the sun, at the season that thou camest forth out of Egypt.

7 And thou shalt roast and eat it in the place which the LORD thy God shall choose: and thou shalt turn in the morning, and go unto thy tents.

8 Six days shalt thou eat unleavened bread: and on the seventh day shall be a solemn assembly to the LORD thy God : thou shalt do no work therein.

9 Seven weeks shalt thou number unto thee: begin to number the seven weeks from such time as thou beginnest to put the sickle to the corn.

10 And thou shalt keep the feast of weeks unto the LORD thy God with a tribute of a freewill offering of thine hand, which thou shalt give unto the LORD thy God, according as the LORD thy God hath blessed thee :

11 And thou shalt rejoice before the LORD thy God, thou, and thy son, and thy daughter, and thy manservant, and thy maidservant, and the Levite that is within thy gates, and the stranger, and the fatherless, and the widow that are among you, in the place which the LORD thy God hath chosen to place his name there.

12 And thou shalt remember that thou wast a bondman in Egypt: and thou shalt observe and do these statutes.

13 Thou shalt observe the feast of tabernacles seven days, after that thou hast gathered in thy corn and thy wine:

14 And thou shalt rejoice on thy feast, thou, and thy son, and thy daughter, and thy manservant, and thy maidservant, and the Levite, the stranger, and the fatherless, and the widow, that are within thy gates.

15 Seven days shalt thou keep a solemn feast unto the LORD thy God in the place which the LORD shall choose : because the LORD thy God shall bless thee in all thine increase, and in all the works of thine hands, therefore thou shalt surely rejoice.

16 Three times in a year shall all thy males appear before the LORD thy God in the place which he shall choose; on the feast of unleavened bread, and on the feast of weeks, and on the feast of tabernacles: and they shall not appear before the LORD empty:

17 Every man shall give as he is able, according to the blessing of the LORD thy God which he hath given thee.

18 Judges and officers shalt thou make thee in all thy gates, which the LORD thy God giveth thee, throughout thy tribes: and they shall judge the people with just judgment.

19 Thou shalt not wrest judgment; thou shalt not respect persons, neither take a gift: for a gift doth blind the eyes of the wise, and pervert the words of the righteous.

20 That which is altogether just shalt thou follow, that thou mayest live, and inherit the land which the LORD thy God giveth thee.

21 Thou shalt not plant thee a grove of any trees near unto the altar of the LORD thy God, which thou shalt make thee.

22 Neither shalt thou set thee up any image; which the LORD thy God hateth.

CHAPTER XVII.

THOU shalt not sacrifice unto the LORD thy God any bullock, or sheep, wherein is blemish, or any evil-favouredness: for that is an abomination unto the LORD thy God.

2 If there be found among you, within any of thy gates which the LORD thy God giveth thee, man or woman, that hath wrought wickedness in the sight of the LORD thy God, in transgressing his covenant,

3 And hath gone and served other gods, and worshipped them, either the sun, or the moon, or any of the host of heaven, which I have not commanded;

4 And it be told thee, and thou hast heard of it, and inquired diligently, and, behold, it be true, and the thing certain, that such abomination is wrought in Israel:

5 Then shalt thou bring forth that man or that woman, which have committed that wicked thing, unto thy gates, even that man or that woman, and shalt stone them with stones, till they die.

6 At the mouth of two witnesses, or three witnesses, shall he that is worthy of death be put to death; but at the mouth of one witness he shall not be put to death.

7 The hands of the witnesses shall be first upon him to put him to death, and afterward the hands of all the people. So thou shalt put the evil away from among you.

8 If there arise a matter too hard for thee in judgment, between blood and blood, between plea and plea, and between stroke and stroke, being matters of controversy within thy gates: then shalt thou arise, and get thee up into the place which the LORD thy God shall choose;

9 And thou shalt come unto the priests the Levites, and unto the judge that shall be in those days, and inquire; and they shall shew thee the sentence of judgment:

10 And thou shalt do according to the sentence, which they of that place which the LORD shall choose shall shew thee; and thou shalt observe to do according to all that they inform thee:

11 According to the sentence of the law which they shall teach thee, and according to the judgment which they shall tell thee, thou shalt do: thou shalt not decline from the sentence which they shall shew thee, to the right hand, nor to the left.

12 And the man that will do presumptuously, and will not hearken unto the priest that standeth to minister there before the LORD thy God, or unto the judge, even that man shall die: and thou shalt put away the evil from Israel.

13 And all the people shall hear, and fear, and do no more presumptuously.

14 When thou art come unto the land which the LORD thy God giveth thee, and shalt possess it, and shalt dwell therein, and shalt say, I will set a king over me, like as all the nations that are about me;

15 Thou mayest surely set a king over thee, whom the LORD thy God shall choose: one from among thy brethren shalt thou set king over thee: thou mayest not set a stranger over thee, which is not thy brother.

16 But he shall not multiply horses to himself, nor cause the people to return to Egypt, to the end that he should multiply horses: forasmuch as the LORD hath said unto you, Ye shall henceforth return no more that way.

17 Neither shall he multiply wives to himself, that his heart turn not away: neither shall he greatly multiply to himself silver and gold.

18 And it shall be, when he sitteth upon the throne of his kingdom, that he shall write him a copy of this law in a book out of that which is before the priests the Levites:

19 And it shall be with him, and he shall read therein all the days of his life; that he may learn to fear the LORD his God, to keep all the words of this law and these statutes, to do them:

20 That his heart be not lifted up above his brethren, and that he turn not aside from the commandment, to the right hand, or to the left: to the end that he may prolong his days in his kingdom, he, and his children, in the midst of Israel.

CHAPTER XVIII.

THE priests the Levites, and all the tribe of Levi, shall have no part nor inheritance with Israel: they shall eat the offerings of the LORD made by fire, and his inheritance.

2 Therefore shall they have no inheritance among their brethren: the Lord is their inheritance, as he hath said unto them.

3 And this shall be the priest's due from the people, from them that offer a sacrifice, whether it be ox or sheep; and they shall give unto the priest the shoulder, and the two cheeks, and the maw.

4 The firstfruit also of thy corn, of thy wine, and of thine oil, and the first of the fleece of thy sheep, shalt thou give him.

5 For the LORD thy God hath chosen him out of all thy tribes, to stand to minister in the name of the LORD, him and his sons for ever.

6 And if a Levite come from any of thy gates out of all Israel, where he sojourned, and come with all the desire of his mind unto the place which the LORD shall choose;

7 Then he shall minister in the name of the LORD his God, as all his brethren the Levites do, which stand there before the LORD.

8 They shall have like portions to eat, besides that which cometh of the sale of his patrimony.

9 When thou art come into the land which the LORD thy God giveth thee, thou shalt not learn to do after the abominations of those nations.

10 There shall not be found among you any one that maketh his son or his daughter to pass through the fire, or that useth divination, or an observer of times, or an enchanter, or a witch,

11 Or a charmer, or a consulter with familiar spirits, or a wizard, or a necromancer.

12 For all that do these things are an abomination unto the LORD: and because of these abominations the LORD thy God doth drive them out from before thee.

13 Thou shalt be perfect with the LORD thy God.

14 For these nations, which thou shalt possess, hearkened unto observers of times, and unto diviners: but as for thee, the LORD thy God hath not suffered thee so to do.

15 The LORD thy God will raise up unto thee a prophet from the midst of thee, of thy brethren, like unto me; unto him ye shall hearken;

16 According to all that thou desiredst of the LORD thy God in Horeb in the day of the assembly, saying, Let me not hear again the voice of the LORD my God, neither let me see this great fire any more, that I die not.

17 And the LORD said unto me, They have well spoken that which they have spoken.

18 I will raise them up a prophet from among their brethren, like unto thee, and will put my words in his

mouth; and he shall speak unto them all that I shall command him.

19 And it shall come to pass, that whosoever will not hearken unto my words which he shall speak in my name, I will require it of him.

20 But the prophet, which shall presume to speak a·word in my name, which I have not commanded him to speak, or that shall speak in the name of other gods, even that prophet shall die.

21 And if thou say in thine heart, How shall we know the word which the LORD hath not spoken?

22 When a prophet speaketh in the name of the LORD, if the thing follow not, nor come to pass, that is the thing which the LORD hath not spoken, but the prophet hath spoken it presumptuously: thou shalt not be afraid of him.

CHAPTER XIX.

WHEN the LORD thy God hath driven out the nations, whose land the LORD thy God giveth thee, and thou succeedest them, and dwellest in their cities, and in their houses;

2 Thou shalt separate three cities for thee in the midst of thy land, which the LORD thy God giveth thee to possess it.

3 Thou shalt prepare thee a way, and divide the coasts of thy land, which the LORD thy God giveth thee to inherit, into three parts, that every slayer may flee thither.

4 And this is the case of the slayer, which shall flee thither, that he may live: Whoso killeth his neighbour ignorantly, whom he hated not in time past;

5 As when a man goeth into the wood with his neighbour to hew wood, and his hand fetcheth a stroke with the axe to cut down the tree, and the head slippeth from the helve, and lighteth upon his neighbour, that he die; he shall flee unto one of those cities, and live:

6 Lest the avenger of the blood pursue the slayer, while his heart is hot, and overtake him, because the way is long and slay him; whereas he was not worthy of death, inasmuch as he hated him not in time past.

7 Wherefore I command thee, saying, Thou shalt separate three cities for thee.

8 And if the LORD thy God enlarge thy coast, as he hath sworn unto thy fathers, and give thee all the land which he promised to give unto thy fathers.

9 If thou shalt keep all these commandments to do them, which I command thee this day, to love the LORD thy God, and to walk ever in his ways; then shalt thou add three cities more for thee, beside these three:

10 That innocent blood be not shed in thy land, which the LORD thy God giveth thee for an inheritance, and so blood be upon thee.

11 But if any man hate his neighbour, and lie in wait for him, and rise up against him, and smite him mortally that he die, and fleeth into one of these cities:

12 Then the elders of his city shall send and fetch him thence, and deliver him into the hand of the avenger of blood, that he may die.

13 Thine eye shall not pity him, but thou shalt put away the guilt of innocent blood from Israel, that it may go well with thee.

14 Thou shalt not remove thy neighbour's landmark, which they of old

time have set in thine inheritance, which thou shalt inherit in the land that the LORD thy God giveth thee to possess it.

15 One witness shall not rise up against a man for any iniquity, or for any sin, in any sin that he sinneth: at the mouth of two witnesses, or at the mouth of three witnesses, shall the matter be established.

16 If a false witness rise up against any man to testify against him that which is wrong;

17 Then both the men, between whom the controversy is, shall stand before the LORD, before the priests and the judges, which shall be in those days;

18 And the judges shall make diligent inquisition: and, behold, if the witness be a false witness, and hath testified falsely against his brother;

19 Then shall ye do unto him, as he had thought to have done unto his brother: so shalt thou put the evil away from among you.

20 And those which remain shall hear, and fear, and shall henceforth commit no more any such evil among you.

21 And thine eye shall not pity; but life shall go for life, eye for eye, tooth for tooth, hand for hand, foot for foot.

CHAPTER XX.

WHEN thou goest out to battle against thine enemies, and seest horses, and chariots, and a people more than thou, be not afraid of them: for the LORD thy God is with thee, which brought thee up out of the land of Egypt.

2 And it shall be, when ye are come nigh unto the battle, that the priest shall approach and speak unto the people,

3 And shall say unto them, Hear, O Israel, ye approach this day unto battle against your enemies: let not your hearts faint, fear not, and do not tremble, neither be ye terrified because of them;

4 For the LORD your God is he that goeth with you, to fight for you against your enemies, to save you.

5 And the officers shall speak unto the people, saying, What man is there that hath built a new house, and hath not dedicated it? let him go and return to his house, lest he die in the battle, and another man dedicate it.

6 And what man is there that hath planted a vineyard, and hath not yet eaten of it? let him also go and return unto his house, lest he die in the battle, and another man eat of it.

7 And what man is there that hath betrothed a wife, and hath not taken her? let him go and return unto his house, lest he die in the battle, and another man take her.

8 And the officers shall speak further unto the people, and they shall say, What man is there that is fearful and fainthearted? let him go and return unto his house, lest his brethren's heart faint as well as his heart.

9 And it shall be, when the officers have made an end of speaking unto the people, that they shall make captains of the armies to lead the people,

10 When thou comest nigh unto a city to fight against it, then proclaim peace unto it.

11 And it shall be, if it make thee answer of peace, and open unto thee, then it shall be, that all the people that is found therein shall be tributaries unto thee, and they shall serve thee.

12 And if it will make no peace

with thee, but will make war against thee, then thou shalt besiege it:

13 And when the LORD thy God hath delivered it into thine hands, thou shalt smite every male thereof with the edge of the sword:

14 But the women, and the little ones, and the cattle, and all that is in the city, even all the spoil thereof, shalt thou take unto thyself; and thou shalt eat the spoil of thine enemies, which the LORD thy God hath given thee.

15 When thou shalt besiege a city a long time, in making war against it to take it, thou shalt not destroy the trees thereof by forcing an axe against them: for thou mayest eat of them, and thou shalt not cut them down; for they are but wood of the field, and not man to war against thee in the siege.

16 Only the trees which thou knowest that they be not trees for meat, thou mayest destroy and cut them down: and thou shalt build bulwarks against the city that maketh war with thee, until it be subdued.

CHAPTER XXI.

IF one be found slain in the land which the LORD thy God giveth thee to possess it, lying in the field, and it be not known who hath slain him:

2 Then thy elders and thy judges shall come forth, and they shall measure unto the cities which are round about him that is slain:

3 And it shall be, that the city which is next unto the slain man, even the elders of that city shall take a heifer, which hath not been wrought with, and which hath not drawn in the yoke;

4 And the elders of that city shall bring down the heifer unto a rough valley, which is neither eared nor sown, and shall strike off the heifer's neck there in the valley.

5 And the priests the sons of Levi shall come near; for them the LORD thy God hath chosen to minister unto him, and to bless in the name of the LORD; and by their word shall every controversy and every stroke be tried:

6 And all the elders of that city, that are next unto the slain man, shall wash their hands over the heifer that is beheaded in the valley:

7 And they shall answer and say, Our hands have not shed this blood, neither have our eyes seen it.

8 Be merciful, O LORD, unto thy people Israel, whom thou hast redeemed, and lay not innocent blood unto thy people Israel's charge. And the blood shall be forgiven them.

9 So shalt thou put away the guilt of innocent blood from among you, when thou shalt do that which is right in the sight of the LORD.

10 When thou goest forth to war against thine enemies, and the LORD thy God hath delivered them into thine hands, and thou hast taken them captive,

11 And seest among the captives a beautiful woman, and thou wouldest have her to thy wife;

12 Then thou shalt bring her home to thine house; and she shall shave her head, and pare her nails;

13 And she shall put the raiment of her captivity from off her, and shall remain in thine house, and bewail her father and her mother a full month: and after that thou shalt take her, and be her husband, and she shall be thy wife.

14 And it shall be, if thou have no delight in her, then thou shalt let her

go whither she will; but thou shalt not sell her at all for money, thou shalt not make merchandise of her, because thou hast humbled her.

15 If a man have two wives, one beloved, and another.hated, and they have borne him children, both the beloved and the hated; and if the firstborn son be hers that was hated:

16 Then it shall be, when he maketh his sons to inherit that which he hath, that he may not make the son of the beloved firstborn before the son of the hated, which is indeed the firstborn:

17 But he shall acknowledge the son of the hated for the firstborn, by giving him a double portion of all that he hath: for he is the beginning of his strength; the right of the firstborn is his.

18 If a man have a stubborn and rebellious son, which will not obey the voice of his father, or the voice of his mother, and that, when they have chastened him, will not hearken unto them:

19 Then shall his father and his mother lay hold on him, and bring him out unto the elders of his city, and unto the gate of his place;

20 And they shall say unto the elders of his city, This our son is stubborn and rebellious, he will not obey our voice; he is a glutton, and a drunkard.

21 And all the men of his city shall stone him with stones, that he die: so shalt thou put evil away from among you; and all Israel shall hear, and fear.

22 And if a man have committed a sin worthy of death, and he is to be put to death, and thou hang him on a tree:

23 His body shall not remain all night upon the.tree, but thou shalt in any wise bury him that day; that thy land be not defiled, which the LORD thy God giveth thee for an inheritance.

CHAPTER XXII.

THOU shalt not see thy brother's ox or his sheep go astray, and hide thyself from them: thou shalt in any case bring them again unto thy brother.

2 And if thy brother be not nigh unto thee, or if thou know him not, then thou shalt bring it unto thine own house, and it shall be with thee until thy brother seek after.it, and thou shalt restore it to him again.

3 In like manner shalt thou do with his ass; and so shalt thou do with his raiment.; and with all lost things of thy brother's, which he hath lost, and thou hast found, shalt thou do likewise: thou mayest not hide thyself.

4 Thou shalt not see thy brother's ass or his ox fall down by the way, and hide thyself from them: thou shalt surely help him to lift them up again.

5 The woman shall not wear that which pertaineth unto a man, neither shall a man put on a woman's garment: for all that do so are an abomination unto the LORD thy God.

6 If a bird's nest chance to be before thee in the way in any tree, or on the ground, whether they be young ones, or eggs, and the dam sitting upon the young, or upon the.eggs, thou shalt not take the dam with the young:

7 But thou shalt in any wise let the dam go, and take the young to thee; that it may be well with thee, and that thou mayest prolong thy days.

8 When thou buildest a house, then thou shalt make a battlement for thy roof, that thou bring not blood upon thine house, if any man fall from thence.

9 Thou shalt not sow thy vineyard with diverse seeds: lest the fruit of thy seed which thou hast sown, and the fruit of thy vineyard, be defiled.

10 Thou shalt not plough with an ox and an ass together.

11 Thou shalt not wear a garment of diverse sorts, as of woolen and linen together.

12 Thou shalt make thee fringes upon the four quarters of thy vesture, wherewith thou coverest thyself.

CHAPTER XXIII.

A N Ammonite or Moabite shall not enter into the congregation of the LORD; even to their tenth generation shall they not enter into the congregation of the LORD for ever:

2 Because they met you not with bread and with water in the way, when ye came forth out of Egypt; and because they hired against thee Balaam the son of Beor of Pethor of Mesopotamia, to curse thee.

3 Nevertheless, the LORD thy God would not hearken unto Balaam; but the LORD thy God turned the curse into a blessing unto thee, because the LORD thy God loved thee.

4 Thou shalt not seek their peace nor their prosperity all thy days for ever.

5 Thou shalt not abhor an Edomite; for he is thy brother: thou shalt not abhor an Egyptian; because thou wast a stranger in his land.

6 The children of them shall enter into the congregation of the LORD in their third generation.

7 When the host goeth forth against thine enemies, then keep thee from every wicked thing.

8 For the LORD thy God walketh in the midst of thy camp, to deliver thee, and to give up thine enemies before thee; therefore shall thy camp be holy.

9 Thou shalt not deliver unto his master the servant which is escaped from his master unto thee:

10 He shall dwell with thee, even among you, in that place which he shall choose in one of thy gates, where it liketh him best: thou shalt not oppress him.

11 Thou shalt not lend upon usury to thy brother; usury of money, usury of victuals, usury of any thing that is lent upon usury:

12 Unto a stranger thou mayest lend upon interest; but unto thy brother thou shalt not lend upon interest: that the LORD thy God may bless thee in all that thou settest thine hand to in the land whither thou goest to possess it.

13 When thou shalt vow a vow unto the LORD thy God, thou shalt not slack to pay it: for the LORD thy God will surely require it of thee; and it would be sin in thee.

14 But if thou shalt forbear to vow, it shall be no sin in thee.

15 That which is gone out of thy lips thou shalt keep and perform: even a freewill offering, according as thou hast vowed unto the LORD thy God, which thou hast promised with thy mouth.

16 When thou comest into thy neighbour's vineyard, then thou mayest eat grapes thy fill at thine own pleasure; but thou shalt not put any in thy vessel.

17 When thou comest into the standing corn of thy neighbour, then thou

mayest pluck the ears with thine hand; but thou shalt not move a sickle unto thy neighbour's standing corn.

CHAPTER XXIV.

WHEN a man hath taken a wife, and married her, and it come to pass that she find no favour in his eyes, because he hath found some disgrace in her: then let him bring her before the judges and write her a bill of divorcement, and give it in her hand, and send her out of his house.

2 And when she is departed out of his house, she may go and be another man's wife.

3 And if the latter husband hate her, and write her a bill of divorcement, and giveth it in her hand, and sendeth her out of his house; or if the latter husband die, which took her to be his wife;

4 Her former husband, which sent her away, may not take her again to be his wife; for that is abomination before the LORD: and thou shalt not cause the land to sin, which the LORD thy God giveth thee for an inheritance.

5 When a man hath taken a new wife, he shall not go out to war, neither shall he be charged with any business: but he shall be free at home one year, and shall cheer up his wife which he hath taken.

6 No man shall take the nether or the upper millstone to pledge: for he taketh a man's life to pledge.

7 If a man be found stealing any of his brethren of the children of Israel, and maketh merchandise of him, or selleth him; then that thief shall die; and thou shalt put evil away from among you.

8 Take heed in the plague of leprosy, hat thou observe diligently, and do according to all that the priests the Levites shall teach you: as I commanded them, so ye shall observe to do.

9 Remember what the LORD thy God did unto Miriam by the way, after that ye were come forth out of Egypt.

10 When thou dost lend thy brother any thing, thou shalt not go into his house to fetch his pledge.

11 Thou shalt stand without, and the man to whom thou dost lend shall bring out the pledge unto thee.

12 And if the man be poor, thou shalt not sleep with his pledge:

13 In any case thou shalt deliver him the pledge again when the sun goeth down, that he may sleep in his own raiment, and bless thee: and it shall be righteousness unto thee before the LORD thy God.

14 Thou shalt not oppress a hired servant that is poor and needy, whether he be of thy brethren, or of thy strangers that are in thy land within thy gates:.

15 At his day thou shalt give him his hire, neither shall the sun go down upon it; for he is poor, and setteth his heart upon it: lest he cry against thee unto the LORD, and it be sin unto thee.

16 The fathers shall not be put to death for the children, neither shall the children be put to death for the fathers: every man shall be put to death for his own sin.

17 Thou shalt not pervert the judgment of the stranger, nor of the fatherless; nor take a widow's raiment to pledge:

18 But thou shalt remember that thou wast a bondman in Egypt, and the LORD thy God redeemed thee

thence: therefore I command thee to do this thing.

19 When thou cuttest down thine harvest in thy field, and hast forgot a sheaf in the field, thou shalt not go again to fetch it: it shall be for the stranger, for the fatherless, and for the widow: that the LORD thy God may bless thee in all the work of thine hands.

20 When thou beatest thine olive tree, thou shalt not go over the boughs again: it shall be for the stranger, for the fatherless, and for the widow.

21 When thou gatherest the grapes of thy vineyard, thou shalt not glean it afterward: it shall be for the stranger, for the fatherless, and for the widow.

22 And thou shalt remember that thou wast a bondman in the land of Egypt: therefore I command thee to do this thing.

CHAPTER XXV.

IF there be a controversy between men, and they come unto judgment, that the judges may judge them; then they shall justify the righteous, and condemn the wicked.

2 And it shall be, if the wicked man be worthy to be beaten, that the judge shall cause him to lie down, and to be beaten before his face, according to his fault, by a certain number.

3 Forty stripes he may give him, and not exceed: lest, if he should exceed, and beat him above these with many stripes, then thy brother should seem altogether vile unto thee.

4 Thou shalt not muzzle the ox when he treadeth out the corn.

5 If brethren dwell together, and one of them die, and have no child, the wife of the dead shall not marry without unto a stranger: her husband's brother shall take her to him to wife.

6 And it shall be, that the firstborn which she beareth shall succeed in the name of his brother which is dead, that his name be not put out of Israel.

7 And if the man like not to take his brother's wife, then let his brother's wife go up to the gate unto the elders, and say, My husband's brother refuseth to raise up unto his brother a name in Israel; he will not take me to wife.

8 Then the elders of his city shall call him, and speak unto him: and if he stand to it, and say, I like not to take her:

9 Then shall his brother's wife come unto him in the presence of the elders, and loose his shoe from off his foot, and spit in his face, and shall answer and say, So shall it be done unto that man that will not build up his brother's house.

10 And his name shall be called in Israel, The house of him that hath his shoe loosed.

11 Thou shalt not have in thy bag diverse weights, a great and a small;

12 Thou shalt not have in thine house diverse measures, a great and a small:

13 But thou shalt have a perfect and just weight, a perfect and just measure shalt thou have: that thy days may be lengthened in the land which the LORD thy God giveth thee.

14 For all that do such things, and all that do unrighteously, are an abomination unto the LORD thy God,

15 Remember what Amalek did unto thee by the way, when ye were come forth out of Egypt;

16 How he met thee by the way,

and smote the hindmost of thee, even all that were feeble behind thee, when thou wast faint and weary; and he feared not God.

17 Therefore it shall be, when the LORD thy God hath given thee rest from all thine enemies round about, in the land which the LORD thy God giveth thee for an inheritance to possess it, that thou shalt blot out the remembrance of Amalek from under heaven ; thou shalt not forget it.

CHAPTER XXVI.

AND it shall be, when thou art come in unto the land which the LORD thy God giveth thee for an inheritance, and possessest it, and dwellest therein;

2 That thou shalt take of the first of all the fruit of the earth, which thou shalt bring of thy land that the LORD thy God giveth thee, and shalt put it in a basket, and shalt go unto the place which the LORD thy God shall choose to place his name there.

3 And thou shalt go unto the priest that shall be in those days, and say unto him, I profess this day unto the LORD thy God, that I am come unto the country which the LORD sware unto our fathers to give unto us.

4 And the priest shall take the basket out of thine hand, and set it down before the altar of the LORD thy God.

5 And thou shalt speak and say before the LORD thy God, A Syrian wanderer was my father; and he went down into Egypt, and sojourned there with few persons, and became there a nation, great, mighty, and populous.

6 And the Egyptians ill-treated us, and afflicted us, and laid upon us hard bondage.

7 And when we cried unto the LORD God of our fathers, the LORD heard our voice, and looked on our affliction, and our labour, and our oppression:

8 And the LORD brought us forth out of Egypt with a mighty hand, and with an outstretched arm, and with great terror, and with signs, and with wonders:

9 And he hath brought us into this place, and hath given us this land, even a land that floweth with milk and honey.

10 And now, behold, I have brought the firstfruits of the land, which thou, O LORD, hast given me. And thou shalt set it before the LORD thy God, and worship before the LORD thy God:

11 And thou shalt rejoice in every good thing which the LORD thy God hath given unto thee, and unto thine house, thou, and the Levite, and the stranger that is among you.

12 When thou hast made an end of tithing all the tithes of thine increase the third year, which is the year of tithing, and hast given it unto the Levite, the stranger, the fatherless, and the widow, that they may eat within thy gates, and be filled;

13 Then thou shalt say before the LORD thy God, I have brought away the hallowed things out of mine house, and also have given them unto the Levite, and unto the stranger, to the fatherless, and to the widow, according to all thy commandments which thou hast commanded me: I have not transgressed thy commandments, neither have I forgotten them:

14 I have not eaten thereof in my mourning, neither have I taken away aught thereof for any unclean use,

nor given aught thereof for the dead: but I have hearkened to the voice of the LORD my God, and have done according to all that thou hast commanded me.

15 Look down from thy holy habitation, from heaven, and bless thy people Israel, and the land which thou hast given us, as thou swarest unto our fathers, a land that floweth with milk and honey.

16 This day the LORD thy God hath commanded thee to do these statutes and judgments: thou shalt therefore keep and do them with all thine heart, and with all thy soul.

17 Thou hast avouched the LORD this day to be thy God, and to walk in his ways, and to keep his statutes, and his commandments, and his judgments, and to hearken unto his voice:

18 And the LORD hath avouched thee this day to be his peculiar people, as he hath promised thee, and that thou shouldest keep all his commandments;

19 And, to make thee high above all nations which he hath made, in praise, and in name, and in honour; and that thou mayest be a holy people unto the LORD thy God, as he hath spoken.

CHAPTER XXVII.

AND Moses with the elders of Israel commanded the people, saying, Keep all the commandments which I command you this day.

2 And it shall be, on the day when ye shall pass over Jordan unto the land which the LORD thy God giveth thee, that thou shalt set thee up great stones, and plaster them with plaster:

3 And thou shalt write upon them all the words of this law, when thou art passed over, that thou mayest go in unto the land which the LORD thy God giveth thee, a land that floweth with milk and honey; as the LORD God of thy fathers hath promised thee.

4 Therefore it shall be when ye be gone over Jordan, that ye shall set up these stones, which I command you this day, in mount Ebal, and thou shalt plaster them with plaster.

5 And there shalt thou build an altar unto the LORD thy God, an altar of stones: thou shalt not lift up any iron tool upon them.

6 Thou shalt build the altar of the LORD thy God of whole stones: and thou shalt offer burnt offerings thereon unto the LORD thy God:

7 And thou shalt offer peace offerings, and shalt eat there, and rejoice before the LORD thy God.

8 And thou shalt write upon the stones all the words of this law very plainly.

9 And Moses and the priests the Levites spake unto all Israel, saying, Take heed, and hearken, O Israel: this day thou art become the people of the LORD thy God.

10 Thou shalt therefore obey the voice of the LORD thy God, and do his commandments and his statutes, which I command thee this day.

11 And Moses charged the people the same day, saying,

12 These shall stand upon mount Gerizim to bless the people, when ye are come over Jordan; Simeon, and Levi, and Judah, and Issachar, and Joseph, and Benjamin:

13 And these shall stand upon mount Ebal to curse; Reuben, Gad, and Asher, and Zebulun, Dan, and Naphtali.

14 And the Levites shall speak, and

say unto all the men of Israel with a loud voice,

15 Cursed be the man that maketh any graven or molten image, an abomination unto the LORD, the work of the hands of the craftsman, and putteth it in a secret place: and all the people shall answer and say, Amen.

16 Cursed be he that setteth light his father or his mother: and all the people shall say, Amen.

17 Cursed be he that removeth his neighbour's landmark: and all the people shall say, Amen.

18 Cursed be he that maketh the blind to stumble on the way: and all the people shall say, Amen.

19 Cursed be he that perverteth the judgment of the stranger, fatherless, and widow: and all the people shall say, Amen.

20 Cursed be he that smiteth his neighbour secretly: and all the people shall say, Amen.

21 Cursed be he that taketh reward to slay an innocent person: and all the people shall say, Amen.

22 Cursed be he that confirmeth not all the words of this law to do them: and all the people shall say, Amen.

CHAPTER XXVIII.

AND it shall come to pass, if thou shalt hearken diligently unto the voice of the LORD thy God, to observe and to do all his commandments which I command thee this day, that the LORD thy God will set thee on high above all nations of the earth:

2 And all these blessings shall come on thee, and overtake thee, if thou shalt hearken unto the voice of the LORD thy God.

3 Blessed shalt thou be in the city, and blessed shalt thou be in the field.

4 Blessed shall be thy issue, and the fruit of thy ground, and the fruit of thy cattle, the increase of thy kine, and the flocks of thy sheep.

5 Blessed shall be thy basket and thy store.

6 Blessed shalt thou be when thou comest in, and blessed shalt thou be when thou goest out.

7 The LORD shall cause thine enemies to be smitten before thy face: they shall come out against thee one way, and flee before thee seven ways.

8 The LORD shall command the blessing upon thee in thy storehouses, and in all that thou settest thine hand unto; and he shall bless thee in the land which the LORD thy God giveth thee.

9 The LORD shall establish thee a holy people unto himself, as he hath sworn unto thee, if thou shalt keep the commandments of the LORD thy God, and walk in his ways.

10 And all the people of the earth shall see that thou art called by the name of the LORD; and they shall be afraid of thee.

11 And the LORD shall make thee plenteous in goods, in thy children, and in the fruit of thy cattle, and in the fruit of thy ground, in the land which the LORD sware unto thy fathers to give thee.

12 The LORD shall open unto thee his good treasure, the heaven, to give the rain unto thy land in his season, and to bless all the work of thine hand: and thou shalt lend unto many nations, and thou shalt not borrow.

13 And the LORD shall make thee the head, and not the tail; and thou shalt be above only, and thou shalt not be beneath; if that thou hearken unto the commandments of the LORD

thy God, which I command thee this day, to observe and to do them:

14 And thou shalt not go aside from any of the words which I command thee this day, to the right hand, or to the left, to go after other gods to serve them.

15 But it shall come to pass, if thou wilt not hearken unto the voice of the LORD thy God, to observe to do all his commandments and his statutes which I command thee this day; that all these curses shall come upon thee, and overtake thee:

16 Cursed shalt thou be in the city, and cursed shalt thou be in the field.

17 Cursed shall be thy basket and thy store.

18 Cursed shall be the fruit of thy land, the increase of thy kine, and the flocks of thy sheep.

19 Cursed shalt thou be when thou comest in, and cursed shalt thou be when thou goest out.

20 The LORD shall cause thee to be smitten before thine enemies: thou shalt go out one way against them, and flee seven ways before them; and shalt be removed into all the kingdoms of the earth.

21 The LORD shall bring thee, and thy king which thou shalt set over thee, unto a nation which neither thou nor thy fathers have known; and there shalt thou serve other gods, wood and stone.

22 And thou shalt become an astonishment, a proverb, and a byword, among all nations whither the LORD shall lead thee.

23 Thou shalt carry much seed out into the field, and shalt gather but little in; for the locust shall consume it.

24 Thou shalt plant vineyards, and dress them, but shalt neither drink of the wine, nor gather the grapes; for the worms shall eat them.

25 Thou shalt have olive trees throughout all thy coasts, but thou shalt not anoint thyself with the oil; for thine olive shall cast his fruit.

26 Thou shalt have sons and daughters, but thou shalt not enjoy them; for they shall go into captivity.

27 All thy trees and fruit of thy land shall the locust consume.

28 The stranger that is within thee shall get up above thee very high; and thou shalt come down very low.

29 He shall lend to thee, and thou shalt not lend to him: he shall be the head, and thou shalt be the tail.

30 Moreover all these curses shall come upon thee, and shall pursue thee, and overtake thee, till thou be destroyed; because thou hearkenedst not unto the voice of the LORD thy God, to keep his commandments and his statutes which he commanded thee.

31 And they shall be upon thee for a sign and for a wonder, and upon thy children for ever.

32 Because thou servedst not the LORD thy God with joyfulness, and with gladness of heart, for the abundance of all things;

33 Therefore shalt thou serve thine enemies, which the LORD shall send against thee, in hunger, and in thirst, and in nakedness, and in want of all things: and he shall put a yoke of iron upon thy neck, until he have destroyed thee.

34 The LORD shall bring a nation against thee from far, from the end of the earth, as swift as the eagle flieth; a nation whose tongue thou shalt not understand;

35 A nation of fierce countenance,

which shall not regard the person of the old, nor shew favour to the young:

36 And he shall eat the fruit of thy cattle, and the fruit of thy land, until thou be destroyed: which also shall not leave thee either corn, wine, or oil, or the increase of thy kine, or flocks of thy sheep, until he have destroyed thee.

37 And he shall besiege thee in all thy gates, until thy high and fenced walls come down, wherein thou trustedst, throughout all thy land: and he shall besiege thee in all thy gates throughout all thy land, which the LORD thy God hath given thee.

38 And thou shalt eat the flesh of thy sons and of thy daughters, which the LORD thy God hath given thee, in the siege, and in the straitness, wherewith thine enemies shall distress thee:

39 So that the man that is tender among you, and very delicate, his eye shall be evil toward his brother, and toward his wife, and toward the remnant of his children which he shall leave ;

40 So that he will not give to any of them of the flesh of his children whom he shall eat: because he hath nothing left him in the siege, and in the straitness, wherewith thine enemies shall distress thee in all thy gates.

41 The tender and delicate woman among you, which would not venture to set the sole of her foot upon the ground for delicateness and tenderness, her eye shall be evil toward her husband, and toward her son, and toward her daughter,

42 And toward her young one, for she shall eat them for want of all things secretly in the siege and straitness, wherewith thine enemy shall distress thee in thy gates.

43 If thou wilt not observe to do all the words of this law that are written in this book, that thou mayest fear this glorious and fearful name, THE ETERNAL THY GOD ;

44 Then the LORD will make thy plagues wonderful, and the plagues of thy children, even great plagues, and of long continuance, and sore sicknesses, and of long continuance.

45 Moreover, he will bring upon thee all the diseases of Egypt, which thou wast afraid of; and they shall cleave unto thee.

46 Also every sickness, and every plague, which is not written in the book of this law, them will the LORD bring upon thee, until thou be destroyed.

47 And ye shall be left few in number, whereas ye were as the stars of heaven for multitude; because thou wouldest not obey the voice of the LORD thy God.

48 And it shall come to pass, that as the LORD rejoiced over you to do you good, and to multiply you; so the LORD will do unto you to destroy you, and to bring you to nought ; and ye shall be plucked from off the land whither thou goest to possess it.

49 And the LORD shall scatter thee among all people, from the one end of the earth even unto the other; and there thou shalt serve other gods, which neither thou nor thy fathers have known, even wood and stone.

50 And among these nations shalt thou find no ease, neither shall the sole of thy foot have rest: but the LORD shall give thee there a trembling heart, and failing of eyes, and sorrow of mind:

51 And thy life shall hang in doubt before thee; and thou shalt fear day and night, and shalt have no assurance of thy life:

52 In the morning thou shalt say, Would God it were even ! and at even thou shalt say, Would God it were morning ! for the fear of thine heart wherewith thou shalt fear, and for the sight of thine eyes which thou shalt see.

53 And the LORD shall bring thee into Egypt again with ships, by the way whereof I spoke unto thee, Thou shalt see it no more again: and there ye shall be sold unto your enemies for bondmen and bondwomen, and no man shall buy you.

CHAPTER XXIX.

THESE are the words of the covenant, which the LORD commanded Moses to make with the children of Israel in the land of Moab, besides the covenant which he made with them in Horeb.

2 And Moses called unto all Israel, and said unto them, Ye have seen all that the LORD did before your eyes in the land of Egypt unto Pharaoh, and unto all his servants, and unto all his land ;

3 The great temptations which thine eyes have seen, the signs, and those great miracles:

4 Yet the LORD hath not given you a heart to perceive, and eyes to see, and ears to hear, unto this day.

5 And I have led you forty years in the wilderness: your clothes are not waxen old upon you, and thy shoe is not waxen old upon thy foot.

6 Ye have not eaten bread, neither have ye drunk wine or strong drink: that ye might know that I am the LORD your God.

7 And when ye came unto this place, Sihon the king of Heshbon, and Og the king of Bashan, came out against us unto battle, and we smote them :

8 And we took their land, and gave it for an inheritance unto the Reubenites, and to the Gadites, and to the half tribe of Manasseh.

9 Keep therefore the words of this covenant, and do them, that ye may prosper in all that ye do.

10 Ye stand this day all of you before the LORD your God; your captains of your tribes, your elders, and your officers, with all the men of Israel,

11 Your little ones, your wives, and thy stranger that is in thy camp, from the hewer of thy wood unto the drawer of thy water :

12 That thou shouldest enter into covenant with the LORD thy God, and into his oath, which the LORD thy God maketh with thee this day:

13 That he may establish thee to day for a people unto himself, and that he may be unto thee a God, as he hath said unto thee, and as he hath sworn unto thy fathers, to Abraham, to Isaac, and to Jacob.

14 Neither with you only do I make this covenant and this oath;

15 But with him that standeth here with us this day before the LORD our God, and also with him that is not here with us this day :

16 Ye know how we have dwelt in the land of Egypt; and how we came through the nations which ye passed by ;

17 And ye have seen their abominations, and their idols, wood and stone, silver and gold, which were among them :

18 Lest there should be among you

man or woman, or family, or tribe, whose heart turneth away this day from the LORD our God, to go and serve the gods of these nations; lest there should be among you a root that beareth gall and wormwood ;

19 And it come to pass, when he heareth the words of this curse, that he bless himself in his heart, saying, I shall have peace, though I walk in the imagination of mine heart, to add drunkenness to thirst:

20 The LORD will not spare him, but then the anger of the LORD and his jealousy shall burn against that man, and all the curses that are written in this book shall lie upon him, and the LORD shall blot out his name from under heaven.

21 And the LORD shall separate him unto evil, out of all the tribes of Israel, according to all the curses of the covenant that are written in this book of the law:

22 So that the generation to come of your children that shall rise up after you, and the stranger that shall come from a far land, shall say, when they see the plagues of that land, and the sicknesses which the LORD hath laid upon it ;

23 And that the whole land thereof is brimstone, and salt, and burning, that it is not sown, nor beareth, nor any grass groweth therein, like the overthrow of Sodom and Gomorrah, Admah and Zeboim, which the LORD overthrew in his anger, and in his wrath :

24 Even all nations shall say, Wherefore hath the LORD done thus unto this land? what meaneth the heat of this great anger?

25 Then men shall say, Because they have forsaken the covenant of the LORD God of their fathers, which he made with them when he brought them forth out of the land of Egypt:

26 For they went and served other gods, and worshipped them, gods whom they knew not, and whom he had not given unto them:

27 And the anger of the LORD was kindled against this land, to bring upon it all the curses that are written in this book:

28 And the LORD rooted them out of their land in anger, and in wrath, and in great indignation, and cast them into another land, as it is this day.

29 The secret things belong unto the LORD our God: but those things which are revealed belong unto us and to our children for ever, that we may do all the words of this law.

CHAPTER XXX.

AND it shall come to pass, when all these things are come upon thee, the blessing and the curse, which I have set before thee, and thou shalt call them to mind among all the nations, whither the LORD thy God hath driven thee,

2 And shalt return unto the LORD thy God, and shalt obey his voice according to all that I command thee this day, thou and thy children, with all thine heart, and with all thy soul;

3 That then the LORD thy God will turn thy captivity, and have compassion upon thee, and will return and gather thee from all the nations, whither the LORD thy God hath scattered thee.

4 If any of thine be driven out unto the outmost parts of heaven, from thence will the LORD thy God gather thee, and from thence will he fetch thee:

5 And the LORD thy God will bring thee into the land which thy fathers possessed, and thou shalt possess it; and he will do thee good, and multiply thee above thy fathers.

6 And the LORD thy God will circumcise thine heart, and the heart of thy children, to love the LORD thy God with all thine heart, and with all thy soul, that thou mayest live.

7 And the LORD thy God will put all these curses upon thine enemies, and on them that hate thee, which persecuted thee.

8 And thou shalt return and obey the voice of the LORD, and do all his commandments which I command thee this day.

9 And the LORD thy God will make thee plenteous in every work of thine hand, in thy population, in the fruit of thy cattle, and in the fruit of thy land, for good: for the LORD will again rejoice over thee for good, as he rejoiced over thy fathers:

10 If thou shalt hearken unto the voice of the LORD thy God, to keep his commandments and his statutes which are written in this book of the law, and if thou turn unto the LORD thy God with all thine heart, and with all thy soul.

11 For this commandment which I command thee this day, it is not hidden from thee, neither is it far off.

12 It is not in heaven, that thou shouldest say, Who shall go up for us to heaven, and bring it unto us, that we may hear it, and do it?

13 Neither is it beyond the sea, that thou shouldest say, Who shall go over the sea for us, and bring it unto us, that we may hear it, and do it?

14 But the word is very nigh unto thee, in thy mouth, and in thy heart, that thou mayest do it.

15 See, I have set before thee this day life and good, and death and evil;

16 In that I command thee this day to love the LORD thy God, to walk in his ways, and to keep his commandments, and his statutes, and his judgments, that thou mayest live and multiply: and the LORD thy God shall bless thee in the land whither thou goest to possess it.

17 But if thine heart turn away, so that thou wilt not hear, but shalt be drawn away, and worship other gods, and serve them;

18 I denounce unto you this day, that ye shall surely perish, and that ye shall not prolong your days upon the land, whither thou passest over Jordan to go to possess it.

19 I call heaven and earth to record this day against you, that I have set before you life and death, blessing and cursing: therefore choose life, that both thou and thy children may live:

20 That thou mayest love the LORD thy God, and that thou mayest obey his voice, and that thou mayest cleave unto him: for he is thy life, and the length of thy days: that thou mayest dwell in the land which the LORD sware unto thy fathers, to Abraham, to Isaac, and to Jacob, to give them.

CHAPTER XXXI.

AND Moses went and spake these words unto all Israel.

2 And he said unto them, I am a hundred and twenty years old this day; I can no more go out and come in: also the LORD hath said unto me, Thou shalt not go over this Jordan.

3 The LORD thy God, he will go

over before thee, and he will fight against these nations, and thou shalt possess them: and Joshua, he shall go over before thee, as the LORD hath said.

4 Be strong and of a good courage, fear not, nor be afraid of them: for the LORD thy God, he it is that doth go with thee; he will not fail thee, nor forsake thee.

5 And Moses called unto Joshua, and said unto him in the sight of all Israel, Be strong and of a good courage: for thou must go with this people unto the land which the LORD hath sworn unto their fathers to give them; and thou shalt cause them to inherit it.

6 And the LORD, he it is that doth go before thee; he will be with thee, he will not fail thee, neither forsake thee: fear not, neither be dismayed.

7 And Moses wrote this law, and delivered it unto the priests the sons of Levi, which bare the ark of the covenant of the LORD, and unto all the elders of Israel.

8 And Moses commanded them, saying, At the end of every seven years, in the solemnity of the year of release, on the feast of tabernacles,

9 When all Israel is come to appear before the LORD thy God in the place which he shall choose, thou shalt read this law before all Israel in their hearing.

10 Gather the people together, men, and women, and children, and thy stranger that is within thy gates, that they may hear, and that they may learn, and fear the LORD your God, and observe to do all the words of this law:

11 And that their children, which have not known any thing, may hear, and learn to fear the LORD your God,

as long as ye live in the land whither ye go over Jordan to possess it.

12 And the LORD said unto Moses, Behold, thy days approach that thou must die: call Joshua and present yourselves in the tabernacle of the congregation, that I may give him a charge. And Moses and Joshua went, and presented themselves in the tabernacle of the congregation.

13 And the LORD appeared in the tabernacle in a pillar of a cloud: and the pillar of the cloud stood over the door of the tabernacle.

14 And the LORD said unto Moses, Behold, thou shalt sleep with thy fathers; and this people will rise up, and go and worship the gods of the strangers of the land, whither they go to be among them, and will forsake me, and break my covenant which I have made with them.

15 Then my anger shall be kindled against them in that day, and I will forsake them, and I will hide my face from them, and they shall be devoured, and many evils and troubles shall befall them; so that they will say in that day, Are not these evils come upon us, because our God is not among us?

16 And I will surely hide my face in that day for all the evils which they shall have wrought, in that they are turned unto other gods.

17 Now therefore write ye this song for you, and teach it the children of Israel: put it in their mouths, that this song may be a witness for me against the children of Israel.

18 For when I shall have brought them into the land which I sware unto their fathers, that floweth with milk and honey; and they shall have eaten and filled themselves, and waxen

fat; then will they turn unto other gods, and serve them, and provoke me, and break my covenant.

19 And it shall come to pass, when many evils and troubles have befallen them, that this song shall testify against them as a witness; for it shall not be forgotten out of the mouths of their children: for I know their imagination which they go about, even now, before I have brought them into the land which I sware.

20 Moses therefore wrote this song the same day, and taught it the children of Israel.

21 And he gave Joshua the son of Nun a charge, and said, Be strong and of a good courage: for thou shalt bring the children of Israel into the land which I sware unto them: and I will be with thee.

22 And it came to pass, when Moses had made an end of writing the words of this law in a book, until they were finished,

23 That Moses commanded the Levites, which bore the ark of the covenant of the LORD, saying,

24 Take this book of the law, and put it in the side of the ark of the covenant of the LORD your God, that it may be there for a witness against thee.

25 For I know thy rebellion, and thy stiff neck: behold, while I am yet alive with you this day, ye have been rebellious against the LORD; and how much more after my death?

26 Gather unto me all the elders of your tribes, and your officers, that I may speak these words in their ears, and call heaven and earth to record against them.

27 For I know that after my death ye will utterly corrupt yourselves, and turn aside from the way which I have commanded you; and evil will befall you in the latter days; because ye will do evil in the sight of the LORD, to provoke him to anger through the work of your hands.

28 And Moses spoke in the ears of all the congregation of Israel the words of this song, until they were ended.

CHAPTER XXXII.

HEAR, ye heavens! I will speak,
listen, O earth, to the words of my
   mouth!
My teaching shall drop as the rain,
my speech shall distill as the dew;
as the showers upon the green herb,
as the torrents upon the grass.
For the name of the LORD I proclaim;
ascribe ye greatness unto our God.
He is the Rock, his work is perfect,
for all his ways are justice;
a faithful God, without iniquity,
just and upright is he.
5 Their corruption is not his fault;
the stain is on his children—
a perverse and deceitful generation!
Do ye thus requite the LORD,
O foolish and unwise people?
Is he not thy Father, thy Master,
thy Maker who established thee?
Remember the days of old,
consider the years of past generations:
ask thy father, he will teach thee,
thy elders, they will tell thee.
When the Highest established the
   nations,
when he apportioned the sons of
   man,
he set the bounds of the people
by the number of the children of
   Israel.
For the portion of the LORD is his
   people;
Jacob is the lot of his inheritance.
10 He found him in the desert land,
in the wilderness' howling waste;
he surrounded him, he cared for
   him,
he kept him as the pupil of the eye.

As an eagle watcheth her nest,
fluttereth over her young ones,
spreadeth out her wings, taketh
them,
bearing them aloft upon her wings;
So the LORD alone led his people,
and there was no strange god with
him.
He let him ascend the heights of the
earth,
and enjoy the increase of the fields,
made him suck honey out of the
rock,
and oil out of the hard flint;
Butter of kine, and milk of sheep,
fat lambs, and rams of Bashan's
breed,
and goats with the marrow of
choicest wheat,
thou drankest the pure blood of
grapes.
15 But Jeshurun waxed fat, and
kicked:
—thou hast grown fat, and thick,
and oppulent—
then he forsook the God, his Creator,
and despised the Rock of his salvation.
They provoked him with strange
gods,
they made him wroth with their
. abominations.
They sacrificed unto devils — no-
gods—
unto gods they knew not, that came
newly up,
whom your fathers did not fear.
Thou thoughtest not of the Rock
that bore thee,
and forgotest the God that formed
thee.
And the LORD saw it and was wroth,
provoked by his sons and his daughters:
20 Saying, I will hide my face from
them,
I will see what their end shall be;
for they are a perverse generation,
children in whom there is no faith.
They have vexed me with their idols,
they provoked me with their vani-
ties;
I shall vex them with unworthy
people,
with a stupid mob will I provoke
them.

For the fire of mine anger is kindled,
it shall burn unto the nethermost
depth,
and consume the earth and her increase,
and inflame the foundation of mountains.
I will heap upon them misfortunes,
and spend all mine arrows upon
them.
Burning hunger and scorching heat,
and ravishing diseases,
the wild beasts' teeth I will send
against them,
with the poison of dust-licking serpents.
25 The sword without, terror within,
shall destroy both young man and
maiden,
the suckling and the gray haired
man.
I said, I will destroy them,
I will erase their memory from men:
If not the enemy's wrath I feared,
lest their adversary boast,
lest they say, Our hand hath triumphed,
and not the LORD hath accomplished
all this.
For it is a nation of evil counsel,
neither have they understanding.
Oh that they were wise and noticed
this:
they would consider their latter end.
30 How should one chase a thousand,
and two put ten thousand to flight,
unless their Rock had sold them,
and the LORD delivered them up?
For their rock is not as our Rock—
let even our enemies be judges.
Their vine is of Sodom's vine,
and of the fields of Gomorrah;
their grapes are grapes of gall,
they bear poisonous clusters;
their wine is made of dragons' rage,
and of the cruel venom of asps.
It is hidden in my counsel,
sealed up in my treasures:
35 Mine is vengeance and recompense,
at the time when their foot shall
slide;
for nigh is the day of their calamity,
their future hasteth upon them.
When the LORD will judge his
people,
and will be mindful of his servants;

when he seeth that their power is
gone
and no fortress or remnant left them:
Then he will say, Where are their
gods?
their rock in whom they trusted?
Who ate the fat of their sacrifices,
and drank the wine of their drink
offerings;
let them rise and help you;
let them be your protection.
See now that I, even I alone, am
God,
and there is no God beside me,
I cause death and life,
I wound and I heal,
and none can deliver out of my
hand.
40 I lift up my hand to heaven,
saying, As I am the Everliving!
When I will whet my glittering sword
and my hand take hold on judgment:
I will render vengeance to mine enemies,
and recompense to those who hate
me.
I will make mine arrows drunk with
blood,
my sword shall devour flesh;
with the blood of the slain and the
captives,
and the uncovered skulls of the enemy.
Rejoice, O ye nations, with his people;
for he will avenge the blood of his
servants,
and render vengeance to his foes;
and is reconciled with the land and
the people.

44 And Moses came and spoke all
the words of this song in the ears of
the people, he, and Hoshea the son
of Nun.

45 And Moses made an end of speaking all these words to all Israel:

46 And he said unto them, Set your
hearts unto all the words which I testify among you this day, which ye
shall command your children to observe
to do, all the words of this law.

47 For it is not a vain thing for
you; because it is your life: and
through this thing ye shall prolong
your days in the land, whither ye go
over Jordan to possess it.

48 And the LORD spake unto Moses
that selfsame day, saying,

49 Get thee up into this mountain
Abarim, unto mount Nebo, which is
in the land of Moab, that is over
against Jericho; and behold the land
of Canaan, which I give unto the children of Israel for a possession:

50 And die in the mount whither
thou goest up, and be gathered unto
thy people; as Aaron thy brother died
in mount Hor, and was gathered unto
his people:

51 Because ye trespassed against me
among the children of Israel at the
waters of Meribath-Kadesh, in the
wilderness of Zin; because ye sanctified me not in the midst of the children of Israel.

52 Yet thou shalt see the land before thee; but thou shalt not go
thither unto the land which I give the
children of Israel.

CHAPTER XXXIII.

THIS is the blessing with which
Moses, the man of God, blessed
the children of Israel before his death,
saying:
The Eternal came from Sinai,
rose in light from Seir to them;
he shone forth from mount Paran,
and advanced from Meribath-
Kadesh;
from his right hand fire flamed for
them.
He loved the tribes—
all the saints were in thy hand;
they lay at thy feet,
received thy words.
Moses commanded us a law,
the inheritance of the congregation
of Jacob.
5 He was king in Jeshurun,

when the heads of the people
    assembled,
all the tribes of Israel.
    Let Reuben live and not die,
nor his men be few.
    Hear, O Lord Simeon's voice,*)
and bring him to his people.
    Thy Truth-and-Light
is with Levi, thy pious man,
whom thou didst prove at Massah,
with whom thou strovest at the
        waters of Meribah ;
who saith of his father and his
    mother,
'I have not seen them' ;
who recognizeth not his brothers,
and knoweth not his sons—
for they keep thy word,
and guard thy covenant.
10 They teach Jacob thy judgments,
Israel thy law ;
they place incense before thee
burnt whole sacrifice upon thine
    altar.
    Judah with his hands fighteth for
        himself,
and thou aidest him against his foes ;
bless his power, O Eternal,
favor the work of his hands ;
crush the loins of his adversaries
of all who hate him, that they rise
        not again.
    Benjamin, the beloved of Lord,
dwelleth in safety ;
he screeneth him all day,
and resteth between his shoulders.
    Joseph's land is blessed of the
        Lord,
for the precious things of heaven
    above,
and of the deep spread out below,
for the precious products of the sun,
and the precious products of the
    moon ;
15 For things from the summits of
        primeval mountains,
and the precious things of everlast-
        ing hills ;
for the precious things of the earth
    and its fullness
and the favor of him who appeared
    in the bush—
all this shall come upon Joseph's
    head,

*) Amended Version according to Heil-
prin: Historical poetry of the Hebrews.

upon the head of the crowned one
    among his brethren.
His firstborn bullock is excellent;
the wild buffalo's horns are his ;
with them he thrusteth the nations,
all the ends of the earth.—
Such are the myriads of Ephraim,
such the thousands of Manasseh.
    Rejoice, O Zebulun, in thy going
        out,
and thou, O Issachar, in thy tents.
They call tribes to the mountain,
and offer there sacrifices of right-
    eousness ;
for they gather the abundance of
    the seas
and the treasures hid in the sand

20 Praised be he who enlarges Gad;
he dwelleth like a lioness,
and teareth arm and crown of head.
He selected a first part for himself,
where the field of the hidden law-
        giver lieth;
and marched at the head of the
    people,
achieving the Lord's victory,
and his judgments for Israel.
    Dan is a lion's whelp,
such as leap forth from Bashan.
    Naphtali is satisfied with favor,
full of the blessings of the Lord
sea and southland conquer thou.
    Blessed above other sons is Asher,
favored among his brethren—
he batheth his foot in oil.
25 Iron and brass is thy bolt,
and long as the days is thy peace.
    There is none like God, O Je-
        shurun,
who rideth on the heavens to aid
    thee,
in triumph above the clouds.
A refuge is the God of old,
a resting place are the everlasting
    arms.
He chased the foe before thee,
and said, "Destroy!"
And Israel dwelleth in safety,
undisturbed is Jacob's fountain ;
in a land of corn and wine
which the heavens bedew.
Happy art thou, O Israel ;
who is like thee,
O people victorious through the
    Lord?

He is thy shield of help,
thy sword of triumph.
Thy enemies cringe before thee,
and thou treadest on their heights.

CHAPTER XXXIV.

AND Moses went up from the plains of Moab unto the mountain of Nebo, to the top of Pisgah, that is over against Jericho: and the LORD shewed him all the land of Gilead, unto Dan,

2 And all Naphtali and the land of Ephraim, and Manasseh, and all the land of Judah, unto the utmost sea,

3 And the south, and the plain of the valley of Jericho, the city of palm trees, unto Zoar.

4 And the LORD said unto him, This is the land which I sware unto Abraham, unto Isaac, and unto Jacob, saying, I will give it unto thy children: I have caused thee to see it with thine eyes, but thou shalt not go over thither.

5 So Moses the servant of the LORD died there in the land of Moab, according to the word of the LORD.

6 And he buried him in a valley in the land of Moab, over against Beth-peor: but no man knoweth of his sepulchre unto this day.

7 And Moses was a hundred and twenty years old when he died: his eye was not dim, nor his natural force abated.

8 And the children of Israel wept for Moses in the plains of Moab thirty days: so the days of weeping · and mourning were ended.

9 And Joshua the son of Nun was full of the spirit of wisdom; for Moses had laid his hands upon him: and the children of Israel hearkened unto him, and did as the LORD commanded Moses.

10 And there arose not a prophet since in Israel like unto Moses, whom the LORD knew face to face,

11 In all the signs and the wonders which the LORD sent him to do in the land of Egypt, to Pharaoh, and to all his servants, and to all his land,

12 And in all that mighty hand, and in all the great power which Moses shewed in the sight of all Israel.

Lightning Source UK Ltd.
Milton Keynes UK
UKHW02f1853240918
329454UK00026B/1281/P